Life and Death of an Oilman

Life and Death of an Oilman
The Career of E. W. Marland

By JOHN JOSEPH MATHEWS

with drawings by J. CRAIG SHEPPARD

UNIVERSITY OF OKLAHOMA PRESS
NORMAN

BOOKS BY JOHN JOSEPH MATHEWS

The Osages: Children of the Middle Waters (Norman, 1961)
Life and Death of an Oilman: The Career of E. W. Marland (Norman, 1951)
Talking to the Moon (Chicago, 1945; Norman, 1981)
Sundown (New York, 1935; Norman, 1988)
Wah'Kon-Tah: The Osage and the White Man's Road (Norman, 1932)

Library of Congress Cataloging-in-Publication Data

Mathews, John Joseph, 1895–
    Life and death of an oilman : the career of E.W. Marland / by John Joseph
Mathews ; with drawings by J. Craig Sheppard.
    p. cm.
    ISBN: 978-0-8061-1238-1 (paper)

    1. Marland, Ernest Whitworth, 1874–1941. 2. Industrialists—United
States—Biography. 3. Petroleum industry and trade—United States—History. I. Title.
    HD9570.M3M3 1992
    338.4'76223382'092—dc20
    [B]   89–70455
                                    CIP

To The People of Ponca City

Preface

This account of the career of an oilman is really a personal impression rather than a biography constructed from documents. Ernest Whitworth Marland was at once a hero—to some, almost a god—and a man who inspired the most intense hatreds. Naturally, the information which I went forth to gather was found, on analysis, to be colored by the points of view of my informants. Nor would I deny that I myself, being entirely and gratefully human, have had my own personal paint box at my side during the writing of this story. Since one distills everything that comes to him through the intricate coils of his own being, there can be no perfect objectivity anyway.

However, since I did depend much upon my own experiences and relations with Marland, I have tried to be very cautious and consciously objective in writing about him. I had to find the human being among the many pictures given me by the people who knew him well—most of them much better than I did. This process involved all of the problems encountered by those who work with living sources: on the one hand, I had to cut off his devil's tail, reshape his cloven hooves, and give him the human quality of sympathy; and on the other, to snip off his wings and throw his nimbus away—in effect, to secularize him. Gossip was everywhere for the taking. Publicity had played upon him like a searchlight, because his life at times had the essentials for Greek drama. Humans are ever eager about the details of love and tragedy, which caused many to offer more than they knew—a kind of dramatized truth rather than an embellishment of it.

But there is nothing profane about warm and living information. Even ancient documents, once thought by scholars to be sacred, are now found not to be derived from God but to have originated with men, who possessed—or suffered from—all the failings of men: blindness and vanity and self-interest. Because a letter was written during an earlier age by a hypocrite, a fanatic, a snob, or an honest man of single conviction and has lain in some archive until yellowed with age does not imbue it with sanctity. The truth is hardly ever single, it is almost always refracted, and that last imperfectly.

It was a rare piece of good fortune which permitted me, during Marland's lifetime, to review with him the story of his failure in both West Virginia and Oklahoma. His failure as governor, I saw. I was not so much attracted by his historical or economic importance, whatever weight either may have, as by his personality. Perhaps I was attracted by the difference between him and other acquisitive builders of an earlier period in the Age of Freedom. He was not a Jim Fisk, a Jay Gould, a Daniel Drew, a Cornelius Vanderbilt; he missed a great deal of being an Andrew Mellon, a Collis P. Huntington, an H.A.W. Tabor, or a John D. Rockefeller, Sr. Not only was he not their equal in stature, but he came upon the scene when the rangeland of economic freedom was being fenced. He saw, in fact, what the other builders never dreamed could happen—the end of the Age of Freedom—and he personalized it in his own end. He saw the barriers closing in and talked about it often.

Marland was the equal of any of the big boys (as he called them) in energy, in dreaming, in cleverness, and in acquisitive capacity, but his ruthlessness was vitiated by the fact that he had been born a gentleman. His father, moreover, had stimulated in him a feeling for the underprivileged, by any measure a weakness in those who create for themselves a single standard of money. He lacked the primitiveness of the others. He had no bitterness, and none of that singleness of purpose which springs from the vindictive in a dark mind. Throughout his life he was too much burdened with artificiality. And if a single inclination could be said to have motivated him, it was hedonism. He not only placed high value in pleasure but sought to make it free and easy for others to acquire.

It is curious that, in view of the value he attached to happiness, E. W. Marland should have been driven to over-reach himself, so that, like a character in a naturalistic novel, he proceeded to disaster from a basic and persistent conflict which he seemed never to analyze. He despised and feared the strength, and admired the well-ordered functioning, of the Standard companies, while at the same time aspiring himself to the direction of "a great integrated company"—good enough to rival, perhaps to supersede, the giant he accused of unfair competition. He was nothing if not vain, but in this he was also blind.

All of these characteristics suggest a biographical treatment freed of the restraints of traditionally written history and the documentation required by graduate schools. Marland's failure was dramatic rather than economic. He failed because of his vanity and a humanitarianism based upon the false premise that pleasure for others is an attainable goal. The one led to business competition for which he had not the requisite shrewdness, and the other to artificiality—the country-club, polo-playing, fox-hunting ornamentation which ruined him, from the point of view of economic struggle, and which destroyed his capacity for humanitarianism because it supplanted it.

It was the literary value of the man that struck one. Here in one man appeared all—or almost all—of the tensions of an age which was, in reality, the end of an age, with many human qualities and weaknesses thrown in for good measure: pride and self-interest, an exaggerated sympathy for the common man, a love of bigness, a materialist conception of happiness, a reckless, plunging ambition coupled with a dark fear of failure, which in the boy caused headlong flight from a mob of jeering youngsters, and in the man the decision to "run" for the United States Senate after two years in the governor's chair.

Whatever the story of E. W. Marland may hold for the future student of the Age of Freedom, these things have attributive significance, and it may indeed be that the human truth they contain will afford a larger reality to history than the merely factual details of industrial success and failure when America was moving precociously from youth to maturity.

JOHN JOSEPH MATHEWS

The Blackjacks
Pawhuska, Oklahoma

Contents

Part I   The Age of Freedom

1

ONE DAY, about the year 1880, a lady in a large house on Mount Washington in Pittsburgh gave a last tug at the kilt in which she had dressed her little boy. She kicked her skirt train to the left deftly as she stood up and moved away to get a better view. The Glengarry was perched at a jaunty angle, the dirk was in place, and the sporran hung straight. The kilt was of his mother's tartan, the McLeod, and she had brought it back to him from her last visit to her old home in Scotland.

The boy's older sisters, smiling indulgently on their glorious little brother, stood ready to make suggestions, but they had no suggestions to make. They could only approve of him with shining eyes. The boy was highly pleased with himself, but he wore an expression of petulance so that the others should not see his pleasure.

He was not embarrassed, nor did he have any feeling of revolt against his mother's dressing him in her family's tartan for the holiday party at the near-by public school. One might expect a little boy to object strenuously to this violation of the unwritten, unspoken standards by which little boys lived. This little boy did not attend the public schools, and perhaps did not know much about such standards. In allowing himself to be dressed in these proud but outlandish clothes, he considered only the secret swelling of his self-esteem and the reflection of his im-

3

portance in the eyes of his mother and sisters. Another little boy might have had a secret pride in such clothes, but remembering the law of the pack would have fought frantically against wearing them out of the house.

The little boy of Mount Washington walked with assurance up the street, and his mother and sisters watched him through the windows with unreasoning pride. He walked in glory; the party, the others who were to attend, the very trees that stood like a guard of honor properly spaced along his way, were nonexistent except as a setting for his magnificence.

From the children at the school he expected praise of his kilts and deference to the important young man from the big house. He mistook the interest in his approach for admiration, and the children's halting in their tracks for the proper recognition of greatness.

The little boys, who had been standing stock-still like surprised deer, soon gathered round him—and for this movement there was only one interpretation by the arrogant little boy, the expected homage.

An exclamation grew into a series of definite taunts, then the taunts grew in volume, and then came the first tentative push. The next push was stronger, inspired by the smugness of the little boy. Pushed and shoved one way and another, the child looked into the faces filled with contempt and ridicule, and the first pallor of fear shone in his own face. Vulgar hands attempted to lift his kilt, and there were lewd remarks, then shouts in his ear.

He turned and primitive fear took complete control. He ran as fast as he could run for home. He had no urge to hit back, nor to stop and bluff his way out. Piece by piece the beautiful kilts were torn from his body. The plaid was torn from the brooch, and the Glengarry went flying. The kilt became ribbons flapping about his legs, and the sporran bounced out in front of him, and from side to side, as his legs hit it.

When he reached home only the sporran was intact.

Little Ernest Whitworth Marland was not upset long over his experience. It was soon forgotten in his daily life at the big

4

house. He was not only the baby of a family of eight, but the only son of an English father and of a mother old enough to be his grandmother.

Since the boy's birth, May 8, 1874, his father had made plans for him. He believed in the law of primogeniture, and his little daughters were early made to realize that something quite holy had come among them that May day when brother arrived.

He was christened Ernest Whitworth Marland because this was the name that shone brightly in the family history back in England. His father, Alfred Marland, was filled with dreams for the new land which was not bound by tradition, and in those dreams of the future greatness of the United States he saw his family name a part of the glory that history would undoubtedly record. So he watched with care the upbringing of his little son, Ernest, and the family was made to encircle him with care and adoration, making their own needs secondary to his. The princeling, whose royal robes were to be, in his father's dreams, the robes of the chief justice of the Supreme Court of the United States, became the object and the center of Alfred Marland's life.

Alfred had been educated by his grandfather, Ernest Whitworth, who was head of the Whitworth School for Boys, in Whitworth Valley, near Manchester, England, and he had taught mathematics and English history in that school. In doing this he was simply carrying on the tradition of an academic family—a tradition that influenced his family, just as traditions of bootmaking, trade, or domestic service influenced others.

Ernest Whitworth, Alfred's grandfather, had academic fame as one of the great mathematicians in all England. But mathematicians, no matter how famous, were restricted by the rule of the patricians in England and did not have the means or the freedom possessed by the landed gentry.

After teaching mathematics and English history in his grandfather's school for a time, Alfred Marland emigrated to America in a sailing ship. He was moved by the Southern cause and came over in the year 1862 with the express purpose of aiding the arms of the South. Like many Englishmen of that period, he

5

was in deep sympathy with the gentlemen of the South, fighting to protect their culture from what he believed to be hordes of Northern tradesmen bent like the Huns on destruction. The trading Yankee was well known in every port in the world. Those who had not known him personally had heard about him. His careless speech and crude manners made him a very interesting subject for conversation and appraisal that was not flattering.

Alfred enlisted in the Southern army. The period of his enlistment is unknown, but apparently it was a short one. He might have suddenly realized that a victory for the South would have meant the dissolution of the United States, or he might have become sympathetic to the plight of the bound black man, or he might have seen a chance to break the academic tradition of his family and remain in the United States.

He was on an Ohio River boat, either during the period of his enlistment or soon after, and he seems to have noted especially and with wonder the throbbing heart to which that great artery was joined, the city of Pittsburgh. He discovered that when the industrialists of the North needed materials which were supposed to be contraband of war, these materials found their way out of the South along the great river and landed in Pittsburgh to be processed or sent on to other points. From the point of view of a logical Englishman, the war might have begun to appear somewhat farcical. His diary of this period was lost; there is only a hint of this attitude. But he seems to have lost his Byronic fervor rather suddenly and to have contracted the Yankee "fever."

He was shocked at the waste he saw in America, seasoned as he was by the tight economy of a mathematician's household in England. He noticed during his days on the Ohio that the cotton bales were carelessly bound and that cotton lint was strewn about. After some thought, he invented an iron band for the economical binding of cotton bales, and with the money he had brought over with him and the money he received as a soldier (if the latter were of any importance) he set up a mill in Pittsburgh to manufacture these iron bands.

6

As soon as his business gave him sufficient profits he went to South Hills, close to Pittsburgh, and bought land. It seemed to his English mind that Americans did not have the proper reverence for land—though admittedly there was no scarcity of it! Here was the best of all commodities. It gave, in England, social dominance to the gentry, whose position for at least two centuries had been impregnable. In America, landowning gave Alfred Marland freedom from the traditions of England. Could the inhabitants of this Western world know what this meant?

When his profits began to mount, Alfred Marland bought more land, this time near the great steel plants belching smoke by day and pillars of fire by night. He divided it into large lots and began to build houses for the polyglot population of laborers working at the mills. He made the divisions large enough so that they could have chickens, vegetables, and cows. He rented his houses as cheaply as possible, or sold them with the smallest profit to himself. The murmurings of the discontented English workmen had been heard in his book-lined rooms, and his sympathy had been aroused. He thought that the people of this new country must have a feeling of security and independence if the country were to attain the glory he believed possible.

What he saw about him was unlike England, and yet like it. Exploitation had merely taken another form here—that of industrialists, sharp, canny men, unendowed with the tradition of English middle-class responsibility. He believed that some day the chaotic period of exploitation would end and the government would be represented by reasonable, cultured, and able men. He could see that every military hero elected to responsible office was not a Washington, and that every backwoodsman born in a cabin was not necessarily a Lincoln. He would head an English family in the new atmosphere, which might through the years produce able jurists, administrators of state, legislators.

He gradually became a rich man, but had no ambition to become a great industrialist, although he did become an ironmaster and a man of industrial property. He got himself elected from South Hills to the state legislature and later to the Select Council of Pittsburgh, where he served for twenty years. He thus began

7

at the bottom to contribute whatever influence he might have to the development of the new country.

He kept a plot of five acres in South Hills for a home, and here he built a twelve-room house on Mount Washington. He planted grapevines, laid out flower plots, and erected stables and barns. He would live as a gentleman ought to live; he would create an unpretentious manor here in the beautiful hills of Pennsylvania.

He was not a young man when he married Sara McLeod, a widow with five children well on their way to maturity. While Alfred had been trained in the traditional academic pattern, Sara had been trained in the military. She had been born at a military establishment on the Island of Skye, and grew up as a soldier's daughter. She had been educated in the army schools. She had a fine sense of humor, and she was religious, "but not unduly so." She was a very attractive woman, and her attractiveness must have been unusual, since Alfred married her with a family of five children and brought up the younger ones, as well as one of her grandsons, as his own.

He established his family on the estate he had built on Mount Washington. When his own children came along, he was happy as the head of a landowning family.

There was Ignatia, then Charlotte, and finally, on May 8, 1874, Ernest Whitworth Marland. The male child was received as an English heir rather a long time in coming; in the dreams of Alfred he was an instrument for the realizations of his hopes for family and nation.

The home was a quiet one, with a large library where Scott's Waverly novels, and Dickens' novels and stories were read aloud by Alfred, at first to his wife's children, later to his own. After the younger children had learned to read with facility, he heard each one of them read selections from what he called "good literature," and carefully criticized the manner of reading and the posture, and especially the diction. He also urged the children to cultivate originality through the invention of their own games. He impressed upon his son an understanding that he was

8

being trained as a gentleman, and warned him constantly that "of him to whom much is given, much is required."

Young Ernest saw little of other children, because Alfred thought that most American children were carelessly brought up and left without proper criteria for their speech and actions. But Ernest did play with some children; he played with the little King boys, who lived on Grandview Avenue, especially. He imposed his family-invented games upon the others, and assumed leadership with unquestionable assurance. He changed games whimsically, and his sisters watching him and knowing him, and ever deferring to him, changed with him, so that he never had the experience of standing alone as a leader without disciples.

But he manifested more than the conscious rights of the English first-born male. He had a complex personality which confused and intrigued, and a very bright mind. He could fire his playmates with his ideas. They were absorbed by the wonderful play and failed to resent the bald egotism of the little boy whom the game was supposed to glorify.

He was a dreamer rather than a boy of action. Some of the dreams were inspired by the books he read in his father's library; many were original creations in which he played the leader, the prince, or the hero.

He cared little about competition since he could not entertain the thought of possible defeat. He ran no foot races on his short legs, and he refused to wrestle or box or play follow-the-leader, for which physical prowess was important. He cared little for mental competition, but assumed leadership through the power of his self-assurance and the fascinating glow of his imagination.

His acquisitive instincts, or better, his gambling instincts, were revealed through his love of marbles. He found tense pleasure in the game of "keeps" whenever he could be sure that his father was not aware of his playing. His love of the game and the intensity with which he played made him clever and he won often. The weight of the sack in which he carried his winnings gave him pleasure, yet he seldom cared to trouble himself by

9

counting the marbles in the sack; the bulge and the weight were sufficient.

This boyhood play seemed to be the only indication that he might someday become a businessman. He read omnivorously, he dreamed, and he wrote poetry and fairy stories. But just as young John D. Rockefeller's little black account book in which he noted his minute little boy's income and expenses became the great philanthropic organization for the donation of millions of dollars, so did little Ernest's sack of marbles become the depository of millions which he refused to abase by prosaic accounting.

Thus did he grow into big-footed boyhood, this princeling of Mount Washington, this future chief justice of his father's dreams. He noted the manners about him but never seemed to question the teachings given him, and he was sure that certain things were not done, and certain things, though known, were never mentioned. He heard names that became magic to him— J. Pierpont Morgan of New York and London, the greatest of the dollar-princes; John D. Rockefeller; and the local princes, Andrew Carnegie and Henry Clay Frick. The latter, when he was pointed out to him by his father, impressed him as "the handsomest man I have ever seen."

Even though his father ever insisted on the fact that money could not possibly make a gentleman, he secretly wished that his father, who liked to have company and talk with men of intelligence and whose house was a meeting place for civilized conversation, would ask these great men to come as well. He would have liked to hear their oracular statements and to watch their every mannerism. But his father found pleasure in inviting men of social and political ideas, and there were many of these who came to his father's house. Most of them failed to impress young Ernest the way the great industrialists did about whom everyone talked.

Sir Thomas Hughes, the author of *Tom Brown's School Days* and *Tom Brown at Oxford*, came often to the Alfred Marland house. He had been a friend of Ernest Whitworth's in England. He was a noted liberal who had come to America with the idea of establishing a colony in the land of freedom, where insecure workers of England, robbed of their human dignity by intensified industrialism, and second sons, victimized by the law of primogeniture, could have freedom to express with full force their latent power.

He established his colony in 1879 on the Cumberland Plateau in Tennessee, after a committee had traveled many hundreds of miles searching for a suitable location. American publishers gave him specially bound volumes for his library to the number of nearly seven thousand, and James Russell Lowell and Charles A. Dana, the famous Dana of the *Sun*, gave both money and encouragement.

When Alfred Marland saw this Cumberland Mountain colony he immediately gave money for its support. Here was freedom and primitive dignity. In the distance was the vague outline of the Great Smokies, and at hand, oak, hickory, poplar, chestnut, maple, pines, and hemlock scented the air. The eager, restless postwar masses of homeseekers were rejecting the mountains for the rich lowlands and the rolling prairie. Here was an island that could be kept as an island, a natural laboratory for a planned society. Anyone who wished could come to the colony on the colony's terms: community co-operation based upon work of the hands as well as of the brains and the spirit.

Houses were built, a commissary and a church imitative of the Gothic towers of Europe and England. The little church stood among the oaks and pines, and no church in England had a more tranquil or beautiful setting. One could look across the area to Tabard Inn, sentimentally named for the old English inn made famous by the *Canterbury Tales*. A town hall was built and later a cannery, and with them other necessary community buildings. All these were constructed of the native pine, processed by the colonists.

The Arnold School was established, named for the headmaster of Rugby School in England, the scene of Hughes's *Tom Brown's School Days*, and the little community was called in honor of the same school, Rugby.

Alfred Marland saw that such an arrangement fitted exactly

with his own ideas, and he placed his children in school there and lived in the little community during the time his son attended the Arnold School. The atmosphere was England's, but the clear, scented air, free from the chemicals and smoke of industry, and from the obsequious cap-touching of weary men, was the breath of freedom. Thomas Hughes dreamed of the day when the worker with his hands could walk with dignity to meet the prince at the gates of the colony.

E. W. Marland liked Rugby—even the Spartan discipline of the Arnold School. Though reckless young second sons, who hunted foxes over the rough mountainous country in traditional costume, lived very importantly in his memory as fascinating novelty, his training at Arnold School was so much like the training his father had received earlier that we may readily assume the one was simply an extension of the other.

He was thrown with other boys here, but there is nothing to indicate that his assumption of leadership was questioned, with the exception of that leadership inherent in successful competition in games. If leadership fell naturally upon the shoulders of the successful athletes, as it does in English public schools, there must have been some rather sharp disappointments for the dreaming little princeling from Mount Washington. Perhaps he felt that he had offset them with his superior marble-playing or with his brilliant inventions.

He received his early training at Rugby's Arnold School before the disintegration of the colony. It seemed doomed from the beginning. Many of the underprivileged from England found the new freedom rather baffling and the unaccustomed tools of agriculture unconquerable. They were like deer kept confined for generations, then suddenly freed to run wild in the forests with the wild bands—deer that would come back from the woods to eat with the cattle, or to beg at the kitchen door.

However, the young second sons, some of whom were remittance men, found the strange wild country interesting, and seem to have inherited that adjustability which the rulers of a pelagic empire must have. They had, still, the common failings as well as the virtues of their class. They hunted foxes and built tennis courts when they should have been co-operating in the building of much-needed houses. Some of them carelessly drank from the still pools which they found in the deep ravines, mistaking them for springs, and died of typhoid.

The young second sons and the workers looked at each other with a mutual understanding which was as strong a tradition as the little Gothic church, the inn called Tabard, and the Arnold School. Despite Thomas Hughes's beautiful theories, the transplanted social stratification had not been disturbed in the least.

Thomas Hughes was not the energetic egoist such a project demands for a leader. He was too gentle and kindly, and his ideas had no power to protect themselves from the selfish actions and expressions of those who wished to make themselves more important in the eyes of all. He had said that "patience, humility, and utter forgetfulness of self are the true royal qualities." Before his death in 1896 he was compelled to call upon all of these qualities, but still his colony failed.

While in Rugby the Marland family lived in Ivey Cottage, and Alfred was constantly contributing to the colony both money and ideas. His plans for the colony were not always carried out to his satisfaction, however. Gradually he became disillusioned about Rugby. An article in the colony paper, *The Rugbeian*, was the occasion of his break with Rugby and the Arnold School.

In August, 1882, he wrote a letter to *The Rugbeian*, in answer to a criticism which the paper had carried concerning Sara Marland's interview on Rugby in the *Pittsburgh Dispatch*. Alfred ended his letter thus: "While Mrs. Marland was very much pained at the published report of the interview as it appeared in the *Dispatch*, for in writing up the interview (as he evidently did in his office) the reporter drew upon his recollection for some portions and upon his imagination for the spice, yet she did not feel so much poignancy over it as she did over the unkind comments of the *Rugbeian* in general, and at the dark insinuation of your 20th in particular [intimating that Mrs. Marland had made only one correct statement], but if it will cure her of Rugby fever, or even mitigate its severity, I, for one, shall be very thankful, and shall ever remain, Your Obedient Servant, [signed] Alfred Marland."

Back in Pittsburgh, Ernest entered Park Institute, graduating in due course at seventeen in 1891. During these later years he had begun to question the teaching of his father. His boyhood interest in the local dollar-princes was now intensified, and added to this interest was an interest in the manifestations of wealth. Certainly he began to think less of his father's admonition that money does not make a gentleman. If money didn't make a gentleman, it gave birth to fascinating developments. The ladies with their parasols, their voluminous skirts, and their leg-o'-mutton sleeves, sitting grandly in carriages whose wheels flashed as they turned behind high-stepping horses, seemed wonderful to the boy. The men who came away from mysterious bars talking jovially with each other, the incense from their expensive cigars floating back over their shoulders, impressed him—men like the fashion plate, Henry Clay Frick, the very rich and ruthless coke and steel man, whom his father criticized for contracting for steerage loads of southern Europeans to work in the mills of Pittsburgh. The interest with which he read of the feasts and the balls of the self-made American royalty in New York would have displeased his father. Alfred thought that wealth and leisure ought to be utilized for the development of a better type of civilization, and not wasted on imitation of the old world. But to young Ernest this was grandeur greater than anything he had read about in books, and therefore wholly desirable.

His father talked constantly of the inexhaustible natural resources and of the new nation that could be developed upon them, free from the economic and social evils of the old world, but he also had begun to see that the national absorption in acquiring riches left the people's government to its own devices, or rather to the devices of the dollar-princes. Noting this development, he believed more and more that it was a gentleman's duty to contribute his thought and strength to the proper growth of that government, so that there might be some guidance of the dollar-mad nation.

Ernest dreamed of his own future greatness as a dollar-prince. Morgan, Rockefeller, Carnegie, and Frick were magic names. Their power and glory could be seen and felt, and in his mind they had begun to push Washington and Lincoln into the realm of make-believe with the Santa Claus of his early childhood.

In his new male glory, Ernest, naturally contemptuous of plodding and cautious middle age, questioned the conservative opinions that had once been the law as expressed by an English father. His father's formality, his personality, and his dignity did not encourage the expression of independent opinions by Ernest—but the opinions were there.

Alfred Marland was not aware that he was losing his future chief justice.

2 ERNEST ENTERED the Law School of the University of
Michigan in 1891. His father had retired as an ironmaster and
had sold his business. In 1891 he sold his home on Mount Washington and traded for some land in West Virginia, back in the
hills from the present Weirton. Sara Marland was chronically
ill, and perhaps he moved here for her health. But it could have
been a move which the need for economy forced upon him.

At Ann Arbor Ernest lived with about twenty young men
at the Sigma Chi fraternity house, and one assumes that they
were all older than he, since he was only seventeen when he entered college. He wore well-made clothes and affected a derby
hat and a large-knot bow tie with ends deftly tucked under the
wings of the high starched collar. He drank beer with his fraternity brothers and joined them in the song and jollity which was
supposed to be in the spirit of the old tavern in Heidelberg.

The fraternity was essentially staggy—there were few dances
or mixed social gatherings. There was much beer-drinking,
poker-playing, and conscious maleness. Of these pastimes, of
course Marland liked poker best. He became a first-rate poker
player; the transition from "keeps" to poker had been natural.
He loved gambling intensely. He had no girl, and he was not
boisterous. No one of his fraternity brothers remembers ever
seeing him even "half-seas-over."

Here at Michigan, Ernest seemed to have no capacity for leadership; at least he manifested none. He took no part in athletics or social activities. His more sophisticated classmates wore Ascot ties, sometimes with wing collars, and they sometimes wore white ties. Those who parted their hair in the center wore derbies on the backs of their heads, especially if the ends of their carefully parted hair had a tendency to curl. Neither these doggy young men nor the more serious students were interested in the imaginative creations of a seventeen-year-old, no matter how they glowed. The subtleties nurtured by his English father and the Arnold School at Rugby, Tennessee, were lost upon the mustachioed young men who sang with deep feeling and volume as they raised steins in the manner of German students. The little boy with the rainbow imagination, whose well-formed and convincing figments had inspired other little boys and fed his own vanity, was now face to face with buck-deer ruggedness, physical competition, and self-absorption. His vanity retreated within himself for protection, and he became silent, self-sufficient, and mechanically friendly.

One of his fraternity brothers described him as "a good looking chap with good color, although his features were somewhat on the coarse, sensual order, with rather heavy eyes—sometimes almost sleepy—that might have given to the casual observer an impression of indolence." And another described him as "a run-of-mine, friendly, 'lumpy' fellow, inclined to plumpness, gregarious in a quiet way and never uproarious."

Charles F. Roehrig, in later years a journalist and a good friend of William Jennings Bryan's, was his roommate at the Sigma Chi house and was probably closer to Marland than any of the others. Roehrig was a Democrat, and Marland, like his father, was a Republican, but Marland was not sufficiently interested in politics to argue about it.

The Sigma Chi house was not a mansion on State Street in those days, but "an unpretentious cottage-type East Huron Street place." The building was rented and there were no meals served in the house. A woman came to clean each day. For a bath there was a sheet metal tub into which the bather ran the water, then lit three Bunsen burners to heat it. Occasionally some brother would forget to turn off the burners, and he would cry out when he stepped into the tub, then fall over the edge, splashing water over the room.

Marland was not a distinguished student, but he was a good poker player, a fair loser, and a modest winner. At Ann Arbor he never gave the impression of excitability over anything. However, when he played poker he was alert, though silent.

In one session a sharpshooter from another part of town, a law student, came to the Sigma Chi house to play. Very soon he had chips piled before him on the table. Then suddenly he stood up, beamed on the others, and said, "I guess I'll check out." As he raked in the money from the banker in exchange for his chips, he said with a smug smile, "The fact is, boys, I need the money."

Marland showed shocked surprise on his usually unreadable face. The expression of incredulity impressed the others, and when the law student had gone with all the money, they bantered him. And at each game thereafter someone at some time, usually after winning a large pot, would say, "The fact is, boys, I need the money."

Thus did the young Marland prepare himself for the Supreme Court of the United States and the head of a Marland dynasty of American gentlemen-statesmen.

He was graduated by the Michigan Law School in June, 1893, and he went back to Pittsburgh to live with his sister Ignatia, who was now married to a Mr. Rittenhouse. Ernest had little money, and he lived with her for the sake of economy.

Alfred had lost his real estate, with the exception of the home in West Virginia, and was seriously affected by the beginning of the depression that was to hold the nation for several years. He was unable to help Ernest, but he did put him into the law offices of his attorney, a Mr. Ralph Bigham. There he was allowed to do only "leg" work, since he was just nineteen and could not be admitted to practice in the state of Pennsylvania until he was twenty-one.

He had no sense of the value of money and made no attempt

to save any part of his salary, or of the small amounts which his sister and his father gave him. He had the idea that he should have money when he needed it, that it would appear as it had always done. There had always been air to breathe, food to eat, and money; he couldn't understand why any of these basic conditions for living should suddenly disappear. He refused to recognize the absence of money.

He was kept busy, since Mr. Bigham had a good practice, but he had time for reading and dreaming. He read the works of Herbert Spencer, and they influenced his thoughts and perhaps his dreams for the rest of his life. He began to notice the strange difference between the lives of people in the streets of Pittsburgh and the lives of people he had known. He began to notice especially the shacks along the river where the "Hunkies" lived who gave their lives so completely to the flame-belching steel plants. His "leg" work carried him into all sorts of holes and crannies, as well as into the imposing business buildings, and he saw for the first time the dog-like eyes that shone from coal-dust-covered faces of the miners as they stood patiently with their dinner pails. Their seemingly crooked bodies and their bovine patience touched him deeply.

He brought them into his dreams. Someday, from the Olympus which he himself would attain, he would help these people to a better life!

But secretly Ernest began to be afraid of the city of Pittsburgh. The feeble daytime lights shining through the windows into the smoke made one who was outside the intimate glow of big business feel hopeless and frustrated. He was afraid of becoming nothing more than an outsider looking in upon that glow. Even to sit on one of the park benches for a few minutes seemed a surrender to the fire-belching world about him. If he made a habit of it, he might be lost.

The security of a small position with an established organization seemed to him a guarantee of insignificance. His vanity chose the freedom of a lone struggle. When he was twenty-one he opened an office of his own on Diamond Street. His feeling of independence was not shaken by the aid his father and sister gave him to make this move possible. He felt free in his little under-the-stairs office. Here he could keep his bright dreams—here the wheel of chance would be allowed full spin.

His sister acted as an office girl while he inspected coal lands for Guffey and Galey, promoters and entrepreneurs. She had legal forms printed for him. She gave him money. His father helped him far more than he could afford.

The physical evidence of the spirit of the age—the frowning, out-of-harmony masses of stone and steel, the smoke, the shrieks of locomotives, the tongues of flame from the steel plants—seemed to kill all Ernest's creative dreams except those which would have as their realization a hard core of material success.

The daytime lights about whose beams the smoke and fog rolled, and the cold, stern buildings from which they shone, were symbolical to him of the power of Big Business. He was sufficiently intelligent to realize that the power symbolized by the yellow light beams could reach out and defeat a young lawyer-promoter in a dark little office on Diamond Street, or by using him could take from him his independence. He did not know for sure that the Mellons—perhaps old Judge Mellon himself—did not own or control the very building in which he had his office.

He feared the cold-eyed men who sat behind the polished desks of T. Mellon & Sons.

"They found the flaw in any scheme of mine immediately," he said. "I could feel their cold eyes on my back, and my footsteps leaving the building sounded like rifle shots."

He carried the fear of bankers all his life. Bankers, he believed, were forever stating gravely that two and two make four, and there was something in him that rebelled against such an inevitable, prosaic conclusion, rebelled against its finality and its smug restrictions. He had the fear that a promoter usually has for precision and fact, and out of this fear grew a deep contempt for the fateful men who build upon them with such grim caution. Their apparent inhumanity annoyed him, and he sneered at these men because he feared them. And yet he seemed, paradoxically, to admire bankers for the very characteristics which he feared, characteristics which he himself lacked.

His symbol of the banker was not, as one might expect, the magnificent J. Pierpont Morgan of New York and London, but an everyday Pittsburgher, old Judge Thomas Mellon, founder of the House of Mellon.

Old Judge Mellon had retired from the bank, from the bench, and from the old-fashioned struggle which was perhaps the true "rugged individualism." His enterprises were the foundation upon which his sons built the Mellon organization—the soft-lighted, protectively colored empire whose control reached from bauxite deposits in South America, across to Europe, and back again across the Atlantic to the Mesabi Iron Range on the Great Lakes, with Pittsburgh as its capital. But Judge Mellon grew into senility with profit ever in his mind. He was determined to remain active when he was actually feeble.

One day while young E. W. Marland was looking through the mortgage records at the courthouse, he noticed a deference in the manner of the grey, shirt-sleeved clerk as he set out some books for an old visitor. The old visitor carried a neatly sheathed umbrella and wore a long black coat. He laid his hat down carefully, then began to fumble through the records with chalky white hands that trembled slightly as he wetted his thumb before turning each page.

"Something came over me," E. W. said. "Here was the great Judge Thomas Mellon looking through the tax books for delinquent taxes—the great banker worth millions, maybe, still trying to make money. I closed my record book and left. The image of that fumbling old man with that eager, grim look in his face will stay with me forever."

When it was suggested that he himself had been up to the same thing, he said, "Oh, no. I had legitimate business there. I was working on mortgages. Besides, that's not the only time I saw Judge Mellon. He used to attend the sheriff's sales."

E. W. was a spender, and he often spent money which he needed for necessities drinking with friends in the bars of Pittsburgh. Making an impression was part of the very nature of the money-maker of the 1890's, and E. W. never failed to assume the grand manner. Money, quite often the objective of his life, was just as often scorned and made to appear unimportant through display of generosity. He used champagne as a symbol of his grandeur, even in the days when his business was nothing more than a series of unimportant windfalls.

He had many schemes for making money. He made some of his expenses on the transfer of mortgages, one of his schemes in the early days of his practice. One day as he was walking with a friend along the street, he suddenly stopped and said, "Say, come up to the courthouse with me. I want to show you something."

He ran his finger down the listings of the mortgages until he came to the name Hostetter as mortgagee. "Look," he said, "here's old Doc Hostetter's estate with all this money out on loan, and more to put out. Guffey and Galey could take over many of these other loans at a cheaper rate of interest, and still make enough. They're interested in real estate, anyhow, and that way they can keep their money working."

According to his friend, he remained there studying the mortgage record.

This particular plan proved profitable to him. He had always felt an admiration for Dr. Hostetter because of the stories he had heard during his extreme youth. The doctor at one stage, about the time of E. W.'s birth, was almost a hero in Pittsburgh— at least the Pittsburgh *Gazette* proclaimed him one, and the independent oil refiners thought of him as a Moses.

John D. Rockefeller had built his great monopoly, the Standard Oil Company of Ohio, on the control of refineries and rail transportation. The city of Pittsburgh had suffered through the understanding between the Standard Oil Company and the Pennsylvania Railroad, much as it had suffered through the rivalry of Cleveland, Ohio. The *Gazette* had been bitter about the treatment which the Standard and the Pennsylvania Railroad had given to Pittsburgh. It pointed out that Cleveland, 150 miles from production, had to bring crude oil that distance, then ship the refined oil 750 miles to the coast, while Pittsburgh, only sixty miles from production, had to ship the refined oil only 350 miles. But Pennsylvania oil at Pittsburgh's door went to Cleveland to be refined, and as a result Cleveland could furnish two-fifths of the entire export of refined oil from the United States. The city's injured pride seemed more effective than the discomfort of the independent refineries of Pittsburgh.

Dr. Hostetter had bought oil production in Butler County from the wealth he had made from Hostetter Bitters, and planned to bring oil to Pittsburgh for refining. He laid a three-inch pipe line of 3,500-barrel capacity from the oil regions to the city, with the idea of having the Baltimore and Ohio Railroad carry the refined product, chiefly kerosene, to the markets in the East.

When his workmen got to a branch of the Pennsylvania Railroad they ran into trouble. The railroad men tore up their pipe, which had been laid under the roadbed. The Hostetter workmen laid it again, and again it was torn out. Then there was warfare of the stick, shovel, and gun type, common enough at the time but nevertheless disturbing to its witnesses.

Hostetter lodged a protest with the state of Pennsylvania, then built on toward Pittsburgh, leaving the gap at the roadbed. When his workmen came to another Pennsylvania roadbed, they ran the pipe along a creek and through a culvert. This brought an armed force of roughnecks paid by the railroad, and they were met by a like armed force paid by Hostetter. They bluffed and called out obscenities to each other. The pipe was not relaid.

The people of Pittsburgh, except those refiners affiliated with Standard, were furious, but their hero had to lease his pipe line to Benson, Hopkins, and McKelvy, who took the oil to the first gap by way of the pipe line, then had it hauled over the roadbed, piping it on the other side to Pittsburgh.

When later the Standard and the Pennsylvania had a disagreement over the Pennsylvania's Empire Pipe Line (the people called it the "battle of the giants"), Hostetter was able to sell his Conduit Pipe Line to Standard for a fair price. This was after Standard had laid a parallel pipe line to serve its refineries.

E. W. had heard much of the claw-and-fang battles among the exploiters of the continent, and this story he remembered well because it was a part of the story of Pittsburgh, and because it had moved his father to bitter pronouncements. He was proud of a connection, even a remote one, with Hostetter.

His work in the field, checking and appraising coal lands for Guffey and Galey, didn't take much of his time. He had an eye out constantly for new possibilities. Every morning he rode to his office on the street railway; when not making plans for profit, he amused himself by reading the cards advertising a diversity of things which were placed between the roof and the windows of the car. They began to worry him. They had the respectable stiffness and superfluity of a Victorian guest room, and he began to wonder if they might not be made more effective.

He developed a new interest in the people who swayed so glumly along the curving, rasping line. He noted, by watching people climb aboard and settle themselves in their seats, that scarcely anyone noticed the cards, but spent the time talking desultorily, reading the paper or gazing listlessly out of the windows on the smoke-smudged houses. He thought that if color and gaiety were ever effective in attracting people's attention they certainly ought to be effective in Pittsburgh on dreary, sun-obscured mornings.

Back in his room, he experimented with lively jingles and phrases. He wanted color, friendliness, and confidential optimism somehow to speak from his cards and inspire in the observer a sense of self-importance and dignity.

Several mornings later, a confused playboy climbed aboard the streetcar. His top hat was at a rakish angle, and he had difficulty with his cane. His smile was vacuous, but his spirit of friendliness was insuppressible. He was extravagantly gallant to the women and Chesterfieldian in his attitude towards the men. The atmosphere was changed upon his entrance. Raw-handed Irish domestics giggled and hid their mouths with their hands, slightly uncomfortable Slovak workmen brightened and looked knowingly at each other, and others put aside their papers to smile indulgently. Even an old bluenose in the back of the car let his face crack into a smile. This incident confirmed E. W.'s theories on advertising.

It seemed to him that most advertising was aimed at the silk-clad ladies who were driven to the stores in their carriages and who diligently read *Godey's Lady's Book*. It was designed to appeal to gentlemen from the Oil Exchange, the business offices, and board rooms. It was stiff and monotonously correct, illustrated with ladies, wasp-waisted and wearing expensive stoles, and with men, correct and dignified in coats fastened by a single button just under the huge knot of their cravats.

This, he reasoned, was class appeal. These people, his fellow passengers, bought things, too. Why not flatter them as well as appeal to the snobbishness of the dollar-chivalry? In spite of all the talk of "independence," he believed the word couldn't be stretched to cover anything more than the political fact. In the dollar-stratification, each class imitated the class above it, and the highest imitated the patricians of England. He wanted no better authority than his father for this observation. But he also believed that in the substrata of America hope had displaced the resignation of the English system. Therefore, it seemed to him that flattery could be applied effectively to all classes in America: flattery, solicitous good humor, and histrionic benevolence, with the constant intimation behind all appeals that "you also can attain this or that"—this or that which once might have seemed to be a prerogative of ladies in carriages and of gentlemen in high-button coats and large cravats.

He thought all day in his office about the "genial clubman," and about the effect he had had on the people of the railway car. By the time he got to his room that night ideas were in flood. He devised cards with color and light and created bright jingles that flattered all potential buyers of a varied merchandise. He attempted to retain the dignity of the old cards but relaxed the stiffness and made the appeal universal.

The profit from his cards was satisfactory and gave him freedom to work out some of his more important plans.

He was interested in children, not as one might be who had

experienced a hard childhood and knew something of children's frustrations and desires in a home where fundamental necessities were of first importance, but with a poetic interest. For a Pittsburgh daily he wrote a column of jingles and fairy stories. But he shrank from being associated with such unbusinesslike folderol. Although his fairy stories were anonymous, he had real fear that friends and acquaintances would discover his apostasy and think of him as unstable. He continually cautioned his sister Ignatia, who knew about these little stories and rhymes, to keep the secret.

He spent some time in Harrisburg, Philadelphia, and New York. The state government at Harrisburg in those days was a likely place for an ambitious young promoter. The politics of Harrisburg and Philadelphia was practical and effective, and a young man who had been taught to live according to the precepts of Christianity and the ways of a gentleman, and had been taught to revere the Constitution and the law soon discovered that, for the purpose of getting along in the world, one took advantage of the carelessness of the people who were so occupied with the exploitation of the continent that they felt no immediate need for standing guard over their rights. Representatives were elected with spasmodic emotion, then left to their own devices in the pursuit of their own interests.

Alfred Marland had been a member of the Pennsylvania legislature. Through his father E. W. had met other legislators, some of whom were of aid to him.

Sam Collins, Sr., was one of these. He had been in the state legislature with Alfred Marland and was one of those canny people who become unit leaders in one or another of the great political machines. He was "street smart." He was genial but he could be stern when it was necessary to "keep the boys in line." Above all he was goodhearted, Irish, and influential in the ward politics of Philadelphia. He never lacked a political job for himself. At the time E. W. was beginning his struggles, Collins was tipstaff at the Superior Court of Pennsylvania.

There seemed to be a bond between him and E. W., even though he was more nearly Alfred's age than E. W.'s, and he often advanced money to the young man and put him in the way of deals that had promotional value.

They often met at Steele's in Philadelphia. The smoke from their expensive cigars would fill the room as they drank and talked. Several of Sam Collins' friends and satellites might be present. As the little company became warmed and mellowed, Sam would recite poetry. He liked Bret Harte, but the poem for which the company called most frequently was Robert Burns's "Holy Willie's Prayer." Sam would oblige with pleasure. His rendition was engaging and in the proper dialect, and his manner seemed to please as much as the poem.

The poetry of Burns seemed to express for E. W. and other young men their disturbed, unsure reaction to the severe, thin-lipped and fist-hammering certainties of the ministers of Christianity. As E. W. grew more and more interested in simple people, he began to feel that their faith was imposed upon for the benefit of the materially more favored.

Sitting at a table at Steele's with glass in hand, he felt that Holy Willie was expressing through the histrionics of Sam Collins that which he and his friends were beginning to assert: that the stars of salvation, already sufficiently bright, must be lowered so as to give earth-stained man confidence in his ability eventually to touch them.

His philosophy, never quite expressed, was that any man not inherently criminal can be a good citizen if he is allowed material security and hope. If a man has nothing to lose in the way of property and must be ever fearful of his material security, and if he is spiritually without hope, then he is dangerous to any established order. The seeds of this philosophy first began to burst when he read Spencer in the poor little room under the stairs in Diamond Street. They were nurtured in the Rabelaisian freedom of Steele's, where Sam Collins' Burns could both fire young manhood and vindicate doubting. E. W. rebelled against the two-plus-two precision in religion as well as in business; he wanted something more romantic, and being naturally religious he set out to bridge the canyon between his home training and the facts which faced him on the streets of Pittsburgh and in its offices. Virtue seemed to be based upon wealth. The dollar-princes seemed to be able to keep an old-fashioned God locked up in the proper room upstairs, away from the brawling of the public rooms below, and they would go up to Him with bowed heads and open purses on His day.

Though E. W. had a deep religious feeling, he was not concerned about walking in the approval of God. He formed his own pattern for action and assumed that God would have no hesitancy in approving it since it was based on the well-being of Charlie, John, and Mary, the common people.

He lacked interest in the theories of Karl Marx and thought of him as a bitter, frustrated little German who wanted to give the underdog control of the machine civilization through revolution. Since this bloody theory didn't fit in with Alfred's idea of the gentleman's responsibility, E. W. also refused to entertain the idea. With other Pittsburghers of established position, he considered such wild and bloodthirsty madness unworthy of serious thought.

He chose to follow Herbert Spencer. He could understand him. He read and digested Spencer as he waited in the little under-the-stairs office. He had adopted Spencer and therefore he intended to defend him.

3

THERE OCCURRED in 1895, when E. W. had been out of law school two years, an opportunity for him to get into the oil business. One of the great but ephemeral booms of the oil industry came right to the city limits of Pittsburgh.

From 1891 through the panic years of 1893 and 1894, the production of oil in Pennsylvania and in the Lima–Indiana field had dropped to something like thirty-six million barrels, and just before the boom in the spring of 1895, to only about thirty million barrels. World demand had not only continued but had grown, and the domestic demand was growing despite the depression, the unfavorable trade relations of the United States, and the lack of gold. American oil had been lighting the world for twenty years with its chief product, kerosene. Oil stoves were becoming popular, and gasoline was in incipient demand.

The price of oil went to $2.70 a barrel. The streets of Pittsburgh became crowded, and the hotels jammed. The speculators overflowed the Oil Exchange into the street; leases were taken around the city. The derrick for a wildcat well went up at the city limits. Old wells were drilled deeper, and wildcat money was easy to obtain. Even the small pumper of five barrels a day became interesting. The Standard Oil Company was leasing and buying land in Pennsylvania, West Virginia, and Tennessee. E. W.'s old school at Rugby was the center of a Standard lease.

E. W. might have begun his life's work here when oil came to the very door of his city. But the days of building a refinery were gone. In his boyhood, a refinery could be set up with quite small capital, and this fact not only hastened the setting up of refineries, but also hastened the absorption of them by the Standard Oil Company. By the time he was a young promoter, Standard did 82 per cent of the refining business of the country, though earlier, just after Standard had completed its organization, as much as 90 per cent. If he had been interested in oil at this time, he might have bought acreage and production for the Standard, as he bought coal for Guffey and Galey.

But he had been taught to believe that the Standard Oil Company, with its rate understanding with the railroads, had done great harm to his home city. He could remember that his father had praised a James H. Hopkins who had offered a legislative bill designed to regulate interstate commerce, along with a resolution for an inquiry into railroad practices concerning rates and rebates. The Standard Oil Company had stopped such nonsense. E. W. held in contempt those who lent themselves, or sold themselves, to the Standard as tools. But he did not criticize the Standard's "guidance" of the federal government. Perhaps what he learned at Steele's and at Harrisburg prejudiced him against the elected representatives of the people.

The oil boom was ephemeral. In June, oil was down to $1.85, but it struck no depression bottom. It remained steady because the Standard continued buying to encourage the production needed to supply the world demand and to compete with the Nobel brothers of the Baku field on the Caspian Sea. Prospecting and producing continued, for interest in oil remained alive, if not frenzied. But E. W. was interested in cabbages at this time.

John G. "Jack" McCaskey was another young promoter of Pittsburgh. Those who knew him said that he would promote anything. About this time he was promoting a certain type of sauerkraut from New York state. He would carry jars of it around to the grocers, insist that they taste it, then talk fast about the soil in which the cabbages had been grown, and about the special minerals that had been found in that particular soil and nowhere else in the whole world. He would have been a perfect peddler of Seneca Oil, the panacea peddled by John D. Rockefeller's father, had he lived forty or fifty years earlier.

His volume of sales depended upon his daily efforts to keep the growers convinced that his sauerkraut did have some special virtue.

One day he talked with E. W. about his product. He said, "If I had the money, I could make big money out of this."

E. W. thought for a minute, then said, "Say, you don't need money. You'd better get a corner on the cabbage up there. You know that when others see your success they'll make kraut from the same cabbage and undersell you. Don't you see?"

E. W. drew up a contract for an option between McCaskey and the farmers of Dutchess County, New York. Naturally the contract favored McCaskey. Soon "Dutchess Sauerkraut" was selling like the well-pushed product it was.

E. W. was often sent by Guffey and Galey to check coal deposits, for which he had the assistance of John Hosack, an able engineer of the Pittsburgh and West Virginia Coal Company, one of E. W.'s promotions.

James M. Guffey and John H. Galey were promoters with money ready for either oil or coal. They later financed Anthony F. Lucas, who brought in the Spindletop well on the Gulf Coast of Texas. When this venture got too big for them, they went to the Mellons, who immediately got control. The company carried Guffey's name for a while, but it was later dropped and the Gulf Oil Company was formed by the Mellons. Guffey had a claim against them which was later adjudicated—he claimed that the Mellons had squeezed him out.

When E. W. spotted a coal opening, or "farmer's bank," no matter how uncommunicative or suspicious the farmer-owner might be, he seems to have had little trouble investigating. "He poked around all over the place. He used to crawl into coal openings on his belly," said Sam Collins, Jr.

The farmers E. W. dealt with were the descendants of Scotch-Irish and German settlers who had moved westward to secure their independence, not only from England and Germany, respectively, but from the proprietors and the patrician-dominated areas of the East. They had their homesteads along the Allegheny and Monongahela rivers and Oil Creek. They were as keen for profit as the coal and oil men. While E. W. had sympathy for the workingman of Pittsburgh and gave him every chance to realize the full value of his labor or his property, he mentioned the independent farmers of western Pennsylvania and West Virginia with a smile. "They were nobody's fools," he said. "They made fools of us sometimes."

Then about the end of the century, the Mellons, bankers of the West, who had been watching the manipulations of the great bankers of the East, apparently decided to do with regional coal what John D. Rockefeller had done with oil refining and transportation. Somehow, and for some reason not quite clear when considered in the light of the public good, the federal government decided to take over the Monongahela Navigation Company, to make the river more navigable for coal and to do away with tolls. This was said to be a Union Trust promotion, and since Andrew Mellon headed the Union Trust, it was therefore a Mellon promotion. The Congressional delegation from Pittsburgh, with the aid of a Senatorial backer, achieved the federal action.

"There were periodic flurries in coal," said E. W. "But this was a big flurry."

Andrew Mellon and his associates (the important one being George I. Whitney of the brokerage house of Whitney & Stephenson of Pittsburgh) sent their agents out to buy coal lands along the Monongahela. Speculators haggled with farmers, and farmers left their plows and went into the business of speculation, until thousands of acres had changed hands, sold, resold, and sold again. "The valley went plumb crazy," said an old timer. This flurry in coal was not as great or extensive as the oil frenzy of the early 1860's; certainly it didn't last as long.

The discovery on Lake Superior of a mountain of haematite, which had been deposited in an old lake basin and subsequently covered with glacial drift, seemed to be another gesture of aid by Nature to the American dollar-prince in realizing his dreams.

32

This drift-covered deposit, the men of the age felt certain, had waited until man was ready for it—like the oil of Oil Creek and the gold of the Yukon River region—and its discovery came in a time of victory in war and of the heady realization that England was no longer the only Anglo-Saxon power. Hopes seemed to be high after the depression of 1893-97.

The Mellon-Whitney organization was completed in the autumn of 1899, and about 1900 E. W. became general counsel for his own promotion, The Pittsburgh Securities and Guaranty Company. He moved from his under-the-stairs office when his promotions took on dignity and importance, first to the Frick Building, then to the Farmer's National Bank Building.

One day a man named McDowell came from Montana to see him. He visited the plush offices but was told that E. W. was in New York, perhaps at the Waldorf-Astoria. McDowell put in a long-distance call, saying that he was very anxious to get in touch with Mr. E. W. Marland of Pittsburgh. The call buzzed into the ear of a lone red-headed operator at the Waldorf, and the people sitting about heard her say, "I'll locate him, sir. He's got to be at the Waldorf. Everybody from Pittsburgh always comes to the Waldorf."

McDowell was representing a Mr. Raines who had twenty acres of copper land, a quartz claim. When E. W. left the telephone, he got in touch with his friend in New York, Gene Waldo, and told him of his idea. They would take an option on the Raines claim, then raise the money and buy it, work it if necessary, or sell to H. H. Rogers and Senator William Andrews Clark, of Montana.

Gene Waldo put up seven thousand dollars for the copper venture. Guffey and Galey put up some money, and E. W., of course, was counted in, but for an unknown amount.

The Raines twenty acres of copper were drained by the Silver Bow River of Montana. North of the acreage was a similar twenty acres owned by the Boston-Montana syndicate, and bordering both units were five acres owned by Frederick Augustus Heinze. Heinze, the political boss of Butte, Montana, was mentioned with H. H. Rogers, William Rockefeller, and

33

Senator Clark as being associated in a copper combination, and subsequently became one of the principal figures in the struggle for control of American copper.

Everything ready, E. W. and his associates began operations. They soon discovered that whatever copper had lain under the Raines claim had previously been exploited by way of a shaft which had its opening outside the Raines boundary.

"We never knew," said Gene, "when or how this had come about, or by whom the shaft had been operated. We just looked sheepishly at each other and smiled. We only knew that there was no copper under the Raines claim, or under the Heinze land, either, for that matter. As I say, we just looked sheepishly at each other. You know how E. W. always grunts when he is uncomfortable? Well, he smiled and grunted. I don't know how much he lost on the deal, but I can tell you it was a tight smile that I smiled over my big—in those days—seven thousand dollars."

But it was a period of optimism and people believed in everything; there was so much happening. Being pessimistic was like being unpatriotic.

The nights were too long for E. W. He was in a fever of anxiety to realize his dreams before something happened—say, the world coming to an end. He felt it was luck that he happened to be in his office one morning when a lawyer acquaintance came in. It was during the period of the Mellon consolidation and the United States Steel activity. The young lawyer had been approached by one of his clients for advice about an option on six thousand acres of coal lands. He thought that E. W. might know the right people to deal with.

After the lawyer had gone, E. W. sat long and studied the leases. He found them on the regional map. The acreage was scattered. Coal deposits in the Pittsburgh area were extensive, and, like all natural resources, the most accessible had been exploited first to supply the industries of the growing city. E. W.'s stubby finger slid from one spot to another on the map before him—spots indicating deposits that might be of special interest now, during the postwar, post-depression flurry in coal.

Before the extensive development of land transportation, coal deposits, navigable rivers, and harbors had determined the location and growth of industrial enterprises and of civilization. Coal had revolutionized industry in England in the seventeenth and eighteenth centuries. And when deposits were found on the new continent, competitive industrialism in America was made possible, once colonial status and its restrictions on trade and industry were shattered by the Revolutionary War. The coal deposits along the Allegheny, the Monongahela, and the Ohio rivers were at least as important as the rivers themselves in the development, though not in the establishment, of Pittsburgh.

E. W. spent some time tracing on his regional map the coal deposits which had been overlooked or had been less accessible in the first growth of industry in Pittsburgh. Perhaps they had been made more valuable by the extension of the city and increased industrial activity. He believed that whatever the Mellon and the United States Steel people did not control in the way of deposits, they might want. He placed the options carefully in his safe, then floated out of his office in a dream, taking his marked regional map with him.

He got his aneroid barometer and other instruments in which he had faith and set out to examine the deposits. He found them; they really existed. Some of them, according to his judgment, were not workable with profit, but almost any coal deposit at that time would have value, even if one group of enterprisers merely held it from others.

Back at the office he wrote to Mark Hanna's secretary about the leases, but the secretary replied that Mark Hanna wanted thirty thousand acres, and would take the acreage at $6.00 an acre if E. W. could get twenty-four thousand acres to go with it.

This was a challenge, and his imagination almost crackled as his self-importance was fired. Mark Hanna of Cleveland was one of the big boys, certainly. He was both a dollar-prince and a political power—everybody knew that he had been the power behind McKinley, newly elected for his second term.

E. W. knew the coal deposits around Pittsburgh, east, south, and across the line in West Virginia, so it didn't take him long to get options on thirty thousand acres of coal lands for Mark Hanna. The deal was consummated, and he received a check in the amount of $180,000. He kept $5,000 for his services and also shared in the profits, which were considerable.

This was the biggest deal to date. He was in high excitement. He put in a call to Gene Waldo in New York and urged him to come to Pittsburgh immediately. He was peremptory. "Never mind," he answered to Gene's request for information, "just get out here."

Gene was also a habitué of Steele's and he and E. W. had met there. He had been born in New York, where he had been brought up. Like E. W., he had attended private school, but after his father's death he had entered public school with grave doubts on the part of his mother. His home training in religion had been much like E. W.'s in Pittsburgh, though he was a Baptist and E. W. was an Episcopalian.

When Gene arrived in Pittsburgh, E. W. said, "Come on. We're gonna make some money."

When he opened his safe and got out the maps, Gene could see that he had drawn little circles here and there. He pushed them toward Gene.

"Know what those circles are for?" he said mysteriously. "Well, I'm gonna let you in on a deal. You're gonna help me get some options on some coal land. Put in something if you want to, but I can handle it."

He smoothed the maps with his hand, then said, "I'll tell you what I want you to do. I want you to introduce me to some of the big steel people. I want you to introduce me to Judge Gary. You know Alex Peacock, don't you?"

"Sure, but—"

"You've been talking about knowing these big men, now let's see what you can do."

Gene looked at the map. It looked like a medical survey map upon which plague spots had been encircled and colored red. The encircled areas represented isolated leases upon which E. W. had already taken options, or upon which he desired to take options, the whole representing thousands of acres.

They drove out over the hills and got options wherever they could get them. They talked with stubborn farmers, whose suspicion and cupidity were immediately aroused when they saw E. W.'s thoroughbred horse and shiny carriage. Gene's special brand of geniality was often necessary to offset E. W.'s dignity. Gene's business good humor had been used so much that it seemed to be a part of his character.

When they finally had their leases ready, Alex Peacock introduced them to Judge Elbert H. Gary, the head of U. S. Steel. He was polite but noncommittal. The young men thought that perhaps they had impressed him.

They worked with nervous enthusiasm, and very likely spent some of the expected profits, but in the end they lost their options through expiration, and with the expiration of the options went E. W.'s recent windfall. He was broke again.

In their innocence they had laid their cards upon the table, and their optioned deposits later came under the control of the great combinations.

E. W.'s vanity and optimism gave him little time for denunciation or indulgence in injured innocence. He was soon lost in the next scheme.

He was arriving, despite his setback, and he could live now in better harmony with his inherent dignity. As general counsel for the Pittsburgh Securities and Guaranty Company, he told the company what it could do and what it could not do to remain within the law, even though the law as written was not necessarily the criterion. His job was often a matter of finding ways to escape the vigilance of the law's guardians, or finding flaws in the law's fabric where threads were missing. While some of the wavering courts which interpreted laws in favor of the dollar-princes were not necessarily sympathetic to such insignificant enterprises as the Pittsburgh Securities and Guaranty Company, the young counsel could always beckon his company to come under the protection of court decisions where some of the big boys had gained their contentions.

E. W. later became president of the Pittsburgh Securities and Guaranty Company, and served as its president until its disintegration about 1904. It seemed to have been one of his glowing ideas. One of many enterprises that sprang up after the Spanish-American War, it was, perhaps, a fungus growth on the drenched prairie of business optimism. The company offices were at 224 Fourth Avenue in Pittsburgh, and there E. W. had offices that befitted a corporation president.

He was now able to live in a manner for which he had at least part of the money. He met powerful men in the business world and spent long vacations with his friend Gene in New York and at the many Eastern resorts. Pittsburghers were very fond of Atlantic City, where many of them went to spend their money and parade as Americans of importance.

In Atlantic City, E. W. found gaiety and freedom from his Pittsburgh conscience, which condoned no idleness or playing. In Pittsburgh, as in other communities of the United States, making money seemed to be one of the Christian obligations.

4   Gene and E. W. had spent some of their pleasantest hours in New York with actresses who were much gayer than the young ladies of Pittsburgh.

E. W. liked the jolly, witty, sparkling girls best, and he found them among the chorus girls of New York. They were ever ready to play and eat, and they could make one feel important through their "ah's" and "oh's" when one ordered champagne. Their eternal hopefulness of gifts gave them a vivacity which inspired one to greater lavishness.

Women never seemed to be very important in his life, either in his youth or during the time of his greatest glory. He seldom spoke of them in connection with romance. He spoke only in romantic memory of "a girl in Memphis."

But later in life, in advanced maturity, he clung to them desperately. The hedonist would have youth and beauty at an age when the shirt-sleeved boys and the still-faced boys were beginning to make friends with God, fearfully and seriously. When he had youth himself, however, women seemed to be of little importance to him. Even later, when he became very wealthy, he was much less sportive than most men in his position. However, he did have an academic interest in their economic and political position. He had a deep feeling for the underdog, and he might have considered women as belonging to that category.

He was short and showed stockiness even before he was graduated by Michigan, but he seemed to fascinate almost everyone he met because of his cocksureness about his own future. It was more than the cocky attitude of a small man; it was more a convincing air of self-importance, nurtured by energy. People took him at face value.

He had a youthful optimism which was much more than a reflection of the background of the time. Optimism, if it is not foolish, is ever attractive to people of prosaic habits of thought, and if it is backed by energy, then it becomes inspirational. Energy in achievement is possibly of more importance than inherent ability. And anyone who could play for big stakes and lose gracefully, even in the days of exhibitionist generosity, was fascinating. By his conscious actions he would be recapitulating the very essence of his being, appealing to sympathy and vicarious interest as fundamental and as universal as sex and murder, since from conception to death one exists through chance.

He seemed to appeal to women, and he must have received great satisfaction from the admiration of lowly little creatures who believed him to be all-powerful and miraculously wealthy.

It was coal that had his full attention at this time. He was constantly studying and applying the latest theories concerning its deposition and its nature. He was becoming a self-taught geologist. He had begun to base his search on geology, and he was coming to the conclusion that the Pittsburgh Vein must outcrop somewhere in the West Virginia Panhandle. His optimism and his supreme confidence in his own conclusions caused him to concentrate his search for unexplored coal deposits in West Virginia. He dreamed of this discovery as any daydreamer might dream of personal heroism. The dream was not only recurring, it existed in the back of his mind, ready to come upstage in his consciousness at any moment.

He had given a champagne party for Gene Waldo and his wife, Helen, on one of their visits to Pittsburgh. There had been a mild rivalry between Gene and E. W. over Helen, an actress, and Gene had won her. E. W.'s entertainment in the grand manner was even more lavish than usual, for Helen's pleasure and admiration.

It was early in the morning when Gene and Helen arrived at their hotel. Gene had scarcely got to sleep, it seemed to him, when E. W. came into the room stealthily and poked him in the ribs. When Gene finally got his eyes focused, E. W. whispered, "Sh-h-h, don't wake Helen. Get dressed."

"Wha-wh-at?"

"Get dressed. I'll wait for you downstairs."

"What for?"

"Never mind. Get dressed—hurry!"

"Well, what the hell!" E. W. put his fingers to his lips and left the room.

When Gene came downstairs he was too sleepy to ask questions, but meekly followed E. W. out into the street. E. W. was in a characteristic mood; under the influence of elation and self-satisfaction he became uncommunicative and domineering, producing an atmosphere of mystery.

E. W. had two tickets to a little station on the Cleveland-Pittsburgh Division Railroad that hugged the bend of the Ohio River and ran down the Ohio side. When they got aboard, the fog followed them inside, in sudden, eager whisps. There were a few drowsy passengers, some of them with dinner pails.

They stopped for some time at East Liverpool, Ohio, then again at Wellsville. When E. W. recognized the tiny Jeremy Run, he punched the sleeping Gene into action, and they only just had time to leap off before the train started again.

E. W. led the way to the edge of the Ohio. Gene slipped down the low bank. He could feel the presence of the river in the fog. "It seemed sinister in the fog," he said, "and E. W.'s plans seemed more and more mysterious."

E. W. felt for a chain attached to a stump, and when he found it, he drew a boat up to the bank and they climbed aboard. They rowed silently across the river. The current, not noticeable from the bank, seemed swift and menacing in the woolly darkness.

On the West Virginia side they tied the boat to a stump, then scrambled up the bank and felt their way to a farm. E. W. disappeared into the barn and came out leading a horse. The rising sun was making the fog milky, and in its light Gene watched E. W. harness the horse, which snorted and looked around at them, shivering when the harness settled about him.

"What's his name? Got a mean eye," said Gene.

"Mack. I paid five hundred for 'im."

"Looks mean."

At another time E. W. would have talked with pride of the virtues of Mack, making Gene feel that he really should know more about horses, but now he looked up through a hole in the fog at a spot on a high ridge where an early morning sunray played. "That's the 'Bulger,' " he said. "We're on the west side of it. They say there is no coal worth while on this side. We'll see."

The "Bulger" is a topographic high that runs from the Ohio River across from East Liverpool, Ohio, in a southwesterly direction to the Ohio River at New Cumberland, West Virginia, where the river changes direction and runs south. It is the backbone of the Grant district of Hancock County of the West Virginia Panhandle. It was thought to be the natural dividing line between the coal deposits of the Pittsburgh area and other areas west of it. Especially was it believed to be the western boundary of the Pittsburgh Vein of coal. E. W., in his search for coal for Guffey and Galey, had already had some experience with the variations of elevation in a single coal vein, and with the aid of geological information had learned about the dip and strike of strata.

What he didn't know was that the topographic feature which he called the "Bulger" was actually the New Cumberland Anticline, a structural high. Had he had this light to throw on the matter, he might have been even more enthusiastic, since he then could have assumed that the "lost" Pittsburgh Vein might have "humped" with the other strata in the anticlinal fold and would appear through the erosive work of the Ohio on its southward flow, or through the erosive process of the runs that flowed into it.

But he did start his investigation at the southwest end of the New Cumberland structure, then proceeded to drive up along its western side in following the contact line between the foot of the Bulger and the alluvium of the river flood plain.

"As we drove along, Mack kept looking back at us with contempt," says Gene. "I think he had the meanest eye I ever saw on a horse." In the weird milky light of the early morning, with the sunray fingers pointing out spots here and there on the Bulger, they rocked and jolted in the buggy. E. W. would pull Mack to a stop periodically and climb up on the side of a run to poke about in a coal hole. He would take the elevation, peer about, then come back to the buggy. Wherever a run cut into the side of the Bulger, E. W. would get out and investigate. The Tomlinson River cut deep into the side of the mountain, but he was more interested in the Dry Run erosion, near Arroyo.

Soon they stopped where they could see a "farmer's bank" above them on the edge of a little run. They hitched Mack to a tree and climbed through the briars to its mouth. There was a rusted track running into it. E. W. peered into the blackness, then turned to Gene and said, "Get that aneroid out of the buggy, and I'll show you how to use it."

He had deep pleasure in his independent scientific research. He felt that he had begun to disprove some of the traditional stories and old wives' tales about coal. He felt quite scientific.

They lighted candles and walked back into the tunnel about four hundred feet. There E. W. pointed to a seam of coal about five or six feet thick. He looked at the aneroid again: "They say the Pittsburgh Vein doesn't run west of the Bulger. Now, there it is."

Gene looked closely at the seam and said, "How long has this place been abandoned?" E. W. brightened at Gene's interest. "That's it!" he said. "Not worked for a long time," and again he looked at Gene with triumph, as though he would say, "You see, the smart boys say that the Pittsburgh doesn't come west of the Bulger. This hole's been worked by farmers, but you and I know that it's the Pittsburgh."

One of the candles sputtered out as a drip from the ceiling hit it, and while E. W. was relighting it Gene turned toward the entrance and said, "I'm getting out of here. That shale's bound to be rotten."

On the way back to the buggy, E. W. was silent. Gene felt that he was disapproving of him.

"He was always looking into old mines and poking around," Gene said. "I believe I heard after I went back to New York that rotten shale had fallen on an engineer E. W. had hired— rotten shale from one of those old farmers' banks along the west side of the Bulger. I believe he was killed."

Near the north end of the Bulger the mountainsides were dotted with clay-mining holes, the clay of which was being used in East Liverpool for the making of sewer pipe and pottery, for which the town was becoming famous. The holes dotted the mountainside like the nest-holes of bank swallows. The clay was lowered to the waiting barges in little cars that were operated by cables, the loaded cars pulling the empty ones up as they themselves descended.

As they drove past one of these operations, a car came rumbling down the mountainside, and Mack's nerves could not tolerate this phenomenon. He snorted and reared, then with long jumps, as though he would outrun the buggy, he ran up the road. "E. W. tried to handle him but I think he must have got his run out of his system and just stopped," said Gene. "He wasn't really scared, he was just a devil."

It was the thing to own a fine horse in those days, and men talked of their horses as they talked about the virtues of their motorcars later. E. W. insisted on the best, not only because men were more or less identified and valued by their horses and their rigs, but also because he had an inherent love for horses. In his search for the Pittsburgh Vein, he drove the best horses he could buy and was proud of the price he had to pay for them. His high-spirited horses were not always the best in wet weather for the clay roads winding up the mountains of West Virginia, but they did much for his self-esteem.

Most of the time he was alone when he took Mack out of the stable at New Cumberland and hitched him to the fancy buggy, thinking, as he arranged the harness mechanically, of the Pittsburgh Vein and of the map showing the coal deposits of Pennsylvania and the Allegheny region.

To him the romance of romances was the story of coal. He liked to study the queer trees that had grown in the steamy air of the Carboniferous swamps, thousands and thousands of years ago. He refused to remember the number of years in the hundreds of thousands and in the millions that geologists assigned to different periods of the earth's history, because he felt that it was the clumsiest kind of guess, and he liked the romance of it unmixed with man's calculations.

This land over which he traveled in the West Virginia Panhandle had been covered by a sea or, more likely, a great swamp, steamy and fetid, where large fern trees grew and the giant Sigillaria pushed fifty feet into the air. All of these millions of trees had completed their life cycles and had fallen and had lain there for thousands of years. The swamp, which had become the graveyard for the great, queer trees and animals, had been covered by the sea again. Then hundreds of feet of sediment had been deposited upon the trees. The weight of the sediment had generated the heat and pressure that were necessary to convert the trees into the coal which men, millions of years later, were utilizing. Upon these remote processes he built his hope for power and glory.

He seemed to think that the surface indications which he sought, on the flanks of the humped Bulger and in the runs that were exposing earth's secrets through constant erosive action, were secrets known only to himself, though he had his latest geological information from the books of Sir Archibald Geikie, F.R.S., thus overlooking the fact that this scholar was obviously sharing his knowledge with the world.

He seemed by his manner, or at least he impressed his associates with such a manner, to have assumed for himself the discovery of new and delightfully romantic fields of knowledge, the contemplation of which would not only strain man's imagination but overwhelm it, like moonlight on an Alpine glacier.

Years later, when he was religiously learning the names of the strata from which he was gaining his great wealth, instructed by his geologist, Dr. Irving Perrine, at Ponca City, Oklahoma, it was to him like putting down the notes to a song he had been singing for several years, since the time when the structural history of the earth first dawned upon him.

The romance of coal grew with his knowledge of the development of the strata with which it was associated, and the little boy of Mount Washington dreamed again as he jolted over the Panhandle of West Virginia, while Mack pranced with thoroughbred delicacy, ever watchful for wind-animated papers or nerve-shattering clay cars.

E. W. was not thinking of oil at this time, if one accepts his own statements. But if one wonders why this was so, since he was so busy impatiently jerking open the gates to the fields of scientific knowledge, the answer may be found in the fact that Standard Oil's power, based upon its monopoly of oil, might have acted as a psychological deterrent to his natural interest. The great power of Standard and the awe in which its founder was held in America must have made E. W. feel small and futile, as the cold buildings of Pittsburgh had during his first years out of college. In coal he might have felt that he was not gambling with his independence, even though the origin of oil and its exploitation would have seemed much more romantic to him than the history of coal. Being a "front runner," his confidence would come with his first oil well.

Filled with the romance of earth's history and his ability to read it, not only for romantic pleasure but for the unlocking of its secret rooms of treasure, he would let Mack have his head back to the familiar stable at New Cumberland. He would mechanically unharness Mack, then row across the Ohio River and catch the train for Pittsburgh, then entrain for Philadelphia to tell Virginia Collins of his dreams.

Virginia was the daughter of Sam Collins, Sr., and a court

stenographer in Philadelphia. She had the alertness of mind and the type of wit that E. W. liked. He was attracted to sparkle and beauty in women, and in Virginia he found both. As a matter of fact, she had all the characteristics which he admired, not the least of which, naturally, was youth. He therefore loved her.

One has a tendency to write that trite phrase, "he loved her in his own way," but there seems to be little or no point in mentioning the fact, since, after all, everyone loves in his own way. If one were to say that Virginia's wit and bright spirit pleased him and that her appearance and alertness actually made brighter his self-esteem, one would be warranted in saying that his love lacked nothing that a young man's love is supposed to have when he meets the right girl.

Virginia was evidently attracted to this self-assured young man who, with his gambler's instinct, seemed to live dangerously—this young man whose presence in a small room immediately dominated the company there.

E. W. Marland and Mary Virginia Collins were married at her home in Philadelphia, November 5, 1903, in a quiet wedding.

5

E. W. KNEW of the big deal concerning the Mesabi Range at the turn of the century, when John D. Rockefeller sold his interest in the iron ore deposit, along with his Lake ore fleet, to J. Pierpont Morgan for $85,000,000. The Mesabi Range became an integrated unit in the United States Steel combination when it was formed in March, 1901.

He saw the Mellon and the Moore coal monopolies of Pittsburgh make the difference between seven and one-half cents a ton and thirty cents a ton profit. These things interested him very much. He could pick up little corners of overlooked coal —bituminous coal, since anthracite could be or had been monopolized. With his overlooked corners he could then demand his own price when the big boys needed it in their business or in their designs for victory over competitors.

There was coal all over the place, and the Mellons' 100 per cent monopoly on the Monongahela was only a monopoly as far as the river deposits were concerned. He would find the big vein west of the Bulger and then sell it to the highest bidder.

He could see that steel was the backbone of the nation's war might, as well as of its peacetime prosperity, and he knew that the nation's coal deposits were of an extent to stagger the imagination. He would find the deposits nearest the industrial centers that depended upon them, hold them until the need was greatest, then control other deposits which were now of little importance, but which would become important with industrial growth.

The Mellons could tie up Monongahela coal and the world's bauxite deposits, and United States Steel could tie up the Mesabi iron deposits, he supposed, but he felt sure that bituminous coal, like oil, could never be fully monopolized. The world was talking about the Spindletop well that had come in on the Gulf Coast in January, 1901. This well, many were saying, would break Standard's grip on the industry, its control of refining and marketing, and its understanding with the railroads. This oil, far away on the Gulf Coast, would be free. And who could say how many more wild wells would come in to break Standard's monopoly?

But even though E. W. was excited about the Spindletop well, he was too absorbed by coal to develop a desire to leave Pittsburgh.

He continued his investigations in West Virginia, pecking about in old farmers' banks, reading the stratigraphy, studying the dips of strata, taking elevations, and inspecting flood-incised fields for hints. Finally he found a farmer's bank on the Brenneman farm on the west side of the Bulger. He decided that the coal worked there must be from the middle Kittanning. He apparently worked out the westward dip of the strata which actually formed the west flank of the later recognized New Cumberland Anticline. He reasoned that the Pittsburgh Vein would be closer to the surface here owing to the erosive work done by the Ohio River.

He decided to do some testing. He made a lease with George Brenneman and got a block of leases around the Brenneman farm. Then he moved with Virginia down to Arroyo, West Virginia, and rented a big frame farmhouse from Hattie Clark.

The Ohio River runs north from its birth at Pittsburgh, which is the joining point of the Allegheny and the Monongahela, then makes an indecisive loop around the end of E. W.'s Bulger, and thereafter decisively flows south to form the boundary between the West Virginia Panhandle and Ohio. Along the

West Virginia side there is a narrow shelf of ancient flood plain which runs up to the foot of the Bulger. On the west flank of the Bulger, running down onto the old flood plain, is the Brenneman land, cut by a small run. At the source of this run, and a little up the right side of the ravine, is the old Brenneman farmer's bank.

It was here, on this nameless little run, just below the coal opening, that E. W. planned to make his test. He seemed to visualize the underground condition as being something like the "tree and well" of a meat platter, where the sauce, oozing from the meat, drains down and collects in the "well." There was the middle Kittanning coal measure and it was dipping toward the river flood plain. The run's tiny gorge below the coal measure, a topographic depression, might be a structural low or even a syncline—the subsurface "well" into which the oozings from the Kittanning coal might flow as the precious hydrocarbon. He was doing more than core boring for the Pittsburgh: he had oil in the back of his mind. Thus he gave himself two chances, based upon his geological theories, to make a strike.

E. W. had read all the geology which he could come by. Like many another of the Age of Freedom, he had intense confidence in the new knowledge and the new inventions of science. He used all the instruments that were available to him and became interested in every instrument usable in geology. In harmony with the age, he was ready to pick up new inventions and consider the possibilities for profit in them. But still he was serious when he asked Margaret Brenneman to drive the stake for the location of the bore, as a gambler might pass the dice to an attractive girl standing by him at the gaming table.

His location was about one hundred feet down the flank of the New Cumberland Anticline, but it is not likely that he knew much about the structure; he knew about the dip of the coal beds, and he expected to find the Pittsburgh closer to the surface here, since the Ohio River had already done most of the work through its erosive processes. This location would fit in well with his theories on the accumulation of hydrocarbons. He believed that oil was the "drippings" from the coal beds, hence would be found somewhere below it, and that gas had the same source. He later sought oil in synclines and drilled in topographic depressions.

He found a local man by the name of Wilkinson, owner of an old Star drilling rig, with whom he made a deal to drill a core well. He watched the operation intently. His attitude was ever that of the gambler waiting for the wheel to stop. He could not leave the complaining, clanking drilling outfit for long at a time; the clank of the tools was music to him and held him as drumbeats hold the primitive worshipper.

His optimism was infectious. He was pleasant and genial, which made him popular with the people of Arroyo, even though their conservatism was disturbed when he acted with characteristic lavishness. They adjudged him a "plunger" and a "sport." One day he came up to the Brenneman house carrying a pie which Virginia had baked. He carried it carefully on a Haviland china plate, and when Margaret Brenneman came to the door, he handed it to her, saying, "Save it for the papa," which amused her very much.

One morning when E. W. came up to the well, Wilkinson looked at him significantly but said nothing. Down to 738 feet, crewmen had kept the log very carefully. The bit had gone through three feet of Lower Kittanning coal at 38 feet, five feet of Clarion coal at 155 feet, and six feet of coal at 231 feet. Then at 564 feet it had plunged into two feet of Squaw sandstone, and when they pulled it out it was stained with oil. Now this morning at 738 feet, they were eight feet into the Berea sandstone. E. W. and the crew sensed something.

They watched as Wilkinson pulled the tools. They examined the bit very carefully; they smelled of it and rubbed their fingers on it, then they rubbed thumb and forefinger together to get the "feel." It was oil and they were at the right depth for possibilities, so Wilkinson began drilling again. E. W. walked up to the Brenneman house to tell Margaret that he had decided to drill an oil well.

When Wilkinson had drilled nine feet deeper into the Berea, at 747 feet, he pulled the tools again. The oil began to well after they loosened the sand with nitroglycerin. There wasn't much pressure, but the oil welled lazily. It oozed over the lip and began to follow the little run down through the orchard toward the Ohio.

"When they shot the well," said Margaret, "it swished up higher than the derrick. Then you know how it sprays when the wind catches it? I tell you it got on everything, on the crib, and the chickens, and all!"

Young John Brenneman watched the oil spray above the derrick and drench the trees along the mountainside. In his joy he caught a calf by the tail, whirled with it like an athlete with a hammer, then threw it over the fence, saying, "There, you sonofabitch! I'll never work for you anymore."

George Brenneman in his excitement tried to water the stock with a basket. "They told us to stay out of the way," said Margaret, "but we didn't have to be told."

The tinkling of the little run was smothered by its new burden now. The oil as it flowed formed into fingers of greenish black which came together in a little ravine. It crept toward the river, carrying bits of sticks and leaves. It spread out on the water of the Ohio and made it iridescent, then crested the current and rode it.

Despite the fact that E. W.'s location was far down on the flank of the New Cumberland Anticline, the striking of oil in his first well by the tinkling little run on the Brenneman farm was the blindest kind of luck. He might as well have used a witch-hazel fork or employed a spiritualist to locate his well. Even if he had known that he was on the flank of the New Cumberland Anticline, the oil deposit he punctured had nothing whatever to do with structure accumulation but was trapped by stratigraphy in what are now called "shoestring" sands. These represented the sands of an ancient Carboniferous (Pennsylvanian) river. Finding such an accumulation was like stabbing a concealed rabbit in a haystack with a harpoon.

The finding of his first oil well, then, was luck, and the details seem important because luck was ever at his shoulder in his future operations. Although he had confidence in science and adopted with faith the later geological theories of the origin and accumulation of hydrocarbons, he insisted on glossing over with romanticism whatever exactitude geology enjoyed. The closer the science came to mathematical precision, the more reluctantly he admired it and the greater the liberties he took with it.

If E. W. had been boring for the Pittsburgh formation, he made no explanation of why he had drilled on down below fair beds of coal, or of why he had not had the tools pulled when he missed the Pittsburgh where he thought he might strike it. One may assume that whether he was seeking coal or actually drilling for oil on his "drippings" theory, he immediately thought of his acreage—his five thousand acres of coal leases. He had no oil leases.

The oil could not be handled; there was not even a catchment basin, nothing. He occupied himself with helping Wilkinson get the flow shut off at the wellhead. There was a flow of 100 barrels a day, which held for a week, then increased to 225 barrels a day, until the third week, when it went back to 100 barrels. At the end of a month the well was making 75 barrels a day.

When the oil from his well reached Steubenville, Ohio, as it rode the current of the river, a cleaner and dyer named Freudenburgh saw "stuff that looked like paraffin" on the water. As he watched, it caught the light just right and there was the telltale iridescence. He waited for nothing more, but hastened up the river as fast as he could go. When he located the source of the oil near Dry Run on the West Virginia side of the river, he got across and hurriedly began making leases and recording them.

Soon others heard of the strike and came to join in the lease excitement. The fact that E. W. had no oil lease confirms his statement that he was actually boring for evidence of coal, not for oil.

He managed, however, to retain the Brenneman lease for oil, and the Buben lease, closer to East Liverpool, Ohio, higher up on the Bulger.

53

Derricks went up quickly, and soon there were other wells producing and selling to Joseph Seep, one of the Standard's pipe line representatives. Seep had a hard-headed honesty, good nature, and constant friendliness, so that he more or less personalized the Standard for many. The Standard's Eureka Pipe took the oil from the field. Naturally, there were many derricks not stained with oil, standing abandoned off the edges of the "shoestring" pool where E. W. had found his oil.

His well, or the E. W. Marland & Co. well, came in during the autumn of 1906, just forty-seven years after the Drake well, which marked the beginning of the oil age, and just five years after the Spindletop well near Beaumont, Texas, on the Gulf Coast, which had inspired E. W. and others with the hope that Standard's shadow was not long enough to cover all the oil in the United States. Standard, controlling the markets with its monopoly on refining, and on rail and pipe transportation, could be quite whimsical with "little oil men" if it chose. It was doubtful if Standard would allow one to build a pipe line to sell oil independently, and certainly Standard did not want to be disturbed by mushroom growths of local refineries of small capacity. The Standard's shadow not only covered E. W. but spread over all of New York, Pennsylvania, Kentucky, Ohio, and Indiana, thence across the continent to California, and even to the Gulf Coast, at the time E. W. stood and watched his oil flow down the nameless little run in 1906.

In December, he drilled two more wells on the Brenneman lease which made 200 and 250 barrels a day, respectively. Well No. 2 was just beyond the yard fence, slightly higher on the flank of the Bulger and near the old clay-rutted road that wriggled up the mountain. This one was so near the house that it sprayed it with oil; E. W. suggested that the Brennemans move out until they could bring it under control, but Mrs. Brenneman refused to leave her chickens.

Number 4 was a "duster." It was practically at the same elevation as No. 2, and the fact that it was dry might have told a modern geologist a significant story. E. W. noted that the wells above his locations were striking oil, so he moved to the

Buben lease, where he got gas. His well for which Margaret Brenneman had set the stake had opened the Congo oil field of West Virginia, and to him is given full credit for the discovery. Even though it was a mere spot on the map of the state, it was important. West Virginia was producing as much as twelve to thirteen million barrels of oil a year during the last years of the nineteenth century, which, for comparison's sake, was only about three million barrels less than the combined output of New York and Pennsylvania.

The discoverer was filled with emotion. When the Eureka Pipe Line Company agreed to take his oil at $1.78 a barrel, he proclaimed with feeling, "God bless the Standard!"

6 E. W. MARLAND MOVED five miles closer to East Liverpool on the Ohio side, but his explorations were still in West Virginia, on the Buben lease. He drilled more and more wells, and soon he had to have a greater outlet for his growing volume of natural gas. In East Liverpool he negotiated to sell gas to individuals and to the pottery factories, perhaps seven or eight of them. His well log near Dry Run had shown eight feet of fire clay at 46 feet, and two feet of clay at 157 feet. This clay and the surface clays were utilized by the potteries of the region.

He was interested in every detail. He watched the sweating men digging the ditch which would carry his pipe to and under the Ohio River. There was no ditching machinery then; he hired day laborers and paid them well. His pride would not have allowed him to pay small wages, even if he hadn't had a feeling for the man who worked with his hands, and even if he hadn't believed implicitly that you get more and better work, and stronger loyalty, from the payment of wages higher than the current scale. His humanity was inherent and sincere.

His fellow feeling for his workmen did not affect his small swaggerings. He dressed well, as an important man might be expected to dress, even in the field, and he enjoyed making Olympian observations.

He stood one day watching a sweating gang of laborers screwing the collars on two lengths of pipe. With the inscrutable obstinacy of inanimate things, the collars refused to be fitted. Foul, terse Anglo-Saxon words exploded from the depths of the exasperated workmen. A red-faced Irishman straightened up and wiped the sweat from his face. He spat over the edge of the ditch, then looked up insolently at E. W. and said, "Goddamit, Fat, give us a hand! We'll pay yuh as much as we pay a man."

His pipe from the Buben lease carried his gas production under the river to the Ohio side, to the potteries as well as to individuals, so he decided to get the franchise from the city of East Liverpool for gas.

He went to the mayor, who seems to have been attracted by E. W.'s youth and personality. He became friendly with the city attorney. But there was another company after the franchise, a subsidiary of the Standard, no less, The Manufacturers Light and Heat Company. E. W. conceived a plan.

He loaded his carryall with whiskey and invited the mayor and the city councilmen to a barbecue at the gas field across the river. He said that he wanted to assure them that he had sufficient pressure and volume. He drove them to the field where the barbecue had been prepared. He had plenty of Old Plantation whiskey and ale at the spot, and on the way he handed his flask about frequently, but it was never emptied. He secretly kept it filled from a jug under the seat. Since the day was cold the flask was appreciated.

At the field he ordered a shut-in gas well opened so councilmen could judge of its pressure. He had kept the well shut in several days to make certain of the proper show of wild whistling and roaring at the proper time. He made a ceremony of it. The councilmen, expectant and pleasantly warm, stood about the well as the men opened the valve. He handed the flask around again, after he had warned them to put out cigars and pipes.

The gas in its screaming escape, with its accompanying impression of an earth-shaking roar, was overwhelming. Words

57

were drowned as if they had not been spoken; no sound could live in this unearthly scream of escaping gas.

The council and their mayor were impressed. By this time they were magnifying their own official importance and their own generosity. The late afternoon was cold, but there was more passing of the inexhaustible flask. E. W. invited the officials to dinner in the sitting room of his suite at an East Liverpool hotel. His old symbol of pride and importance was there in ice-filled tubs; the champagne was guzzled like beer. After dinner the tables were arranged for poker, with bottles of Overholt placed about handily.

"Luck" went against the young oil and gas producer. As he lost steadily, it seemed that each of the other participants was winning. They started with a dollar limit, then the mayor suggested that they raise the ante to five dollars, but still E. W. lost. The next day he got his franchise.

The council was cajoled by the competing company, which had a limited franchise with the city and an exclusive one with some of the residents, but the council favored young Marland.

But there had been too much competitive drilling in the West Virginia fields. It was not long before the pressure at E. W.'s wells was weakened. His original pressure had enabled the pottery manufacturers who bought his gas to bake their wares in less time than before. The offset drilling in the fields soon reduced pressure, with the result that one day the pottery manufacturers found they had kilns of half-baked pottery on their hands. They talked of complaining to the courts, but, since reduced pressure was beyond E. W.'s control to rectify, the case was never brought.

The pottery people were more prone to sue at this time because of the national business depression. The sale of pottery had suddenly fallen off, banks began to fail, and the boom following the Spanish-American War was clearly ending. Again the United States Treasury offered bonds to increase its deposits—$150,000,000 of bonds this time. J. P. Morgan and Company got busy and prepared to handle them. John D. Rockefeller made a $10,000,000 deposit in the Union Trust

Company of New York and offered to give half his wealth to "restore the balance."

It had happened again under American optimism and enthusiasm there had been overexpansion, inflated credits, and watering of stocks. It was suggested by some that the Rooseveltian earnestness in seeking the dissolution of the trusts had undermined national confidence, and that the muckrakers had brought about lack of confidence through the disillusionment of the people.

E. W. thought such economic depressions were brought about through the indifference of the dollar-princes toward their responsibilities to the public. The reality of the national catastrophe was not missed upon him, for he lost his home in the city and watched his grandeur vanish. When Gene Waldo came to visit E. W. in the little farmhouse which he used for an office, he asked, "How you getting along?"

E. W. pointed to a bill hook on the wall by the desk. "There, on that hook, one hundred and fifty thousand dollars worth of unpaid bills."

"We drank a lot in those months of depression," said Gene. "We met in the bar of the old Henry Hotel and just sat and drank. The spirit was gone." The room was gloomy and the fog and soft coal smoke swirled at the windows and seemed intent on entering the lighted room. The gloom that surrounded the place made it snug, and there was a certain security in the very fact that they were shut in by the dullness of the smoke. There was cheer in the bottle. Shut in by the greyness they felt temporarily safe from the immaterial menace that prowled the land.

It was a terrible thing to go broke in the Age of Freedom, when wealth was everything. The Panic of 1907 was like an act of God. The world had temporarily come to an end again. His first oil well had given E. W. the independence he required. He had put behind him his promotions, his fairy stories, and his jingles, to become an oil producer. Now he had lost a million dollars and had nothing left.

He and Virginia sent their furniture into storage and went back to Pittsburgh. The city had issued certificates worth two dollars, which were honored by the street railways, but he and Sam Collins, Jr., who had lived with the Marlands in the field, walked to work to save carfare. The fine horses and specially made carriages had gone to pay debts.

E. W. sent forth a new idea for each one that met with defeat. He polished his offerings and let each one show its best face, as a shrewd grocer places the more worthy oranges in a crate of uninspiring average. He took his promoter's ideas to gamblers like himself, rather than to the still-faced boys who had such detestable ways of figuring possible profit and the interest to the penny.

E. W. didn't have a nickel, but he made a prosperous appearance. He seemed to think that if he never created a model of defeat in himself, nor allowed the crystallization of one thought of dejection, then there would be nothing to attract the attention of the old hag, Fate. His fine quality clothes wore well, and he bought a new silk hat. He also bought a new house in the Mellon-developed residential section, Squirrel Hill. He must have bought it with his dignity and self-assurance. It was another gesture to Fate, and, of course, he soon lost the house.

For the first time in his life, E. W. thought seriously about democratic government. He had voted for Theodore Roosevelt in 1904 because he was a Republican. Now, no longer a contented man with a million dollars and bright hopes for many more, E. W. was surprised and intrigued by Roosevelt's "trust busting." He felt that the dollar-princes had failed in their responsibilities to the people and deserved censure. They had even contributed to the conditions which caused his own ruin!

Roosevelt was the very spirit of America—young, optimistic, aggressive, and unaware of the stark bitterness of struggle. His shouting against the trusts, against the British, the French, and the German Empire expressed that which was in the American heart. He became the symbol of American democracy, just as his antagonist, John D. Rockefeller, became the symbol of monopoly, selfish interest, and sinister practice. The Standard Oil Company of New Jersey supplied the test case of the Prince *vs.* the People.

Roosevelt's enthusiasm stirred a nation which was quite ready to be stirred. Times were difficult and the people were in full cry before the towers of the princes, egged on by both politicians and muckrakers. The Age of Freedom was coming to an end.

It was not until much later that E. W. realized that an Age of Freedom had existed. For the first time in history, perhaps since men joined together in a herd or pack for protection, a unit of society had the freedom for which men had fought and died through the centuries—religious, social, and political freedom—and he, E. W. Marland, had been born into it.

In 1907 E. W. was thinking of ways to keep his dignity and independence until he could get back into the oil business and make another million. He projected himself beyond current difficulties by faith in the whimsicalities and lavishness of Petrolia, and by faith in the progressive development of the horseless carriage. The "auto-mobel" was already weaving in numbers up and down Fifth Avenue, and now there were no flunkeys walking in front with red flags to warn horsemen. The refineries had begun to stress the production of gasoline, the old waste which the first Standard refineries in Cleveland had allowed to float out onto the waters of the lake, where bargemen had set it afire for fun. They were now adjusting their mechanisms for its production in greater and greater quantities. Petrolia was ready to do for transportation what transportation had done for her.

E. W. had faith in the horseless carriage because, like most Americans, he had faith in mechanisms in general, in scientific inventions, and in a future glory, vague but thrilling.

In his search for some flame of hope in the cold fog of depression, he spent hours with bent, serious men, whose faces were lit with eager certainty when they showed him their crude machinery in the back room of a shack, store, or home, or in a crib room of some abandoned stable. Some worked on perpetual motion, others on engines which would receive power from the air. All they needed was money for promotion, money for the building of proper models. If they had money they could revolutionize industry.

Sometimes he went to these tinkers with ideas he had worked out during a sleepless night—complete mechanisms of fancy, of which every cell was to be replaced by the proper metal to give it structure.

His friends advanced him money to live on. Oscar Ainsley, chef at the Boyer Hotel, helped him. In the good days of E. W.'s promotions, Ainsley used to come to his office and repeat conversations which he had overheard from the big boys, with whom he was popular. He, like others, admired the atmosphere of E. W.'s office during the days of prosperity. It seemed to have the same attractiveness that smokehouses have, that clubs and bars often have, where men talk of horse racing, boxing, and baseball. There was ever an air of expectancy in the office, of things about to happen, bringing sudden profits or thrilling uncertainties.

A Mr. Kerns bought an interest in almost everything that E. W. promoted. And a man named Stevens, a retired chair manufacturer and spiritualist, encouraged him with financial assistance. E. W. had, mysteriously, some money from the Anchor Bank in Pittsburgh, and, since he had no assets, one assumes that some daring official at the bank had become intrigued by the varicolored explosion of one of his ideas.

But no opportunity arose in Pittsburgh for E. W. to get back into the oil business. He began to believe that he could realize his dreams only if he could get out of the symbolic smoke of Pittsburgh and into the sunlight of the Mid-Continent.

On the winds from the Southwest came the scent for which he quested. It came burdened with romance and the possibilities of riches, like the spice-laden breezes from the East to the captain of a lifeboat whose sunken treasure ship had left him bobbing on a limitless sea.

A far view of the new land was brought to him by his nephew, Lieutenant Franklin Rockefeller Kenney, who visited periodically on the famous Miller Brothers' 101 Ranch, near Ponca City, Oklahoma.

Part II   The Cherokee Outlet

7

FRANKLIN KENNEY was the son of E. W.'s half sister, Sara's daughter by her first marriage. Young Kenney had lived with his grandparents, E. W.'s father and mother, at Mount Washington. Since he and E. W. were about the same age, there had been much boyhood rivalry between the two.

Young Kenney had left home to join the army, and in the natural course of events took part in the Spanish-American War. After the war he was commissioned a second lieutenant in the regular army and was stationed at Fort Sill, Oklahoma. In Oklahoma he met George Miller, who introduced him to ranch life on his and his brothers' sprawling domain. The Miller Brothers' 101 Ranch was just entering the circus business. Soon the world would be plastered with its notices.

George Washington Miller, the founder of the ranch, was an old-time cowman who had brought up his three sons in the tradition of cattle and Indian leases. After his death the sons built ranch headquarters called the "White House," which seemed a brash white anomaly on the wild, limitless plains.

The brothers could not themselves fail to attract attention. Joe, George, and Zack Miller had different characteristics, but in combination they were acquisitive, lavish, generous, humane, high-spirited, and sensational, with a touch of frontier histrionics thrown in for good measure.

They were typical Southwesterners whose spirit and lavishness knew only the boundaries which their eyes recognized, the place where the earth and sky met on the Red Bed plains—a line so distant and so immaterial and so mobile that it only hinted at limitations and restrictions.

George W. Miller left some authority in the hands of his widow, and apparently Mrs. Miller liked her son George's friend, the personable army officer, Franklin Kenney. She agreed, on his suggestion, to lease certain lands of the 101 Ranch, and he communicated with his half uncle, E. W. Marland, in Pittsburgh.

E. W. was anxious to escape the smoke of Pittsburgh. He loved the comforts which Eastern industry had produced, but without money these unattainable comforts made life incredibly stark. The difference between the comforts of wealth and the discomforts of poverty were startling. For him the fog and smoke of Pittsburgh had symbolically enveloped the metallic brightness of the Age of Freedom.

He hadn't sufficient funds for streetcar transportation. How could he find sufficient funds to carry him halfway across the continent? His mind worked feverishly and schemes passed through it like lantern slides. The idea which he settled upon was one based upon the sure-fire American lure—a big name. The 101 Ranch was famous, and people had heard of the Miller Brothers' 101 Wild West Show. Perhaps the very name might coax a few dollars from the reluctant hands of people with a few dollars and a degree of optimism left over from the pre-panic days.

He and Sam Collins, Jr., walked to the offices of the Pittsburgh papers and inserted advertisements appealing to both greed and hope. E. W. had worked over the proper wording. The 101 Ranch Gas Company would drill wells on the famous 101 Ranch, out in romantic and untouched Oklahoma, land upon which the advertisers had the exclusive rights, land filled with the glorious possibilities for great riches.

They walked back on their tired feet and waited. This advertisement attracted no attention. E. W. and Sam between them couldn't even pay for the ad.

Somehow E. W. did raise some money. Perhaps his father, an old man now, doting more than ever upon his only son, gave him money, and most certainly his "angels," Ainsley, Kerns, and Stevens helped him. Perhaps also the Anchor Bank and Jack McCaskey.

At any rate, he set out for the new state and the ranch of the Miller brothers on the edge of the Red Bed plains.

As the Gothic towers of Europe loom above the cities, and the great, fire-belching chimneys loom above Pittsburgh, so do the rounded towers of the grain elevators loom above the towns of the old Cherokee Outlet, symbols of faith and progress.

There were no mountains or river gorges to claim E. W.'s attention when he descended from his coach; there were only the sky, a few buildings, and a few surprisingly fine residences. To one from Pittsburgh, the little cattle and wheat town seemed somnolent and the people passively inquisitive in their casual glances. The little town lay shining in the sun, unprotected from nature's tantrums. It was a geometrical figure, cross hatched with monotonously straight streets which terminated suddenly in a limitless plain of close-growing grass, yellow or tawny with the autumnal change or emerald green like a carpet when the winter wheat had sprouted. To the east, however, the streets stopped abruptly at the edge of the Arkansas River flood plain.

Immediately south of the little town was the Ponca Indian Reservation, where the Salt Fork of the Arkansas cut the plain with its growth of cottonwood and elm and its tangle of vines and thickets. Dotting the plain were the small houses of the Ponca, with their brush-covered structures close by.

On the banks of the Salt Fork, a short distance above the mouth, where the Osage once crossed on their way to the Salt Plains to hunt the herds of migrating buffalo, was the "White House" of the Miller Brothers' 101 Ranch. It gleamed with abruptness and inspired interest as whiteness ever does in the

Temperate Zone. It was the center of activity and stood among the other buildings like a white peacock in a flock of ducks.

Buffalo stood and looked stupidly at the passer-by through a game fence, and out on the tawny swells camels grazed, blending so perfectly in this strange habitat that they could scarcely be seen. Circus wagons stood immobilized among the manure and mud-stained workaday wagons. Along the railroad siding stood the circus cars, less gaudy than the wagons.

South of the Ponca Reservation was the reservation of the Otoe and the Missouria, and east of them, seeming by pressure toward their old home to push the Arkansas River into an unnatural and unaccustomed bend, was the old reservation of the Pawnee. North of the Pawnee and east of the Ponca and Otoe-Missouria reservations, and east of the town of Ponca, was the large reservation of the Osage, a Siouan tribe that once claimed all the land from the Arkansas River to the Missouri River, and from the Mississippi to an indefinite line on the Great Plains.

West of the town of Ponca was the old reservation of the Nez Percé. They had been brought to this restricted reservation in 1878 but had found their way back to their old hunting grounds in the north. Their land had been given to the Tonkawa, who had a strange history south of the Red River, which is the present boundary between Oklahoma and Texas.

These tribes were settled here after the treaties of 1866. This area, in the north-central and the northwestern parts of what is now Oklahoma, was called the Cherokee Outlet. It extended from the ninety-sixth meridian, which is the eastern boundary of the Osage Reservation, to the one hundredth meridian, which was the western boundary of the United States after the Spanish-American agreement of 1819. The north line was the southern boundary of the state of Kansas. From this line to the southern boundary of the Outlet was a distance of about sixty miles—the width of this great original grant to the Cherokee.

When the first Cherokee came to the region now known as the state of Arkansas, the Osage began to make war upon them and added them to their other enemies, the Pawnee and the Caddo tribes of the Red River, as well as white hunters, squat-

68

ters, and many refugees from state and federal laws. Gradually, however, the Osage were forced to yield their lands to the United States government through a series of treaties from 1808 to 1866. These lands were turned over by the government to white settlers in Missouri, Kansas, and Arkansas, and to the Cherokee and other immigrant tribes for reservations.

By the terms of the treaty between the United States and the Cherokee, the latter were to be given lands west of the Mississippi equal in area to the lands they had claimed in the states of North Carolina, Georgia, Alabama, and Tennessee. By the treaty of 1828 they were removed west of the present boundary line between Oklahoma and Arkansas, and this land, ceded by the Osage, was turned over to them.

Thus were the Cherokee given the land with an "outlet to the setting sun" which they had requested. The Creek, Seminole, and the Choctaw-Chickasaw were also given outlets to the west. This arrangement was not only the fulfillment of a promise made to them by the government, but was supposed to be of benefit to the government, since these outlets to the west would give the Indians access to the millions of buffalo that migrated from the upper Missouri and Milk rivers in the autumn to the headwaters of the Red and Brazos rivers and returned northward in the spring. Thus would the government have less responsibility for these tribes, who numbered in the thousands.

The coming of the Cherokee was a mass invasion under artificial pressure, and could result only in chaos. The wars between the Osage and the Cherokee were bloody and continual. A lone warrior was no longer safe; when the hunters set out for the upper Cimarron on their buffalo hunts they had to take their women, children, and old men along.

The Cherokee Outlet was only Cherokee in name. As far as the plains warriors and hunters were concerned, the western part belonged to them, no matter what men in Washington had willed. It was a skirmish area among the strong tribes, who continued to keep a balance there. The Cherokee wars with the Osage were restricted to another part of the Outlet, its eastern extremity, but the development of the Outlet was long delayed by the warfare prevailing in both its eastern and western parts.

After the Civil War, the United States government made new treaties with the Indian tribes. The fact that the Cherokee and the Osage had been divided in their loyalties between the North and South, and that parts of each tribe had fought with the Union armies, had little significance to men bent on house cleaning. They forced the Cherokee to cede parts of the Outlet, and they placed thereon, in diminished reservations, the Osage, Pawnee, Ponca, Otoe, Missouria, Nez Percé (later Tonkawa), and the Kansa.

In the 1870's, great cattle herds were driven across the Outlet from Texas to the railroad terminals in Kansas. Thousands of longhorns plodded to market over the Abilene Trail (more popularly known as the Chisholm Trail) and the Western Trail. In dry weather, when there was no water in the Cimarron or the Salt Fork, the dust clouds reached high into the steel-blue sky, and the cowboys tied bandannas over their mouths and noses to keep from choking. But when there had been much rain, the red-tinted waters of the rivers swirled and foamed, forcing stopovers upon the cowboys and their impatient, bawling cattle. At night when the lightning made luminous trees in the black sky, the trail men had to watch their herds carefully to keep them from stampeding.

They must also watch out for the Cherokee, and even the Osage, who would demand toll for the crossing. The Osage, having no longer any claim to their old hunting grounds, would leave their reservation east of the Arkansas on their hunting trips to the Cimarron, and were ever ready to resent any activity which might disturb their hunt.

Later this great expanse of range was leased from the Cherokee by cattlemen. One year, the winter of 1886, cold blasts from the arctic swept across the Outlet, driving sleet and snow horizontally before them, rolling the tumbleweeds like balls and piling them into ravines or packing them against the huddled cattle. The next spring, when cowboys rode over the plains, they found thousands of skeletons with only the ragged hide and sinews clinging to the bones, as they had been left by coyotes and wolves the winter before. They also found cattle still alive, moving about grotesquely on the stumps of their legs.

It was shortly after this that the old familiar cry arose again on the Red plains: "Open the unassigned lands to settlement!" The lands to which people referred were located roughly in the center of present Oklahoma and had been ceded by the Creek and Seminole tribes to the United States for the settlement of other tribes after the Civil War. They had not yet been assigned, hence their popular designation.

The unassigned lands were finally opened to white settlement in the spring of 1889 and later given the name Territory of Oklahoma, to differentiate the area from the Indian Territory, which surrounded it on all sides. This white enclave had a common boundary with the Cherokee Outlet on the north, and soon some of the disappointed claim seekers were squatting on the Cherokee land. Other whites were slipping into the Outlet from across the Kansas border. Some of the new settlers, struggling against the savagery of the plains, came across the boundary from the newly settled lands to the Cherokee Outlet to gather the bones of blizzard-killed cattle for shipment east for fertilizer, just as others were gathering the bones of slaughtered buffalo all over the plains. The newcomers killed prairie chickens for the market, and antelope, deer, and wild turkey, which found their way to the tables of the wealthy in the East.

Soon the cry was heard again. This time the homeseekers said that the cattlemen who leased range land from the Cherokee were keeping free Americans from their natural rights in a free country. When the Territory of Oklahoma was organized in 1890 and a form of government given the new owners of the old unassigned lands, the federal government allowed the Cherokee Strip Livestock Association, principal lessee of the Outlet, a certain length of time to get its members' cattle off the range. It also urged the Cherokee and the other tribes it had placed in the Outlet, under the terms of the treaty with the Cherokee, to accept allotment and sell the surplus land to the government to be turned over to white settlers. The Cherokee, Osage, Kansa, Ponca, and Otoe refused. But the cutting off of the rentals from the cattlemen made the Cherokee more flexible, and they finally agreed to sell the remainder of their Outlet.

The Pawnee and the Tonkawa were allotted lands from their reservations in severalty, and the surplus was thrown open to settlement, along with the recently purchased Cherokee part of the Outlet.

In September, 1893, this great wind-swept land, which touched the woodland area of post oaks and blackjacks to the east along the line of the Arkansas River, and reached to the "apron" of the Rocky Mountain uplift in the west, was opened for settlement. It was a wild, temperamental land of red gashes, buttes with shining bands of gypsum, hills sparkling with selenite chips, and salt beds that seemed to float in the distance. Little dervish winds picked up the sand from the dry beds of the Cimarron and the Salt Fork and swirled it into pale smoke.

It had been a drought year, and the September grass was as dry as excelsior. The soldiers set fire to it, then the wind, which always stirs on the plains, rushed the flames across the shimmering, drought-cracked land. The "Sooners," who had been hiding in the ravines and in the long grass, were smoked out, and they cursed the government for the outrage. The people waiting patiently at the borders, however, felt smug and self-righteous.

When at last carbines were fired, signaling the opening of the Outlet, the race started over the charred grass. Sweat made little lines through the black dust on the strained faces. Little whirlwinds raced playfully with, or athwart, the runners. Wagons were tipped over and their contents spilled on the black plains. Sweating race horses, their nostrils distended, their barrels moving like bellows, their heads high with nervous excitement, whinnied to each other across the acrid plain or trotted off with dragging reins while their owners pounded their stakes or disputed a claim.

Much has been written about the opening of the "Cherokee Strip." Since there were many types of people who made the run on that September day, or followed upon the heels of those who did, almost everything that has been written might have some basis in fact. Certainly there were mild idealists, sporting adventurers, opportunistic young lawyers and doctors and teachers, independent young women weary of Victorian restrictions, gamblers, boisterous would-be bad men and quiet, cold-eyed bad men, jobless mechanics and laborers, hopeful young married couples, businessmen and real estate speculators, an occasional apologetic Negro, and stern-faced immigrant Germans, along with pimps, professional women, swindlers, and quarrel-lusting murderers.

In this cross section of America was every type and profession, except those who felt no economic necessity to run madly over a burnt plain—the dollar-princes, the well-established politicians and successful professional men, the scholars and gentlemen of New England and the Old South. But despite these exceptions, there was probably represented in the run every virtue and every vice in the nation. The land itself brought out the dominant virtues of courage and thy-brother's-keeper Christianity, as war brings out these virtues. The unaccustomed settlers were faced at once with the purposeful hostility of the savage Red plains in one of their cyclical droughts.

The Osage no longer rode, his more than six-foot body projecting above his Kiowa pony, the plains sun shining on his bare and hairless upper frame. His scalplock, from which the wind-spun eagle feather protruded, was no longer a challenge and an insult to his enemies. He was no longer the painted demon who understood the fear he inspired.

When the Outlet was opened he sat on his reservation east of the Arkansas and talked of the vanished days and the vanished buffalo. He talked sadly of Mo'n Sho'n, Mother Earth, who had become a shriveled old woman now, although white men measured his reservation at a little less than a million and a half acres.

The enemy of the settlers in the Cherokee Outlet was the land itself. The hot winds tore the soil from their ploughed fields, screamed around the corners of their sod houses, and hissed over their dugouts. There was no rain. Even the arctic winds which sent tumbleweeds across the plain like animated things, piling them against their houses and imprisoning them in the rude fences, brought little moisture.

Sometimes the settlers succeeded in raising a little kaffir or grain sorghum, upon which they had to depend or throw themselves upon the laxity or the generosity of the men who had opened little stores in the village communities. When the plains snarled, the mobile Indians had left the region to take refuge in the Cross Timbers, the Wichita Mountains, or the Ozarks. But these settlers were white men, and they became attached to their little geometrical bits of earth, expecting much from their labors and their prayers. They had little understanding of the land to which they had anchored themselves.

In the battle with nature, no one was exempt or secure. Like soldiers, all were equally vulnerable, and they faced the common enemy with soldierly dependence upon each other.

It was not until 1897 that the rains and the large-flaked snows came again, and the rich ferric soil of the Red Beds produced wheat and kaffir in abundance, and the native grasses came forth again from their refuge in the earth.

Not until still many years later, about the time of E. W. Marland's arrival, were the energies and thoughts of the people freed from the constant battle with the plains.

The exploitation of oil, the prodigal source of hydrocarbons, had begun on the lands of the Cherokee, the Creek, and the Osage before statehood, but the Osage lands were closed to exploitation west of a certain range by the Department of the Interior. There had been only tentative development on the edge of the plains across the river from this closed area. Gas had been found, and a member of the Osage tribe, A. J. Soldani, and his associates had supplied the little town of Ponca from their wells, but this was a long jump from proven oil territory in the eastern part of the state. Exploration for oil seemed to be little more than optimism. E. W. was to have a free hand in unproven territory.

8

THE TWO communities in the Outlet were Ponca City on the edge of the Ponca and Osage reservations at the extreme eastern edge, and Enid in the center of the great Permian syncline, where the red sandstone, clays, and friable limestones were thousands of feet deep.

By nightfall of September 16, 1893, there were hundreds of people camped on the plains where the town of Cross was to grow. The Santa Fe Railroad, which had been built across the Outlet in the eighties, recognized the concentration of people called Cross, and had trains stop there.

On this memorable day, a train chuffed across the boundary at the signal and labored along its line, with people all over it, like some encrustation warmed into squirming life. Men clung to the cowcatcher, sat on the roofs of the cars, and stood on the steps.

Some of the men jumped off the cautiously moving train to stake claims along the way, and many cursed its slowness, fearing that the eager town builders from across the Kansas border might get to the future town of Cross before them. When the train entered the Otoe Reservation and then the Ponca, where there could be no claim-staking, they had to stay with the overloaded conveyance and grow more and more impatient.

When the train arrived at Cross the eager town builders found that rival enterprisers had set up machinery for the drawing of lots. B. S. Barnes, one of the leaders of the town builders from south of the Outlet, decided to move three miles below Cross and lay out a townsite on the high ground at the edge of the Ponca Reservation. He called it New Ponca, and a rivalry between New Ponca and Cross began. The excited men of New Ponca protested to the Santa Fe when its trains were not allowed to stop at their town; at New Ponca they began whistling and slowing up for the stop at Cross. Later, however, Barnes and his associates got an order for the train to stop at New Ponca, an event over which the people made much. They boasted that New Ponca and Chicago had much in common, since trains stopped at both places.

An enterprising lot owner in New Ponca spread a large tent and started the first hotel. He charged twenty-five cents for a bed under his canvas. Many eating places opened, and doctors, lawyers, and blacksmiths put up their signs, their tents, or hastily thrown-together buildings. There were builders, planners, people eager to start a new life.

The gamblers came, as did the professional women who flourish during times of displacement, adjustment, and confusion. The poseur came, dressed in outlandish Western costume with a gun at each hip and a head full of ideas taken from magazines of the Wild West. Refugees from justice came, whose exhibitionism had lain too long dormant in the Indian country where it had not been appreciated. With notches on their guns and a few words of Cherokee or Osage, they grasped the opportunity to strut before the sedentary homeseekers.

Cowboys, out of a job or in town to "hit" the Miller brothers for one, often escaped dull waiting by getting drunk. Because of the stimulant, or because of contempt for the town builders, they would ride at full run through the streets, firing their guns into the air, later escaping into the Ponca Reservation.

High-spirited French-Osage mixed bloods from across the Arkansas came into the little town to escape the boring tranquillity of a "dry" reservation. They could drink at the bars and dance with the bespangled and sweet-smelling blonds of the dance halls. One night several of them lay abed in the tent hotel and vied with each other in shooting recognizable moonlit designs in the tent top.

As the soil of the plains was turned and wheat planted, and especially after the rains came again in 1897, the little town began to grow. It also became a cattle town. As the Millers and their ranch became more and more famous, scholars, artists, adventurers, cowboys from all over the country, and tourists came to the growing town. It became the market for the long yellow corn which the French-Osage mixed bloods raised in their river-bottom soil, as well as for hogs and cattle.

Not only was the time propitious for E. W.'s arrival at Ponca City, but the spirit of the people was in harmony with his own. The let-the-sky-be-the-limit attitude of the Millers and the playful acquisitiveness of the French-Osage were much different from the hardheaded, stolid conservatism of the people back on the Monongahela, the Allegheny, and in the West Virginia Panhandle.

The people of the plains took pride in their generosity and were more interested in working out a rhythm for chance than in basing their hopes on the constancy of agriculture. One gambled on wheat and cattle in the early days in the Outlet. One soon learned to laugh at his own pitiful activities on the great red, wind-swept land.

Their struggles on the plains were against nature. There had been no tariff to protect them against the hot winds of drought, or against hailstones as large as small balls which smashed through their roofs and crushed their wheat and killed their calves, against the funnel-shaped clouds that descended to earth and danced whimsically across the plains, or against the blizzards that froze their cattle. There was no obstacle to the screaming winds that came down from the arctic or to the dog-breath air that rolled in from the Gulf, displacing each other within a few minutes' time and giving birth to elemental drama.

Even after the land was divided into geometrical patterns,

and roads followed dutifully the section lines, and insurance companies gave them comfort, their lives and their fortunes were still under the wide sky of the plains, making them eternally conscious of their vulnerability. There were no mountains, river gorges, or protective forests, no high buildings to give them real or fancied protection from the fury of the elements, nor were there crowds of people to give them herd comfort.

This consciousness of their position and the memory of their struggles, often ridiculous in retrospect, would not allow of smugness or hauteur in the successful ones; they must remain folksy in a small community whose members had run onto and against the plains on an equal basis in September of 1893.

When E. W. began to find his footing among these people, he felt comfortable with them. They promised the flexibility necessary for the immediate adjustment to his fantastic dreams. The stage was large but the cast was small, and he could be the unquestioned hero, as he had been in the large house on Mount Washington back in Pittsburgh.

But E. W. paid little attention to the mores and the traditions of the people of the Red Beds. There is a picture of him out on the range of the 101 Ranch with George Miller, wearing what was known in those days as "knickerbockers" and a Norfolk jacket with a belt. But this was not all: he wore spats. This getup would have meant little to the Miller brothers, for they were accustomed to the clothes, manners, and whimsicalities of the visiting artists, actresses, musicians, and foreign travelers who were often guests at the "White House," but it was fortunate for E. W. that he dealt with the Millers and the Ponca Indians for his leases. The conventional religious claim-staker would have believed his intentions to be as outlandish as his clothes.

E. W. was pleased to see that the plains were gently undulating and formed long swells like a lazy sea. These, to a self-taught geologist, were structural as well as topographic. He immediately concluded confidently and a bit too eagerly that all were anticlines.

After his first inspection trip over the ranch with George

Miller, he was anxious to get started exploiting this untouched land. Among these live-and-let-live people, busy with their cattle and well-ordered patches of earth, he became confident and probably felt like a trained swordsman among oafs.

His 101 Ranch Oil Company was organized to explore whatever lay below these prairies, but unmistakably it was oil for which he searched and of which he dreamed. Oil was becoming more and more important. The demand was growing because the horseless carriage had come to stay. To become a man of great importance he must find oil. But the 101 Ranch had a hundred thousand acres.

The first well attempted was near the ranch buildings, and George Miller hammered the stake as his mother, his wife, and E. W. stood by. This well, instead of being another Congo discovery well, was continually harrassed by the hag Fate. The equipment was not adequate to the task, nor were the finances. But the driller was V. H. Waldo, an old Pennsylvania hand who had been recommended to E. W. by the Oil Well Supply Company, with whom he had credit for his tools. He had returned pipe and other equipment to them after his failure in West Virginia, and he now took advantage of that credit. Waldo, who was paid $6.00 a day, had instructions from E. W. to pay the hands every two weeks. For this E. W. had deposited one thousand dollars in the First National Bank—apparently all he had left from his Pittsburgh promotions. Anyway, he left Waldo with these admonitions about paying the men and went back to Pittsburgh to raise more money.

The second time Waldo drew on the account, the check "bounced." E. W. had got into a poker game in Pittsburgh and had drawn a check against the deposit to pay his losses.

This well was finally abandoned. The next seven wells found gas, but they inspired little interest. Gas had been found there before. The very term "Red Beds" was associated with the absence of oil bearing formation because of the nature of their deposition many geological years before, and everyone knew that E. W.'s explorations were on the Permian, even though they were only a short distance west of the contact line between the oil-bearing Pennsylvanian formations and the Permian.

Sometime during this frustrating search for oil, E. W. and his associates got in touch with W. H. McFadden, a retired Carnegie Steel executive who had quit Pittsburgh to go to Hot Springs, Arkansas, to regain his health. E. W. and George Miller went to visit him there for the express purpose of talking him into financing at least one well in the Ponca field. McFadden had been sent south by his doctors to die, and the idea presented to him by these two personable and optimistic men gave him new interest in life. George Miller and E. W. got the money. This financing came in 1910, and it is possible that the sick steel executive's aid made the first oil well possible.

McFadden and E. W. had not known each other in Pittsburgh; one was the successful steel executive and the other a coal and oil promoter. However, this meeting meant much to both of them. The sick man became well, and from the first oil well in the Ponca field he and E. W. were closely associated in play, work, and in the headlines. One seemed to complement the other. "Mac" had the force, sanguine expression, and earthy conservatism that E. W. needed, while E. W., on the other hand, seemed to inspire Mac with his glowing imagination, his mystical good luck, and his smug assurance.

Before starting the next well E. W. made a reconnaissance. There was an isolated, solidified sea swell that attracted his attention. One day he and George Miller reined their horses toward it. It was within the 101 Ranch lease with the Ponca, on the allotment of one Willie-Crys-for-War. It was also sacred ground. Because it was conspicuous, the Great Mysteries of the Ponca could see it very well without troubling Himself, and His children left there would be unable to lose direction when their spirits set out on the long journey "home." Here the Ponca had left their dead, high on a swell of the plains. It lifted above the land, then slanted off, and on its lower edge, on the trough side, was the line of trees that marked "Bodark" Creek, a tributary of the Salt Fork of the Arkansas which the French had called Bois d'Arc.

The Ponca, like the Osage, had never buried their dead until persuaded to do so by the white man. The Ponca had bound them and laid them upon scaffolds, or swung them into trees where they could be seen by the Great Mysteries. The Osage had placed their dead in cairns. There was also a practical reason for this, since the coyotes and the wolves hunted constantly.

When George Miller and E. W. dismounted at the top of the hill, E. W. began to examine the cemetery. It was interesting to a Pittsburgher to see the well-wrapped bodies, swung onto braided mats supported by four poles. But the silent Poncans awaiting the call of the Great Mysteries did not hold E. W.'s interest long. After perfunctory wonderment at the burial customs of the Ponca, he examined the hill. He said much later, "I noticed by the outcropping rock that the hill was a geological as well as a topographical high."

What he really noticed was a hill, elongated and isolated, and he assumed that it was a geological high, since he could not know definitely after a cursory examination of a few outcropping rocks that the hill was an anticline. But the reality of the hill excited him, and he decided to drill for oil just down from the crest toward Bodark Creek—down from the crest of the hill to escape the defiling of the Poncan dead.

But first he had to get a lease, and he had to get it from the Indians on their hallowed hill. George Miller had great influence with the Ponca. For years the tribe had found comfort in the humanity and understanding of the Millers. But here was a matter of supernatural importance, and, knowing and respecting Ponca traditions, Miller found the situation delicate. But E. W. did get his lease, and there was no prejudice in the heart of White Eagle, Chief of the Ponca, against E. W.'s clothes. There was only a great fear that he might have done the wrong thing by agreeing to a lease on the sacred land, even though his friends the Millers thought that it would be all right. He told E. W. that he was making bad medicine, not only for White Eagle and his people, but for himself.

Preparations went ahead for drilling. The equipment had to be brought to the location from the railroad, and there were no trucks to roar and skid and splash through the red and black mud.

When the derrick was built and the boiler set, the bit and other drilling equipment had to be hauled to the spot by teams, and E. W. had to lend a hand. When the plains lay under a heavy sky and the rain fell for days, horses couldn't keep their feet, and oxen were borrowed from the 101 Ranch. With yokes creaking and loud coughs, they drew the load to the lease.

E. W. couldn't afford to hire help except for the few people who were absolutely necessary. Sometimes he could borrow men from the ranch. However, since cowboys insist upon doing everything from horseback, they were of little aid.

Spattered with mud, he walked alongside the three yoke of oxen and cracked the long driver's whip, hoping fervently that the lumbering oxen would not suddenly decide to go no farther, a decision which their every disinterested movement suggested to him. They seemed terribly slow, and time was very important to him.

When the derrick was up, rising, it would seem, overnight like some fungus growth, E. W. again felt alone and less sure of himself. Always on the first materialization of his plans he felt this way. He slept at the derrick and worked and ate to the clank-CLUNK, clank-CLUNK, clank-CLUNK of the drilling tools. When he ran out of money, he gave Mrs. Rhoades, owner of the Arcade Hotel, promises, and she, a realistic, kindly, profanely compassionate soldier in the ranks of men against the temperamental plains, allowed him credit.

He bought cheap onions, third-grade potatoes, cheap chuck roast, and, when they were not too expensive, carrots. He took them out to the well, and in an old can well scoured with gasoline, he cooked his mulligan stew.

While the clank-CLUNK, clank-CLUNK was music to him, it was sometimes like the drum of the Ponca medicine man in its rhythm: in its fateful, unbreakable rhythm were drumbeats sounding the last hours of a dying tribesman. And there were days when the dry winds screamed in the derrick's top and the unseasonable heat of early spring, the dog's breath from the

Gulf, inspired dejection and hinted of disaster. On such days the rhythm of the drilling tools was a monotonous warning of inescapable fate.

He said that the water pump kept saying, "dollar, dollar, dollar, dollar," so insistently that he felt compelled to get up from his pallet on the derrick floor and walk out under the stars, seeking encouragement from the dark, wild space. Once as he walked he heard a wolf howl, and he climbed the slope to the funeral scaffolds and sat down, thinking he might hear it again.

The dark forms of the Ponca, raised on their platforms against a starlit sky, eternally waiting, drew his thoughts into strange fields of philosophy where he lost both his fear and himself, only to be brought back to reality by the sudden "dollar, dollar, dollar, dollar" of the pump as the plains breeze grew whimsical. The breeze would change direction, the sound would die, and all would be silent again after this reminder.

However, most times when the pumps disturbed his sleep with their hateful "dollar, dollar" talk, he would walk out into the darkness and abandon himself to his fear of losing his independence. He saw himself with a dinner pail working for someone else, because he knew that he couldn't squeeze another penny out of Pittsburgh if he failed to strike oil. He felt that he had staked his future on a hole in the ground, for which he would not be able to pay if oil didn't ooze up and flow to make it an oil well. Even on cool nights he sweated at the thought of being a nobody. Might as well be lying on a wicker platform, as he called the funeral scaffolds, as be unknown among the millions of unknown.

Then the rains would come. Lightning would descend from the clouds like fire along a crinkled fuse, and the roar of the thunder would drown the rhythmic clank-CLUNK of the tools. Men would run about the derrick floor shouting to each other, their mobile lips the only indication that they were attempting to convey thoughts and ideas. The wooden derrick was the highest point within miles, and it stood challenging the lightning.

At such times E. W. would slosh about in wet clothing and often sleep without pulling off his boots. In the last freeze of the season his wet clothing froze on him and crackled when he bent over his mulligan stew.

Sometimes the days came veiled with clouds and whipped by sharp, fresh winds. And sometimes the days were thrashed by a high south wind that carried dust, enervating heat, and an intangible menace. Then days would come when the air was almost still, and the sun shone benignly, and the song of the meadowlark could be heard far across the plain, silly but cheerful and filled with hope that inspired hope.

Then one day the monotonous clank-CLUNK stopped, not for the bailer this time or for tool dressing. The log showed about 1,500 feet. The men smelled of the bit, swung aside for the moment above the derrick floor. The tools were lowered again, and again the laboring rhythm of clank-CLUNK, clank-CLUNK, clank-CLUNK was carried over the earth.

When the first oil in the Ponca field was discovered, E. W. was down the Salt Fork, in the middle of it, as a matter of fact, with his pants off. He was helping his crew lay a pipe line for gas across to the Ponca Indian Agency at White Eagle.

An excited man hurried to tell George Miller that oil was showing at the new well. He and Lew Wentz, then associated with the McCaskey interest in the 101 Ranch Oil Company, rushed to the livery stable for a team and went in search of E. W. When they found him in the middle of the river, they could scarcely wait for him to get his pants on. They drove at a lope to the well. E. W. had the tools pulled and advised oilmen from the old Cherokee fields and the eastern Osage that he had found oil in the Red Beds. When they gathered, the well was drilled in.

The plains breeze was playing with a blackish spray, carrying it across the rolling land and tinting everything with it. The air smelled of sulphur. E. W.'s hands trembled a little, and he said some silly things in his emotion, but he couldn't remember what he had said. Men did rather wild and childish things in such circumstances, throwing their hats into the spray, bathing in it with their clothes on, slapping people on the back, shaking hands with the driller repeatedly.

Later E. W. said, "I am sorry for the man who has missed the big thrill that comes to the wildcatter when his well, on which he has worked night after night and day after day, comes in a gusher."

9

E. W. HAD STRUCK OIL on the plains, but his bonanza had scarcely taken shape when the well-established truism of his day assailed his thinking. Oil had to be transported to be of value. He had brought in the discovery well of what might—probably would—become a great new Southwestern field, and he knew it. Those who controlled transportation could profit from their discoveries.

Petrolia began her industrial life in the mud, with horse transportation, leaky barrels, swearing teamsters, and bumping barges that bridged the streams. Transportation and Petrolia grew up together and are dependent upon each other. Their development together brought about the most amazing period in the history of industry and warfare.

E. W. knew about transportation. He had seen the Standard use it to discourage competition. He knew that if he became the producer he proposed to become he might eventually be compelled to have an outlet on the Gulf of Mexico. It was at this stage only a fleeting idea, but it was there. Day-dreaming, he had got ahead of himself. First he must build his company. He would attempt to consume his own oil by building a refinery. It was all right to think about an "integrated company that would compete with the Standard oil Companies," but that was for a more distant future.

Actually, it seemed never to occur to him that the monster he feared and despised was the model upon which he built his dreams.

With every oil well in the Ponca field—and within three years he had opened two more pools in the Ponca area in Kay County—E. W. became more self-confident and arrogant. The little boy of Mount Washington was once more well aware of his importance. His thoughts of his own greatness were, as ever, mixed with his schemes for helping the common man to a better life. His plans for his company and his plans for the people of Ponca, the town of his adoption, were blended and indistinguishable.

He was impatient of every necessity which delayed the translation of his dreams. He was especially impatient when an expected oil well came in a gasser. What to do with all the gas was a constant problem. His wells supplied by franchise the towns of Tonkawa, Newkirk, and Ponca. One of the great gas wells of the area came in near Newkirk, and one of the greatest gas fields in the world came in at Blackwell in 1913. E. W. built a pipe line to the Chilocco Indian School on the Kansas–Oklahoma border and on into southern Kansas.

E. W. didn't like to have his success called luck. He insisted that he was far in advance of others in the new science of geology —this was his "secret." He felt he was a sort of custodian, if not the spring-source, of the practical application of geological science.

It is true that most oil producers in the area put about as much confidence in a witch hazel or a peach fork as they did in the geological facts of the earth's history. But E. W., who himself had not long abandoned his "drippings from coal" theory, was now scientifically searching for anticlines on the Red Beds. He was drilling on the crests of the plain's swells.

He was on the edge of the Permian, which geologists were saying could not contain reservoirs of oil and gas because the Permian had been deposited under desert conditions, where salt water, trapped by the receding sea, lay heavy and sterile in the hot sun hundreds of thousands of years ago. The sun and

87

drought had oxidized the soil and it now appeared in grades of red. The trapped sea water had disappeared, leaving white salt deposits that seemed from a distance to float above the plain.

He realized that his oil was coming from reservoirs underlying the Permian deposits—from the Pennsylvanian, perhaps—a series of strata coeval with the strata from which he got his oil and coal in West Virginia. The oil had been trapped in the Pennsylvanian strata where it had originated. Many places, where the strata had been formed into anticlines and other structures by lateral pressure in the earth's crust, the superimposed Permian had reproduced such structure on the plains.

In November, 1912, E. W. met a real geologist from the University of Oklahoma. The state geologist, D. W. Ohern, had run into difficulty in mapping certain elevations near Newkirk, and Professor Irving Perrine and his assistant, L. E. Trout, came to Ponca City from the University. E. W. kept Dr. Perrine talking far into the night nearly every evening in the lobby of the Arcade Hotel.

Dr. Perrine taught him the divisions of geological history, the systems, the series, formations, and the members and local names of the strata, and the nature of the sands of the area. Dr. Perrine was surprised at E. W.'s sharpness and his memory for detail.

The traveling salesmen would one by one leave for bed. The soundlessness of those days can scarcely be imagined. A horse's hooves thudding the dust, or the creaking of a late wagon, occasionally the shout of a drunken Ponca or a cowboy, nothing more. Lights would go out all over the little plains town, except for a few gas street lights, and only the night breeze of the plains would be astir as the two men sat and talked of the wonders of the geological past and the formation of the Red Beds, upon the thin edges of which their hotel stood.

Dr. Perrine would lose himself in the deserts of the Permian or the steamy swamps of the Pennsylvanian, while E. W. would not only feel the wonder of the earth, but the possibilities it held which could make real his dreams of wealth and power and princedom. The whole extent of the Cherokee Outlet became to him, under the magic of Dr. Perrine's disclosures, a book

88

completely illustrated and open before him. His strange poetic mind, excited by the romance of the primitive trees and swamps which he had visualized as he drove behind Mack in West Virginia, now became more restive as he visualized with Dr. Perrine the land abandoned by the sea, lying with its entrapped salt waters under a desert sun.

The urge for expression was intense, but his instruments of expression were not the pen, canvas and paints, or music, but the tall derricks—now like hesitant forests creeping onto the plains from east to west as if they had sprung from seeds blown across the river from the edge of the woodland.

Stirred by the talks with Dr. Perrine, he often lay awake planning, dreaming, and waiting impatiently for daylight, so that he could drive out over the plains in the new car he had acquired. The shimmering plains in their immensity seemed to challenge him as they had challenged the claim staker. The state and federal governments were working out the geology of the region, but he was impatient to find structures that they might have missed.

In November, 1914, he sent to the University for Dr. Perrine and asked him to work out the structure as far to the south as the town of Perry. This was the beginning of his geological department. In the spring of 1915, Dr. Perrine, W. C. Kite, a student of geology at the University, and L. E. Trout became his department. They came up from the University on week ends and on holidays. They worked near Morrison and in the Osage, west of the little town of Hardy.

As Easter approached, E. W. felt especially princely over his success. His attitude of deference to Dr. Perrine was changing slightly, as though, having absorbed knowledge from his teacher to satiety, he had risen from the position at Dr. Perrine's feet and was standing erect. It was the prince who asked Dr. Perrine to bring to Ponca as many members of his classes as might wish to work during Easter vacation, and he would pay them well. "I want them to have the benefits of working here in the field—to learn from the best teacher, the earth," he said.

When Dr. Perrine asked how many he might bring, he said, "As many as you like. Use your own judgment."

"We spent the entire vacation teaching the seniors and juniors how to run the alidade, hold the rod, and study the surface outcrops," said Dr. Perrine. "Of those fifteen students, 'Cap' Kite and 'Spot' Geyer later became Marland's chief geologists in turn."

E. W. had learned from Dr. Perrine that the Permian beds of the Cherokee Outlet formed a great syncline, and that as one went west from Ponca City, the beds first dipped to the west then to the east. He conceived the idea that if the Permian beds grew thicker as one went west, there would be less and less chance that the Permian deposits might be affected by the deeper Pennsylvanian structure. He didn't doubt that the structures were there. There was nothing but space from Ponca to the Rocky Mountains—and he saw in this great expanse of land a gambler's chance for a great oil field. Like most acquisitive men, untouched nature, especially that which they might call wasteland, challenged him, and at such time the gambler pushed aside the geologist.

If one were to find oil on the limb of Dr. Perrine's syncline, which plunged deeper and deeper as he went west, he must find the local folding in the Pennsylvanian, which would not be indicated on the Permian surface, through methods other than the key rock method of current exploration.

Already, when he had scarcely begun to exploit them, he began to feel the limitations of the old methods, and like other American industrialists began to turn his eyes to the mechanical inventions of Europe, especially of Germany. There were new mechanical devices constantly being employed in the study of the folding, reverse folding, underthrusting, overthrusting, and plunging of the Alps. Many of these mechanical aids for working out the intricate geology of the Alps could be used, he thought, for oil exploration by the energetic and acquisitive American.

West of Kay County, where the Red Beds became progressively deeper, he began to concentrate his interest. The land, utilized for kaffir, wheat, and other upland grains, seemed to him empty and awaiting exploitation. The tranquillity of waving grain did not interest him. There was no activity there, no clanking excitement. It was still as empty to him as if the indigenous grasses remained.

His great, round reservoir tanks began to spring up on the plains like mammoth toadstools, and his pipe lines running from the wells to fill them were like some queer asymmetrical venous system. The heart was a refinery, west and south of Ponca.

There was constant activity. At first E. W. seemed to be afraid to explore too far off the crests of the anticlines, and this meant that he was producing more gas than he knew how to utilize. The 101 Ranch Oil Company was really in the gas business until he brought in a few oil wells in the Ponca field.

Three of his early associates were old friends from Pittsburgh. One was the promoter, McCaskey, with whom he was associated in the Dutchess County cabbage deal, another the steel executive, W. L. McFadden, the third his brother-in-law, Sam Collins, Jr.

Now associated with him in the 101 Ranch Oil Company were Lieutenant (later Colonel) Franklin Kenney, George Miller of the 101 Ranch, and another local man of importance in banking and politics, Jim McGraw.

Their first office building in Ponca was a nondescript frame building of one story with a "store front." There were four iron bars across the lower parts of the windows and across the glass on the door. It was one of those architectural by-products of pioneer exploitation which cluttered the continent. It might have been used by a harness maker, a storekeeper, a doctor, or a lawyer.

This gambler's company called the 101 Ranch Oil Company was absorbed by the Marland Refining Company, and the Kay County Gas Company took over the seemingly endless gas production—twenty-eight wells in the Blackwell area alone.

Later the Marland Refining Company had a brick building for headquarters, and then, ultimately, the great winged building that loomed on the plains much more importantly than the wheat elevators.

E. W.'s 101 Ranch Oil Company had not only developed a new field but had proved that, by drilling through the Permian Red Beds along their eastern edges, one could reach the producing sands of the Pennsylvanian strata. This oil in the Cherokee Outlet indicated that the Osage Reservation across the Arkansas River might be one of the great oil reservoirs of the Mid-Continent area, and might become a very important field when the restrictions were taken off it by the Department of the Interior. The Permian thinned into nothingness at the western edge of the Osage, like the ultimate ripples of a sea along a sandy coast line, so that the swollen prairie plain of the reservation was of the Pennsylvanian Series of strata. These prairie–plain swells of the Osage were not the indolent undulations of a placid sea, but the menacing swells of restlessness, just before the whitecaps gleam.

E. W. and his associates were ready for the opening of the Osage to exploitation. From atop one of the tanks of the refinery, one could look across the river to the undeveloped western Osage; one could stand there and dream dreams that had no two-plus-two restrictions. One could turn and look to the south and there see the derricks and the pipe lines. And then one would be attracted to the movement far away, and soon a long line of tank cars would crawl across the plains, like some reptile from the beginning of the age of reptiles, with the magic *Marland* on each segment.

E. W. had picked up a local young man, John S. Alcorn, a handsome opportunist, and had made him his right-hand man. John was quick, aggressive, and able, and he drove the Cadillac to carry E. W. and Dr. Perrine across the wind-singing prairie of the western Osage.

The data which they gathered was carefully put away in the safe until time should arrive for its use. This was in 1915, and E. W. believed that he would be compelled to wait until 1921, approximately five years, for the opening of the western Osage to exploitation. By that time there would be a new president in the White House at Washington, and he would be a Republican. The people were anxious for a change from the Schoolmaster, Wilson, but it might be necessary to do a little "guiding" to make sure that there would be a government in sympathy with his hopes and with the hopes of the growing oil industry. He was especially interested in the Department of the Interior, which had control over the Osage Reservation, and in the return of a sympathetic Congress. He would make a contribution to the Republican campaign fund, and he knew he would have a word in the naming of the Secretary of the Interior.

In the meantime, everything was in his favor. He could spend that five years in the further development of the Ponca, Newkirk, and Blackwell areas, and of his property in the Garber field, which came in later, in 1917. Then he must compete in the Billings Field, which was to produce from structure mapped by the state and federal governments.

Billings was west and south of the Ponca field, and E. W. wondered about this production. According to the dip of the Red Beds, the producing sands of the Pennsylvanian should have been deeper than where they were found. Garber, however, still farther west down the structural slope of the great Permian syncline, was producing from sands that failed to indicate the depths which Dr. Perrine had suggested. Also there was the interesting fact that Garber produced from sands of varying depths, and this interested him tremendously. If Garber, with its derricks like a bunched growth of planted locust trees, could produce oil from sands of varying depths, why not the Ponca field?

E. W. sent his chief geologist, W. C. ("Cap") Kite, who was still an undergraduate at the University of Oklahoma, striding across the prairie plains of the Osage and scrambling along the escarpments made by the Chickaskia River north and west of Blackwell.

Like Garber, where the oil producing sands were found at various depths, and like Billings, where they appeared early and were found at a shallower depth than anticipated, there was something strange at Blackwell also. The depth of the producing

93

members did not fit in with E. W.'s conception of the subsurface conditions here either, nor did the production dutifully follow the conditions of normal anticlinal folding which he carried as a image in his mind. He thought there might be a fault there, one of those long, deep, strain fractures in the earth's crust, sometimes upthrusting under lateral pressure. He reasoned that the oil- and gas-bearing sands might be sealed up against some impervious member of the fractured displacement of strata series. He would have liked, in his vanity, to find an unusual condition, even though it bothered him slightly to have his visualized structural conditions disturbed by one of Nature's subsurface whims at this particularly busy time.

More than in the new tank cars with *Marland Refining Company* painted on their sides, more than the construction of the big house on Grand Avenue and the laying out of a field across from the new house for a strange, not very strenuous game called golf, he was interested in Cap Kite's findings. He wanted Kite to reconcile the simple theory of anticlinal structure with the fact of shallow oil deposits as well as deep ones.

Each day when Cap returned to Ponca City, hot, tired, and discouraged, E. W. would ask anxiously, "Well, how did you make out? Find anything?" Cap would shake his head dejectedly. E. W. would then pat him on the shoulder and say, "That's all right, keep trying."

He inspired young men with his genuine interest in them and his visible belief in them. The young geologists on his staff, often treated by other oil men with the condescension which is at once maddening and disillusioning, felt grateful to him for his confidence in geology and in their efforts.

10

IN 1912, E. W. made a move which was the subject of political attacks on him by many a "champion of the people." He had learned in West Virginia that owners of large tracts of land were willing to gamble to prove the worth of their holdings. His Oklahoma options had been made with the 101 Ranch and the Ponca Indians—owners of vast areas. Now, believing that he could find other fields if he could get acreage west of the line of contact between the Permian and the Pennsylvanian, he was confronted with the necessity of dealing with the home steaders of "Old Oklahoma," the former unassigned lands, as well as those of the Cherokee Outlet, each of whom owned only a quarter section. The idea whereby he might secure a blanket lease in several counties south and west of the Ponca field either was suggested to him by a member of the state School Land Commission or, as he said, it just came to him.

When the former Kiowa and Comanche Indian lands had been turned over to the white settlers, two sections in each township were set aside for school purposes, and these lands were placed under the guardianship of a commission, of which the state superintendent of public instruction was a member.

In the summer of 1912, E. W. went to Oklahoma City and suggested to the School Land Commission, or to certain members of the Commission, that he might be given leases on the school lands for the purpose of exploring for oil.

95

He got three leases, on March 4, on May 6, and a blanket lease on August 14. Thus he became the lessee of approximately 137,700 acres of state land. The first lease, a single section in Kay County within the area of his explorations, he got for a fifty-dollar bonus, and the second lease of May 6, he got for a one-hundred dollar bonus. The latter lease contained approximately 17,700 acres in Kay, Pawnee, and Kiowa counties. The final lease of about 120,000 acres, spread over nine counties, he got for a fifty-dollar bonus.

These leases were to run for five years, "with one-eighth royalty of all gas and oil produced, and with the obligation upon the lessee to put down twenty test wells within the period of two years, no less than one well to be drilled in any one county, and no more than one of the twenty test wells to be on any one section, the well to be of sufficient depth to fully test the territory where drilled, and with further obligation upon the lessee to drill sufficient number of wells to offset wells on any adjacent properties of other operators, and to follow up the test wells with such developments of said lands as the law requires and as may be required by the rules and regulations of the Board, and to develop and operate all producing lands as fully and as completely as the tests justify."

Some of the leases in Kay, Pawnee, and Kiowa counties were almost within proven territory, and E. W. subleased two quarters of a section in Pawnee County for a bonus of two thousand dollars each. Leases close to one school section in Kiowa County were bringing bonuses of from five hundred to four thousand dollars per quarter-section.

Thus did the transplanted princeling make a deal worthy of the Standard, the Pennsylvania Railroad, or the Mellons. He might have been too late for the struggle in the East, but here in the naïve Southwest he could make good use of his early training. He had no intention of stealing from the school children of Oklahoma, as politicians later intimated. He hadn't given the public a thought. He had seen an opportunity to advance his plans, and he seized it.

The first political storm over his maneuver came in the

spring of the next year. The last political storm would rear and threaten during his campaign for the governorship of Oklahoma in 1934.

In the spring of 1913 a general investigation was called by the state House of Representatives. The investigating committee found no chicanery on the part of E. W.; they found only that the Commission's agreement to E. W.'s plan was "imprudent."

"We find that leases have been made to E. W. Marland within the last twelve or fourteen months, the first being made March 4, 1912, on section 13, township 26, range 2, east, Kay County, for $50 with one-eighth royalty . . . We find this section of land to be proven territory and of more than ordinary value, being surrounded by lands rich in production at the time the lease was made."

Further: "We find that since the approval of this lease on August 14th, Mr. Marland has subleased to several different people or companies small portions of this territory, ranging from one-half to full sections of the lease for the consideration of his said sublessee drilling one of the twenty test wells which his lease obligates him to drill within eighteen months. The evidence shows that he had procured probably as many as seven or eight wells to be drilled in this manner." Then the conclusions: "In the opinion of the committee the lease bearing date of August 14, 1912, made by the School Land Commission to E. W. Marland, does not contain all the conditions provided by statute for protection of the state.

"It should never be forgotten that we hold in trust for the people of the generation and for the generations yet unborn, these natural resources, which are really the gift of nature for all the people, and that a careless and reckless policy which leads to a dissipation of these resources through unequal contracts or through one-sided contracts by which the rights of the people are lost sight of, and the fortunes of shrewd and cunning individuals are promoted, needs to be discouraged rather than encouraged. The problem of dealing with these great public interests may be involved in a great many difficulties, but the true solution of that problem certainly does not lie in the direction of giving a free hand to any individual or corporation with these natural resources held by us for the benefit of all."

The committee then recommended that the laws of the state be "so amended so as to reserve to the state forever all oil and gas and other minerals connected with state lands, and that the surface or agricultural rights of same only be sold with appropriate provisions to safeguard the state, or its mineral leases in entering the land so sold for the purpose of prospecting and mining of the minerals connected therewith and reserved to the state."

Following this report, E. W. went to officials of the state government and agreed to cancel the blanket lease, but for some reason it was not canceled.

In 1914, when Robert L. Williams became a candidate for governor of the state, he drew his Jacksonian sword in defense of the people's rights, but E. W. Marland did not become his Biddle. He charged his own party's political machine with guilt in co-operating with "the holders of this lease, [who] are in a position to acquire vast riches without a particle of work."

Judge Williams was elected governor. An effort was made in the legislature to carry out another investigation of the leases in the year 1915, but nothing came of it. When the five-year leasing period was to expire, in 1917, some of the members of the School Land Commission met and approved a resolution which was highly satisfactory to the "shrewd and cunning" oil man from Ponca City.

The resolution provided "for reimbursement for money spent in drilling producing wells on school lands, to be made a part of the appraised value of the property of lessee on the tract; so that if any other company or individual should obtain the renewal the original lessee must be paid for all of his expense of drilling." It was put in the form of a contract to which lessees might subscribe. E. W. subscribed and thus had a contract with the state guaranteeing his investments as well as preference rights on producing leases.

In July, 1917, the Commission decided to advertise for bids on the Marland leases. Governor Williams warned that the state might lose as much as two million dollars in school funds if the Commission failed both to fix a minimum for bids and to get an appraisal of the value of the leases. Out of his contingent fund Governor Williams employed Charles C. Brown, who, with the state oil and gas inspector, appraised each tract in the blanket lease and reported to the governor.

When the Commission met to consider bids, E. W. and his legal and geological advisers were present. They rejected about sixty thousand acres of the land and agreed to pay the state a bonus of $1,400,000 for the rest.

E. W. said much later that he was sure his contract had been the principal impetus to the discovery of oil on the school sections. His actions, moreover, had furnished Robert L. Williams with the strongest plank in his platform as a gubernatorial candidate in 1914, with the consequence that the new state got an outstanding Jacksonian as its third governor. "Therefore," he smiled whimsically, "I really made quite a contribution to my adopted state."

But he had not been hurt financially by the school land settlement. The phenomenal success of his over-all operations now made it possible for him to indulge a social whim dating from his Pittsburgh days. He would play the god on Olympus to his ever-increasing employees, soon to number six thousand. Since he had been responsible for their concentration in Ponca City, he was responsible for their happiness. He devised a plan whereby employees could come to the company and borrow money at 5 per cent to build, as he liked to say, "tight little four-room houses, and have chickens." He bought land and dedicated it to the homes of his employees, just as his father had done for the steel-mill employees in Pittsburgh. He had the idea that chickens and cows and "maybe a hog or two" on his own bit of earth would make a man a better citizen and a better worker. He believed that if his employees had adequate wages and security they would have the dignity and self-assurance which his father and Thomas Hughes had dreamed of at Rugby Colony in Tennessee. He would go even further—he would bring beauty to Ponca City so that the common man might be able to appreciate the beauty of the world without traveling a great distance to see it.

But these dreams, born in the flash of inspiration, had to be worked out slowly, and many of them were not realized until after the War of 1914–18 and the opening of the western part of the Osage Reservation to the oil industry. However, he began at once the building of "tight little four-room houses," and at the same time his own imposing house on Grand Avenue.

Moreover, he made a gesture toward protecting Charlie, John, and Mary against the bankers, the "still-faced boys," as he called them. The Southwest interest rates were 8 and 10 per cent, in some instances more. He bought a bank, the Security State Bank of Ponca City, and hired L. K. Meek from the little town of Mulhall as cashier. He made the interest rate 6 per cent. He did this, he said later, to help the "one-gallus boys—give them a Chinaman's chance." McFadden was a partner with him in this venture, but they soon found that their time was so completely absorbed by the building of an oil empire that they couldn't be bothered by the details of the bank. Three years after they had bought the bank, they sold their controlling stock to the cashier whom they had brought up from Mulhall in 1918. It was said that E. W. couldn't bear having people come to him about foreclosures on some "poor devil's only team."

He had begun to think more often now about creating beauty. East of the new house on Grand Avenue, he built his garden. He bought eighty acres at first, then added to it until he had a total of about four hundred acres. He utilized eighty acres for the landscaping of his formal garden and his golf course. The remaining 320 acres he improved, or intended to improve, as a model farm. "The eighty-acre tract was, at the time I bought it, a corn field with rows and stubble, and had not a tree, shrub, or blade of grass. The central part of what is now the golf course was the town dump, and refuse from the city and the city barns was disposed there."

He laid out very carefully the plan of his garden with reference to the house. He located all the little avenues, and planted three miles of Amur River privet hedge around the golf course and the garden, then transplanted from the Arkansas River valley four hundred trees from ten to twelve inches in diameter. The second year he put in concrete walks. Then shrubs, especially evergreens of wide variety, were brought in from many parts of the United States.

He had to cover his trees from the north to protect them from the burning sun of the plains and the oven-hot winds from the south. He loved magnolias, which he considered a symbol of manorial dignity, and had twenty half-grown ones shipped from Avery Island in Louisiana. He had special houses built to protect them against the other extreme of Oklahoma climate, the razor-sharp winds of winter.

He made a beautiful park of his golf course. He transformed the rough into flower beds and shrubbery, and planted his fairways to the tenacious Bermuda grass. The water hazards were lily ponds, where plopping golf balls made the frogs leap from their hunting stations.

He was proud to show doubters that any flower or shrub grown in the United States could be grown in Oklahoma if given proper care. He let the golf course and the beautiful garden, which was sixteen hundred feet long and four hundred feet wide, provide substantiation for his visitors. Sightseers were welcome, and everyone was urged to walk among the flowers and play golf. Golf clubs were available and free, as were instructions by his professional, Sandy McDonald. He wrote with pride: "In the past six years the material and labor used in planting the garden and the golf course has exceeded a quarter of a million dollars, and it now requires an average of thirty men throughout the year to keep the garden and the golf course in condition."

When a number of business and professional men of the city met with a group of Marland employees for the purpose of aiding E. W. in the maintenance of the golf course, he requested that the association be disbanded. He said, "If I permit some of my friends to subscribe toward the maintenance, then the remainder of our citizens will not feel free to use the grounds."

When being interviewed by a staff correspondent of the *Kansas City Star* on his bringing polo, hunting, and the horsey atmosphere to Ponca City, he said rashly, "If a man is a good horseman, he is an efficient employee." Then he added, "If a man or a woman learns to love a good horse, he learns to be a good and helpful citizen. There is more to industry than the making of money and the mechanics of refining oil. We are going to pay dividends in happiness to the community."

He assumed that the great wealth coming from the earth to the Marland Company was the property not only of the stockholders and executives, but of those who had made that wealth possible, who as human beings had certain rights to the earth and its fruits. As a matter of fact, after the war, when the flood of wealth from the Osage and the Tonkawa fields poured into his companies, he gave stock to his employees, to members of his family, to his secretary, and to a duck-hunting partner.

Assuming that that wealth belonged to all, he would take from the company any amount he might need for the carrying out of his ideas to make the pursuit of happiness easier for the people of Ponca City. He never hesitated to use the company's money when he needed it.

As E. W. watched the big house being built, and the fairways and greens of his golf course being sodded, he had no idea that he was not the Marland Refining Company and the Kay County Gas Company, but it also never occurred to him that the swimming pool, which was a part of the new house, was really private. Employees would be asked to come and appreciate the beauty of the gardens, enjoy a swim in the pool, and play golf. He never questioned his right to make gifts to the community or to make more pleasant the lives of those who had helped him take his wealth from the plains and maintain his empire. They had helped him with typewriters, drafting tools, log books, alidades, wrenches and mauls and picks, teams and trucks and scout cars, with their shrewdness, their youth and personality, leadership and executive ability, and even with their flattery and their own hopes of wealth.

He said, "I think the division of the profits of industry and capital is immensely unfair and unjust. I cannot conceive that capital should expect or be permitted to earn extremely large dividends—and give no share of the earnings of the enterprise to the employees whose intelligence, experience, and honesty have made these large earnings."

Already there was the hint of those mannerisms that were to become the outstanding characteristics of his personality as a prince—mannerisms which grew more apparent with his growth in wealth and power.

Even while he held tight conferences with his executive officers—with the dynamic, intense McFadden, the mercurial and convincing John S. Alcorn, and his new chief geologist, "Spot" Geyer, mentioning only these three for the sake of noting the diversity of personalities in the men around him—while he frowned over problems with them, listening, weighing, encouraging, he had begun in general to assume an air of having bestowed a blessing upon them, to hint at an obligation on their part to take from him, the prince, the unpleasant details of mundane business.

Even with millions, some of the company's departments periodically would be running in red ink because of his Olympian use of company money. When a department head would come to his office to lay a problem before him, E. W. would brush him aside with a weary remark, which was at once a rebuke for human frailty and a criticism for approaching Olympus with details that had been delegated to him as head of the department.

Once he put his thick finger on a deficit showing in his treasurer's report and said, "What's this red ink?" His treasurer replied, "Why E. W., that's it. We're in the red—the week-end payroll's coming up." E. W. ran his finger down the column of figures, then looked up suddenly at his treasurer and said, "You'll hafta to do better than that! We can't be in the red this way. You'll hafta do something about it. You're the treasurer."

Thus he dealt with the baffled treasurer as an Oriental ruler might dismiss the bringer of an unpleasant message before ordering his decapitation.

When the United States declared its neutrality in the War of 1914–18, E. W.'s first worry was that such neutrality might affect the flow of his oil production to markets. But his worry never reached definite form, for soon his business interest in sending oil to war and his patriotic fervor went hand in hand with happy enthusiasm.

The automobile was in mass production now, and cars were being spawned like salmon by Henry Ford. With his oil going to war for democracy's salvation, and going in vast quantity also to run Henry Ford's famous automobile, and with his war-bond buying and organizational activities, he felt that he was meeting his responsibilities as a prince.

He felt without qualification, along with his contemporaries, that the dark, moldy, and fetid corners of Europe would be swept clean by the energetic and creative broom of democracy, and that people all over the world, once they saw how it worked in America, would adopt democracy and live happily ever afterward, as handsome cowboys and pretty range land schoolteachers did in the cinema.

He approved of the high-sounding, beautiful rhetoric of the high-minded president, and supplied oil for the engine of war; he sent the rich product of the Cherokee Outlet to the struggle for the balance of power four thousand miles away across the Atlantic, and waited until things should become settled again after the war, until the lands of Osage Nation should be opened by a Republican secretary of the interior, and the red triangle, which was his trade-mark, should be displayed all over America.

He was the Outlet's outstanding citizen now, and his range of influence would be recognized by Frank Phillips, W. G. Skelly, Harry Sinclair, and the Prairie Pipe Line Company, Standard's invariable carrier and price-setter. Each would recognize the other's range, as grizzly bears and cougars of equal power recognize each other's range. The only disturbance was among national units far across the sea.

He and his family lived in the big house on Grand Avenue, with its swimming pool and its cool, tranquil rooms that were the first man-made things in the Outlet to challenge and frustrate the purposeful heat of the plains summers.

His sister Lottie was living with him now, as well as George and Lydie Roberts Marland, who had come out from Pennsylvania to live with him and Virginia in 1912. He had adopted them in 1916. "I want the kids to grow up here in the great Southwest," he said, "where there's freedom and space to develop in. They'll have a chance out here."

After Sara Marland's death, Alfred had come out to live at the Arcade Hotel. He had died there suddenly in April, 1914.

E. W. was sorry that his father had not lived to see his great glory. He had come to Oklahoma against Alfred's wishes, and he had disappointed his father in not striving for the robes of a Supreme Court justice. He was very fond of his father, had been greatly influenced by him, and naturally he wanted not only to vindicate himself in his eyes, but to mend his disappointment in a flood of glory. His father died only a few years too soon.

Almost his last words were, "Oh, if Ernest had not gone after strange gods!"

Part III   Decade of Illusion

11

AFTER THE WAR there was a demand for oil at more than three dollars a barrel. It was in keeping with the Marland luck that E. W. had the Tonkawa and the Osage fields to flood him with the precious hydrocarbons.

There was hope and eagerness in the air, not only on the plains but all over the nation. The soldiers came back from France wondering if they were still in time to have a share in the prosperity of the country. Only a few disillusioned idealists sought sanctuary on Pacific islands or went back to France to deplore the stuffiness, the narrowness, and the hypocrisy of the Middle Western towns. Most of the doughboys could scarcely wait to get their ugly, bobtailed blouses off and their leggings upwrapped, to forget that they had ever been a part of the war to end wars and to make the world safe for democracy.

To the young soldiers who came back to the plains, E. W. and his fabulous company became the stuff of their sanguine hopes. E. W., for his part, attempted to take care of all of them, whether he needed them or not. Among their lot he got some of the cleverest young men in the country, men who would follow his fantastic activity without question.

E. W. seemed to believe with many others that the supply would never catch up with the demand, and that the people would always have "crazy money" to spend. He was only concerned that the days were too short, that there was insufficient time in which to work out his plans.

It meant little to him that the cattle-and-wheat depression came within three years of the end of the war, because he didn't feel it. When he traveled in the western part of the Outlet, he noted that fields which had been scratched in the buffalo grass to supply war wheat were now abandoned. Thousands of these sores in the earth, which should never have been plowed in the first place, would form the sources of future dust storms. These were the troubles of the mediocre; he, the prince, had nothing to worry about since there would soon be no more of Wilsonian foolishness, and one could see to it that another Wilson did not enter the White House. It would be quite simple to return to the good old days with a sensible Republican president. The country could then resume the tranquillity of the period following the Civil War and forget the Big Stick of Theodore Roosevelt and the silly talk about the New Freedom of Woodrow Wilson.

He had already been approached by the "big boys," who by their enterprise had gained the right to run the country. This was flattering recognition of his importance. He agreed with Harry Sinclair and others that the secretary of the interior ought to be an oilman and an Oklahoman, since Oklahoma had more Indians than any other state in the union and Indians were the business of the secretary of the interior. The fact that the Indians were sitting on the richest oil deposits of the state was, naturally, of secondary consideration to the fact that an Oklahoman would certainly know about Indians. There was also the patriotic aspect of a young state which might now be capable of producing a cabinet member.

When they came to him for his contribution, he was like a successful gold miner being asked to drop money into the hat for the aid of some widows and orphans—a flushed and important miner who could turn from his poker hand and say, "Sure, how much ya need?"

He had a part in the selection of Warren G. Harding as a Republican candidate for nomination for president. His good friend, Lincoln Steffens, intimated that he was later ashamed of his role. But certainly, at the time, the selection suited him perfectly. He definitely wanted an administration in 1921 that knew its place, and he wanted a secretary of the interior who understood the problems of the oil business. The Mid-Continent oil operators were not yet particularly interested in the secretary of state, except for the Standard companies, and even they were not interested in the president's difficulties with Congress over the League of Nations. Wilson, who lost an immortality unequalled by any other human because he failed to die at the right time, was also being disowned by biology. Virile America was not ready to become interested in the world. It had its own continent to explore and utilize. There were not yet too many people to the square mile; the continent was not yet fully exploited. There were still frontiers, especially technological frontiers. Self-absorption is a natural biological consequence of such conditions. Now that the war was over, what did it matter if America joined a League of Nations or not? Americans had done their part to win the war for the old-fashioned, ambitionless peoples of Europe. They would now take off the trappings of war and get into comfortable dress for the business of making money.

Thus it was that the people, though motivated by different reasons, felt as E. W. felt: they would go along with him in finding Warren G. Harding the perfect president. He even looked like a history-book president, and his slogan, "back to normalcy," implied to them quiet, shady streets, tranquil fields of corn, wheat, and cotton, and cars for everybody. It implied that young sons would stay at home, go to college, marry their sweethearts, and continue the traditions of peaceful America, safe from the evil world of intrigue and war. The slogan seemed to express a refuge from the Big Four, the Hall of Mirrors, and covenants "openly arrived at," and the uncomfortable appeal of cold, beautifully enunciated English. Their history-book president would talk pleasantly and with serenity. He would talk a little boastfully of America and the American people, and they were sufficiently prosperous to agree with him.

The war, however, with its demands upon the oil of the great Mid-Continent field, had made the opening of the western part of the Osage Reservation for exploitation seem proper to the secretary of the interior two years before the coming of the new national administration. On November 9, 1918, the western Osage was opened for leasing, an event which occupied E. W.'s mind completely. The Kay County Gas Company got its maps from the safe and leased from the Osage Tribe 192,048 acres covering the extreme western part of the reservation. For oil leases, the Marland Refining Company had to await the day when it could bid on the tracts it wanted in open competition with others at the Osage agency.

E. W., Spot Geyer, and their staff of geologists, land men, and scouts, sat with their well-marked, finger-soiled maps among oilmen from England, Mexico, Holland, New York, Pennsylvania, Kansas, Texas, and California, under an elm tree on the Osage Tribal Reserve in the town of Pawhuska, to bid for 160-acre tracts as they were put up for sale by a colorful auctioneer, one Colonel E. E. Walters.

"You could stand on the edge of the crowd and see two or three of the biggest names in America squatting there on the grass, as common as an old shoe," said a bystander at the first sale, "and when they raised their hands it meant millions. That's a fact! I saw a fella raise his hand to scratch his head and he had himself a million-dollar lease."

The Marland Refining Company and the Kay County Gas Company made an attempt to get all the acreage they could in the western Osage, since E. W., with others, believed that it might become a tremendous gas field, if not an important oil field. Thus the Kay County Gas Company got its lease through contract, and the Refining Company bid at the periodic sales against competition from all over the country. At the second lease sale in May, 1919, the Marland buyers believed that they had paid more for leases than any other company or independent bidder. E. W. was very proud as he drove home with his young men. He had bid against Dutch Shell and a Standard company.

He was aware that the bystanders, people who were lured

by the talk of millions and seemed to receive some feeling of vicarious importance as they watched the big boys raise their forefingers nonchalantly, were now pointing him out to others with some awe, and with proprietary pride. He enjoyed intensely the taut moments when, the focus of all eyes, he bid into the hundreds of thousands, moments when he could hear his neighbor's belt squeak with each breath, moments when Colonel Walters, the auctioneer, abandoned his raucous chant and leaned over him to ask softly and with respect if he would raise the bid to $700,000, $900,000, or even a million. There were twenty tracts of 160 acres each in the western Osage oil field, called Burbank field, for which bonuses exceeding a million dollars each were paid, while one of them brought a prodigious $1,990,000.

After the Osage lease sale of the autumn of 1919, E. W. felt that he was really beginning to compete with the Standard companies, even though he was then just building his integrated company. His attitude, or at least an attitude which he condoned, was expressed in his own house organ, the *Marland News*. It was one of vindictive glee, boastfulness, and championship of independents against the great Standard. His *Marland News* said cockily: "Independent oil producers and refiners made history at the Osage land leases sale at Pawhuska Monday when they bucked the Standard Oil in the bidding and beat them in every instance where the going got real warm.

"It is said to be the first time in history that the independents were able to make the Standard stop. It was the general conviction among those at the sale at Pawhuska that the cause of the failure of the Standard, through its subsidiary, the Carter Oil Company, to get the big leases at the sale was the fact that 'they sent some boys to the mill with a limit on price and the independents had the money to beat them.'

". . . It was evident that the Carter was unprepared for the readiness of the independents to meet the limit that they had set on the big pieces. The Carter people quit when they reached their limit and the independents beat them with five- and ten-thousand-dollar bids at the top.

"E. W. Marland led the onslaught of the independents on the plans of the Carter people who were bidding on the big pieces offered. When Mr. Marland, bidding on tract No. 79, ran the price to $600,000 there was a momentary break in the Carter competition, but they made it $610,000 before it was knocked down. When Mr. Marland bid $620,000 the Standard representatives left the arena, beaten because they couldn't go above the limit that had been set for them."

This was not the attitude of the poker player who won or lost with good sportsmanship and in silence. E. W. was never the heckling player or the overbearing winner. It was the expression of his hatred of, and his disgust with, a penny-pinching, business mechanism that made men into cogs and ratchets, allowing them no freedom for initiative or imagination. Perhaps also his success and his dreams were making him a little arrogant.

With the Kay County Gas Company holding 192,048 acres leased from the Osage in 1918, and 153,640 acres leased by supplementary contract with the tribe, and with the Marland Refining Company obtaining leases for oil on the 160-acre tracts for which it bid at the auctions, E. W. felt that the Burbank field was his, or would be if he could get around the Interior Department regulations which restricted each operating company to a maximum acreage. There were ways of doing just that. Besides the Comar Oil Company, which bought leases in the Osage later, there were three companies which had their own identities but had offices in the Marland office building. One was the Tom James Oil Company, named for Colonel Tom James, a capitalist friend of E. W.'s from Charleston, South Carolina; another, the Kenney-Cleary Oil Company, named for E. W.'s nephew, Franklin R. Kenney, and Jack Cleary; and another, just come into the group in 1919, was the Francoma Oil Company. This last company was organized by D. R. Francis, Jr., son of the former Ambassador to Russia, and was formed in time to bid with the other companies at the Osage lease sale of October, 1919.

In 1922, these companies were absorbed into the Marland Oil Company, and into the Marland Oil Company came their executives and officers, P. B. Lowrance, Robert E. Clark, and Charles F. Martin.

There was also the very interesting John S. Alcorn Oil Company, which took leases and drilled wells, then sold both to the mother company.

Although the western Osage had been painstakingly surveyed by the United States Geological Survey as well as by the Oklahoma Geological Survey, E. W. had his own structure maps of the area. He felt he knew the subsurface conditions.

There were better geologists than E. Park Geyer, who was called "Spot," chief of his department at the time, but Geyer was a "business" geologist. E. W. had studied with Dr. Perrine, and he had admired the ability of Trout and Kite very much. As a matter of fact he had urged Cap Kite to stay with him when Cap decided to go back to the University to get his B.A. degree. This man Geyer, however, was one of the best traders in leases E. W. had ever known, and he seemed to ignore the limitation that two and two make four as readily as E. W. himself had always ignored this bothersome fact. He and Geyer would take the maps worked out by others, the maps of the subsurface structure of the area, and study them in the light of their own gamblers' instincts. They slid their forefingers off the crests of the anticlines and located their wells as though Petrolia herself was at their shoulders whispering to her favorites.

Spot Geyer had been fullback on the University of Oklahoma football team, and had gained much publicity in 1915 by a record forward pass to End Howard McCaslin. Later, like many of the University's geology majors, he was lured to Ponca City by the Marland name. Geyer was a fellow gambler, with horse-trading instincts, a man who could hardly have failed to appeal to E. W. Although E. W. had for his chiefs some of the greatest geological minds in America, or in the world for that matter, he always associated Geyer with the period of his greatest glory. "Spot," said a contemporary, "may not have been the country's greatest oil geologist, but he sure was the country's greatest poker-playing oil geologist!"

The Kay County Gas Company started a well on its lease in

western Osage on December 2, 1919. The wagons crawled across the swells like migrating beetles, then disappeared into the canyons as if they were sliding into concealing cracks in the earth, only to appear again. The exposed limestone rang and the drivers cursed. Trucks supplemented the wagons in hauling the timbers and the tools to the location in Section 36, part of which had been allotted to Bertha Hickman, a member of the Osage tribe.

Only the surface belonged to the allottee; all minerals lying under it belonged to the tribe, and the royalties and bonus would be paid into the tribal treasury to be distributed per capita.

After five feet of surface mold, the crew spudded into the hard, white, Foraker limestone. Then the clank-CLUNK of the drilling tools began on the wild prairie-plains that had known only the pulsing of the earth and the rhythm of the seasons.

The ranchers' half-wild steers, with nervous stupidity, formed into groups and watched the activity from a distance, ready to run but held almost against their wills by the familiar animals with their familiar voices, miraculously separated from their horses.

Dodge roadsters, with their tops down and with *Marland Refining Co.* painted on their doors, found their way over ringing limestone and across canyons to the well location. There the drivers sat with notebooks and pencils for a few minutes, then started out again across the trackless prairie, attempting to follow their seemingly whimsical tire-trail back to the dusty road.

An Osage, looking for his horses one cold December day, wrapped his blanket about his head and held it against the icy wind. He sat motionless and unseen and watched the activity about the new well. His only comment was, "Them white mens ack like tomorrow they ain't gonna be no more worl'."

The geologists, expecting gas, had suggested this location, but on May 14, 1920, at 2,965 feet, the crew struck an oil sand and produced 680 barrels of oil the first twenty-four hours. The Kay County Gas Company had no oil lease; and so, according to agreement, they turned the well over to the Marland Refining Company.

This was the discovery well of the famous Burbank field. Oilmen came from all over the world to the new "play." Soon, where there had been no sound except the doleful whistle of the upland plover, the nuptial booming of the prairie chicken, the prairie winds that had many voices, the coyotes questioning the moon about the mystery of existence, and the bawling of the impatient, pettish steers, there developed the metallic rhythms of drilling, the coughing of pumps, and the explosive laboring of trucks stuck in the mud.

It was, of course, the structure of the strata which first lured men to the western Osage and brought about the discovery of the Burbank field. But what they found almost three thousand feet below the surface were offshore sand bars, left by a Carboniferous sea known to geologists, appropriately, as the ancient Cherokee Sea of the Pennsylvanian Series. The bars had been left thousands of years ago—hundreds of thousands of years— and oil had been stored in them through time unimaginable, to be tapped by a drilling bit in 1920. The sand-bar reservoirs seemed to be independent of the folding of the strata that had taken place above them. They lay under the strata in such a manner that when one drilled on the structure one might hit a sand bar and release the imprisoned oil.

E. W. had been very lucky in hitting the limited shoestring sands in the Congo field of West Virginia. Here in the Burbank, the sands were more extensive. E. W. and Spot Geyer could have moved their mystical fingers all over the structure map of the Burbank area, and their angel, Petrolia, could have stayed their fingers on an anticlinal dome, a structural basin, an anticlinal nose, or a syncline, and still their drill might have pierced one of the sand bars left by the ancient Cherokee Sea. If there had been synclinal structure of great importance in the area, E. W. would not have drilled; he shunned these structures after he gave up his coal drippings theory and the tree-and-well accumulation idea.

E. W. had also drilled the discovery well in the area which became the very important Tonkawa field, whereas, just across a barbed-wire fence, the Prairie Oil and Gas Company in its offset well drilled a dry hole. This is the type of whimsy on the part of a playful fate that brought respect for E. W. Even some of the earthiest realists began to question.

The South Ponca field had been exploited, and the shallow sands were becoming exhausted, when E. W. got the idea that there were deeper sands. In 1918 he drilled deeper on the Mollie Miller lease and on the Willie-Crys-for-War land, both within the Ponca Reservation. He struck a deep sand at almost four thousand feet, which was considered in those days to be a very deep well. In these deep sands he found another large reservoir. Soon the derricks surrounding the burial ridge of the Ponca looked like a veritable forest, with wells close together producing from several levels. People shook their heads and said, "E. W. just can't miss."

A. E. Fath wrote a paper for the Geological Survey on the origin of the faults, anticlines, and the buried "granite ridge" in the northern part of the Mid-Continent oil and gas field. It was revealed by Fath and others that there was a subterranean granite ridge running southwestward into the Cherokee Outlet from Kansas. The Blackwell field lay along this ridge, and so did the Garber field.

It immediately became clear to E. W. why oil-bearing sands of the Pennsylvanian series were to be found at unexpectedly shallow depths as far west on the Red Beds as Garber. The Blackwell production had followed the northeasterly-southwesterly trend of this ridge, which is the granitic core of an ancient mountain that had caused the swelling of the Pennsylvanian and the Permian deposits above it, and had sealed the strata against its sides. Also it had caused anticlinal "humping" above its crest. The hydrocarbons in the sealed-off sand strata and the hydrocarbons in the sands of the humps were thus trapped.

This ridge is called the Ne-Ma-Ha, which in Osage means "Water Mountain." In eastern Kansas, where the Osage settled after the treaty of 1825, they found that the granite ridge came quite close to the surface and formed topographic features.

Here the water-bearing sand strata were eroded, so that water came out in springs, hence, Water Mountain, or Ne-Ma-Ha.

Later, when this "ridge," this ancient mountain core, was traced through Oklahoma, it was found to make a long-bow arc just as it leaves the old Cherokee Outlet, by swinging in a southeasterly direction. The Edmond field was much later found along its axis, as was the phenomenal Oklahoma City field, whose derricks sprang up around the state capitol in the 1930's.

The depth of the producing sand at Garber differed little from the depth of the Ponca field's first sand, despite the fact that it occurred farther west on the westerly dipping, and therefore deepening, Permian Red Beds. That the depth at Garber was not greater had upset E. W., because conditions did not harmonize with his image of the regional subsurface conditions. The information on the Ne-Ma-Ha ridge not only made the whole thing clear to him but appealed to his feeling for the romantic. The subsequent tracing of the ridge occupied his mind more than it occupied the thoughts of his geological department.

12

E. W. HAD BEEN INTERESTED in Mexico for some time. In 1919, after he had taken the options on an oil concession in the Republic of San Salvador, he decided to sail there by way of Tampico, Mexico, and the Panama Canal.

He had sent a reconnaissance party of three of his young men and his brother-in-law, C. E. Olden. They had taken boat from San Francisco in October. In December, E. W., Colonel Kenney, and W. H. McFadden embarked in their chartered yacht, the *Oneida*, at New Orleans.

He was close enough to the oilmen who had determined to elect a Republican president in 1920 to know that the air was filled with great enterprises for expansion in foreign fields. Woodrow Wilson had believed that foreign concessions were the root of revolution, especially in Mexico, where there had been attempts by the concessionaires to make and control presidents.

E. W. realized that the struggle among the big boys in Mexico might be too strenuous for him. He knew that, in another oil-rich area, Venezuela, the Mellons, with the Gulf Oil Company formed on his friend Guffey's interest in the Spindletop well—the company that had taken the best locations on the Gulf Coast—were establishing themselves firmly. But he saw his chance in the concession which he had tentatively bought from the concessionaire of San Salvador oil, Sr. Don Amelio Mosanyi.

It was for the purpose of inspecting the San Salvador concession, for which he was to pay $25,000, that he had sent his geologists, Spot Geyer, C. E. Hyde, and Grant Blanchard by boat from San Francisco as a reconnaissance party.

E. W. and his associates put in at Tampico, Mexico. Then in Mexico City he spent some time investigating the possibilities for taking over a blanket lease. The latter he soon found, though he only took over the control of the stock in the Franco-Española Oil Company. This lease consisted of about 275,000 acres, a block which had been built up by the Franco-Española Company lying just north of the Pánuco River, inland. The river was already well known along the coast in connection with the Tampico oil region.

The Pánuco lease lay along a fault reaching up into the mountains; this made the possibilities for trapped oil deposits very interesting. E. W. was very pleased indeed.

"Companies owned by the European capitalists and by the national banks of European governments were already in control of the most productive areas of Mexico and South America and were constantly increasing their holdings against the weak competition that was being offered by the American oil companies, unsupported and not even encouraged by their own government," he said sarcastically, thinking of Wilsonian policy. But he was encouraged by the belief that the fault, tending westward from the exploited areas of the Europeans, meant that he could extend the production fifteen miles inland. He took some pleasure in the thought that the Franco-Española had 275,000 acres. And he felt that only the great Dutch Shell geologists excelled his own in ability.

With the Franco-Española Company stock control, he got, besides the acreage that lay along the north bank of the Pánuco, more than sixty thousand acres in the states of Tabasco and Chiapas. This gave him almost 350,000 acres on the Isthmus of Tehuantepec. The Dutch Shell had got some production in Tabasco and Chiapas.

The two fields along the Gulf Coast and at the mouth of the Pánuco were at this time world wonders for production. The Tampico-Túxpam region had two highly productive fields. The south field, forty miles in length and a mile wide, extended in a north-south direction from Alamo to Dos Bocas, and the Topila-Pánuco-Ebano field, southwest of Tampico, extended for seventeen miles in length, and from one-half to four miles in width. Except for this intense production from fracture cavities in limestone, which was always in danger from water flooding, the whole Gulf Coast line, from Matamoros to Yucatán, was terra incognita as far as oil production was concerned.

E. W. realized the possibilities here on the Gulf Coast, but he had that old feeling that the big boys were in command and that the very atmosphere was charged with their power—not the power of the big boys of the East, but the power of cold, European diplomacy and trickery. Certainly Standard was holding its own there, as it ever did, but the great Standard had been a unit as mighty as a national political unit as long as he could remember.

Edward L. Doheny was there as well, the enterprising man who had started his career digging at the seepages with a spade where the once-sleepy village of Los Angeles, California, stood.

What could he do against European governments that seemed to control Mexico, and against what he considered the timid, foolish policy of his own government. Again, as he did in the Osage, he felt that perhaps there would be a great change in 1921, when the Republicans would end the nonsense of the Schoolmaster. Now was the time to prepare for that future, even as he had prepared for the opening of the Osage through his geological reconnaissance.

He had not enough money to compete against governments, not enough money to bid against European nations, but he felt instinctively that he didn't care to do his business that way. He went directly to the then president of the Republic of Mexico, Carranza.

The meetings with Carranza filled him with a sense of his own importance again. This man was not a peasant or a wild, hill-bandit adventurer. He was a gentleman, a *hacendado*, and when he bowed in a courtly manner to the gentleman of Pittsburgh, the prince of the Cherokee Outlet, E. W. returned the bow and felt that confidence which he always felt when he was free from the obligations of talking down. He felt that the very manner in which he gestured and sat and talked would be understood by the *hacendado* who sat opposite him.

E. W. knew sufficient geology to know that the potential oil-bearing strata would be found along the coast, not in the fractured strata of the Sierra Madre Mountains, or on the plateaus shining with volcanic disintegrations. With this in mind, he asked Carranza for millions of acres along the coast of Sonora, Sinaloa, and Lower California, and the President made vast concessions.

These millions of acres in Mexico, five million in Sonora alone, and some incredible millions in Lower California, as well as the approximately 350,000 acres on the Gulf Coast, were just areas of unproven territory. On the Gulf Coast, the general impression was of a jungle floor dappled by the hot light of the sun; of banana leaves waving like the ears of elephants; of palms reaching from the tangle of jungle growth into the sunlight; and of lagoons at the headwaters of hundreds of feeder creeks of the great Pánuco, like the fruits on the roots of a potato plant. A great half-lighted jungle, where the air is like the air of a Turkish bath, where vapors look poisonous, and to which the early Spaniards first gave the name *mal-airia*.

On the West Coast, one had to find fresh water for existence. Water was a prerequisite to any plan of man's. Here, except where the Gulf of California protected the land, the Pacific seemed to be ever charging the land, foaming along the coast. There were short, periodically-flowing streams, and there was flora in pockets along the west flank of the mountains, but mostly it was arid, shimmering land. The disintegrated volcanic material sparkled in the sun and ever gave the impression of wealth in precious gems.

Here, in his millions of acres, E. W. had the blanket lease of all blanket leases up to this time, but oil, he knew, would be found in some isolated structure, indicating an oil reservoir of only a few square miles perhaps. There might be a series of these spots in all this immensity of savage land. His geologists must cover this land with donkeys for pack animals, and must always be influenced by the available water.

He is supposed to have paid only $1,060,168 for these leases and concessions, the total area of which was equal to that of the entire state of West Virginia. He felt his importance. Never had any individual or company been granted such large concessions by the Mexican government, he felt sure.

He could sit at breakfast in Sanborn's now and enjoy that intangible, thrilling sensation created by people's whispers about him.

The menacing nights of Tampico thrilled him. The women who moved like predaceous, feline animals in the darkness, the men who sat or loafed, detached from both the joys and the ills of the world, intrigued him. The jungles, where there seemed to be no one in sight but where you constantly felt the presence of men, men as silent and as watchful as jaguars, seemed always ready for drama. The politeness of men with *jarros* on their backs, showing their white teeth, moving along the jungle paths with their easy coyote trot, their sandaled feet cracked and hardened like the epidermis of some reptile, inspired in him an urge to help them, yet gave him pleasure in their picturesqueness.

He was impressed in some paradoxical, primitive manner when he stood and watched the arrival of a boatload of blond Danish girls. He watched the black eyes of the bystanders. He was both a little nauseated and filled with a protective urge, yet there was something unaccountable in his feeling too, a shameful approbation. An entrepreneur had brought competition for the harlots of Tampico and inspiration for the blond-worshipping Mexican male.

His success and his good feeling toward the gentleman who was the president of Mexico downed entirely the former sensation of insignificance among the men who represented European interests in Mexico. He even forgot that he had come to

Mexico as an exploiter of petroleum deposits, and forgot also that the *Oneida* was not his own yacht. In fact, he felt that he himself personalized the wedge of American progress and enterprise in foreign lands. After an interview with him, a United Press staff correspondent wrote: "Romance and big business need not be strangers and there has always been romance in the oil business. It is the quest for hidden treasure—backed by the belief that America must explore the four ends of the world if she is to maintain her position in the international struggle for that treasure—that explains the ocean cruise of E. W. Marland, millionaire producer of Ponca City and Pittsburgh, head of the Marland Refining Company and other interests.

"Petroleum is the hidden treasure that prompted the voyage of the steam yacht *Oneida*. Traveling on his own private yacht, Marland and several of his associates lifted anchor here this week bound for the tropical waters of Latin America."

In talking of the lease on the West Coast, E. W. assured his interviewer that he had "deep faith in the oil possibilities of the Mexican states of Sonora and Sinaloa—faith so deep that in these states he plans to establish two or three geology camps, comprising about two hundred men, of whom twenty to fifty will be expert geologists. Here romance and adventure again appear upon the screen, for in Sonora the hunt for petroleum will be made partially in country that is infested with bands of Yaqui Indians, one of the wildest and fiercest Indian tribes alive today."

Before E. W. raised anchor to sail to Colón to pick up his geologists and from Colón to Colombia and Venezuela, he met John Hale. This was one of the important chance meetings in E. W.'s career.

John Hale was the secretary of an American businessman in Mexico, one Judge Haff. Hale had seen Zapata lead *paisanos* in from Guerrero in the south, and Villa lead his horsemen in from the north after the downfall of Huerta, and he had seen the two meet, like two grizzly bears respecting the prowess of each other, and decide to share the rule of the Republic, while Carranza and Obregón planned and waited.

Young John Hale had a special mixture for his pipe and could talk about wine and food and books and art, as well as about Mexico's kaleidoscopic changes in masters. He could talk interestingly of the days when a man carried his rosary in his hands whenever he took even a short train trip, of the days when a traveler could look out of his train window into the deep gorges and gashes of the Sierra Madre Oriental Mountains, along the railroad between Vera Cruz and Mexico City, and see whole trains lying crushed, like maimed, outlandish monsters, partly covered by subjungle growth.

E. W. and John Hale met in a cafe. After studying John for some time, E. W. said, "Please order dinner for me. I can only say '*huevos rancheros.*' "

They met again at Sanborn's, where E. W. went for breakfast. He moved over to John's table and said impishly, "Would Haff lend you to me to go as translator to South America?"

John asked, "Lend?"

E. W., "Yes."

John, "No."

The next day E. W. came to John's table, smiling pleasantly, and after finishing his breakfast said, "Would Haff let you go with me to South America as my interpreter?"

John, "Lend?"

E. W., "No."

They sat smoking for sometime, E. W. blowing the smoke from his cigarette toward the ornate ceiling, and John puffing at his large-bowled pipe.

The agreement was made that John would come with E. W. on his way back from South America as his private secretary. Neither realized that they had placidly formed an association which was to last until the end of E. W.'s days. John brought into his life a civilized kindliness, mellow companionship, efficiency, and loyalty that are rare. John, as his private secretary, was to see him move to the heights of glory, then watch him as his world slipped from under his feet. However, through it all, the thermometer of John's loyalty remained the same, unaffected. John was like another self, the self who knows where papers are, how much money is in the bank account—the efficient adjuster of annoying circumstances while the other self is occupied with dreams.

Spot Geyer, Grant Blanchard, and C. E. Hyde had nothing favorable to report on Salvador when E. W. picked them up at Colón. It was, they said, a rugged country of volcanic cones and necks like the ventilators of hell. They had ridden mules over the volcanic country and had found little except fracturing of the sedimentary rocks. They had found a seepage of oil, but they could not conceive of the earth's holding an intact reservoir there in that fractured land.

On to Colombia, but he made no leases. They looked over the possibilities in the Lago Maracaibo region of Venezuela, where E. W. was offered important leases, but for some reason he was unable to take them. It was thought that he had begun to worry about a cablegram from his treasurer at Ponca City. Here again it seemed that Petrolia was pulling at his sleeve. The lake of Maracaibo later became famous for its oil production.

They stopped at Caracas, where E. W. stood in wonder before an extravagant mass of Bougainvillaea. Here was a vine he wanted for his garden in Ponca City, but the fact that it could not thrive in the latitude of Ponca gave him a feeling of frustration. He always believed that he might have been a happier man if he could have had Bougainvillaea growing up the sides of the house on Grand Avenue where he could see it when he had breakfast.

He cared little for a lone red rose against a white wall, or a single, symmetrical, plume-like tree, but he loved the Red Bed plains that seemed to have no end, the bombardment of extravagant beauty from his gardens on Grand Avenue. He loved the wild forest and the Rocky Mountains of Colorado. Thus did the Bougainvillaea, that might climb over and eventually smother a whole tropical village with its beauty, appeal to him.

On his return to Ponca City he met with the directors of his Marland Refining Company and made statements which indicated that he would await a change in administrations in 1921 before making definite plans about his concessions in Mexico.

His attitude in the presence of his directors was conservative, "I have no statement to make regarding the policies of Marland Refining Company and Kay County Gas Company in connection with the development of the acreage recently acquired by me in Mexico. Whether these companies will enter that field will depend largely upon the attitude that may be assumed by our government toward American oil companies seeking sources of supply outside the United States.

"While in Mexico, I found in my visits to President Carranza and the ministers of the various departments, as well as minor government officials, a consistent government policy in regard to development of oil in that country. That policy in my judgment is sound and reasonable and not inimical to the interest of the American oil companies."

He said that he found a hostile attitude in his own government toward oil companies. "I cannot in justice to my friends, partners, and stockholders in my business employ their capital in this enterprise until I know fully whether our government intends to confiscate the oil produced by American companies or to buy it at a price warranted by the laws of supply and demand. I am not afraid of what the Mexican government may do, but I am afraid of conditions in Washington and what my own government might do, and I must wait until things are more settled in Washington before I will take any steps toward the development of this property."

E. W. sent Earl Oliver down to Mexico City to take charge of the Marland Oil Company of Mexico, later to be followed by Chester Westfall as manager. Others from the Ponca City office also went down in various capacities. For several months before the elections of 1920 there were indications that he was preparing for rather definite operations on his concessions. He had his economic department, under C. C. Osbon, set up classes in Mexican constitutional and commercial law for employees who might be sent to Mexico. He had dealt with a gentleman, and he would act as a gentleman. He had the classes in Mexican law stress the study of the Constitution of 1917, wherein was to be found the already famous Article 27, Section 2, which allowed only Mexicans, by birth or naturalization, and Mexican companies to acquire ownership in leases or to obtain concessions to develop mines, waters, or mineral fuels in the republic. The republic would grant the same rights to foreigners, provided they would agree to be considered Mexicans in respect to such property, and "accordingly not to involve the protection of the government in respect of same."

E. W. had no fear of Article 27, Section 2, of the Constitution of 1917, since he sincerely believed that he would treat the Mexican workers as he treated workers in Ponca City. The Mexicans would have his paternal interest; he would bring dignity and freedom to them. Also, he had noted that Carranza was conservative and that Article 27 had not been mentioned in their conversation.

13

BACK HOME, E. W. had more oil now than he ever dreamed of having. Because of the demand, the price was better than he ever hoped it might be. Now what could he do with all this oil? His refinery would have to be enlarged to take care of the oil from the Osage and Tonkawa fields. He had to have transportation, both by pipe line and by tank car, to market his oil and his refined product, gasoline, and many by-products. What if the local markets became glutted?

The Prairie Pipe Line Company set the price for oil, just as Standard companies had always set the price for oil. The water outlet which he had thought about when he first began to see the possibilities of important production from the Osage and areas farther west, he began to think of again. The ship canal from Houston to the Gulf of Mexico would have been the answer. That was the way the Spindletop Dome companies got away from the control of the Standard, he believed. They were close to the Gulf, and they ran their lines to the Gulf immediately. They had their outlet before the Standard could reach them with its long arm. He believed that this had saved the independence of the Gulf Oil Company and the great Texas Company.

He couldn't go down to investigate himself, but in 1919 he had sent Chester Westfall down. Chester had just come to him from Governor Williams' office in January, 1919. Most of E.

W.'s young men, Dr. Irving Perrine, L. E. Trout, Fritz Aurin, W. C. Kite, C. E. Hyde, Alvin Moncrief, Grant Blanchard, Spot Geyer, Seward Sheldon, and many others, had come to him direct from the University. Chester was not a geologist, nor had he done anything after leaving the University that might prepare him for the oil business. He had been outstanding at the University, where he had worked his way through the four years.

Chester was brilliant and eager. The fact that he knew little about the oil business seemed to matter very little to E. W., who was assured by Chester's sharp mind and energy. Youth and certain mental characteristics were sufficient qualifications for E. W., and if a young man with an alert mind also happened to be tall and handsome, E. W. would champion him against logic and the opinions of his friends. However, Chester was not tall, nor was he ever in need of E. W.'s championing.

Chester looked over the Gulf Coast for an outlet, but everything seemed to have been taken, either by Gulf Oil or by the Texas Company. Aransas Pass was open, but he decided that such a location would be too far away from the Ponca City headquarters and the Oklahoma production. He began to explore the Buffalo Bayou ship canal. He took his time. He knew that the outlet for which he sought was really for a future need, since the refinery at Ponca City at the time was only of about five hundred barrels capacity.

He finally found some land which was divided into many interests. He had a contract to purchase drawn up, a "service" contract, as distinguished from a contract for speculation. He then made a deposit of ten thousand dollars on the million-dollar property.

He had no idea what type of land might be needed for the indefinite outlet which E. W. had sent him to acquire—indefinite because E. W. didn't know what he wanted either. E. W.'s instinct for independence had demanded the outlet on the Gulf, but he was vague in his thinking about the nature of such a convenience.

The land had both high and low areas on it, but was on the

canal, which was as good as a location on the Gulf itself, they both believed. When Chester had left Ponca City for Texas, E. W. gave him few instructions; in his too-important-for-details manner he had said, "See what you can do down there."

When the payments fell due on the land by the canal, there was no money to send, and E. W. was away on the yacht cruise to Venezuela. Chester knew about the telegram that the Marland treasurer had sent to E. W. concerning the payment of salaries and about the message received in reply indicating that it was up to the treasurer to do something about it. He, E. W., would take care of the business at that end, the yacht end.

The ten thousand dollars had to be saved. The only way Chester could effect this was by the well-known business dodge of "injured party." In the attorney's offices at Dallas he became histrionically discouraged over the many individual interests in the land, which, of course, he had known about all the time. He appeared so injured and frustrated that he got the ten-thousand dollar deposit back for the company. Only a few years later the land was worth perhaps ten million dollars.

However, E. W. got his outlet on the Gulf in 1922 through which he could send his refined products all over the world. The capacity was adequate, but this outlet at Texas City, Texas, had to be bought from the United States Texas Corporation for $141,000. Included with the outlet was a thirty-year lease from the Texas City Terminal Company for rights-of-way, wharfage, and pipe lines. This was less than a compromise with the dream of 1919. There was a direct line of the Santa Fe Railroad between Ponca City and the Gulf port. But to depend upon either the Santa Fe or elbow room at the busy, crowded terminal was not his idea of strict independence.

His increased production made enlargements of his tank storage and of his refinery imperative. He ordered twenty-four storage tanks of 80,000 barrels capacity, which would increase his storage capacity 1,920,000 barrels. The addition to his refinery would cost $1,600,000, increasing its capacity from about 8,000 to 14,000 barrels daily.

On January 6, 1920, he opened his first retail outlet for

gasoline, a service station at Pawhuska. Sam Collins, Jr., had charge of the sales department of the company. He and E. W. had differing opinions about the color and general appearance of the stations that were to be built. In the British Isles and Scotland, when E. W. had stopped to fill his car tank with petrol, he had been rather struck by the fact that the petrol was brought out in cans. But there had been little effort to make this service a means for advertising a company's products. He knew that attractive filling stations would create a demand for Marland products. His announced policy was: "If we break even at our filling stations we are making money."

But he wanted to use the red triangle symbol as a motif in the designs of the stations, even if it meant the sacrifice of comfort to the customer. It was suggested that if he were allowed to carry out some of his ideas, the stations would look like fire houses. His sense of advertising was acute, yet that red triangle symbol was like his own name—he wanted to see it on everything.

It was really intoxicating to be a great man. When the famed geologist, W. A. J. M. van Waterschoot van der Gracht, joined him from the admired Royal Dutch Shell Oil Company, where he had been the chief engineer of the entire corporation, E. W. felt that he now had an important link with Europe and England, where he could undoubtedly make contacts to sell his products.

Van Waterschoot van der Gracht made a report for him on the value of his producing properties and his oil reserves, exclusive of the Mexican concession. It was encouraging to know that such a scientific research gave his properties and reserves, as of 1922, a valuation of $109,750,000, based upon oil at two dollars a barrel for 1922, $2.50 a barrel for 1923, and $3.00 for the future year of 1924.

Geology was gaining general recognition now, but E. W. felt that the time had arrived for new methods. He was still searching for a mechanism which would aid him in his search for more oil deposits. Then he thought of the core drills used to determine the thickness of coal beds in Pennsylvania and West Virginia. A short time thereafter, he and Spot Geyer started core drilling for evidence of saturated sands where the structure was not definite or, if present, not convincing. They would core drill to determine if the trouble and the expense of drilling a well were warranted. He was very proud of his secret knowledge and the use of new methods before others discovered them.

He said, "We introduced and succeeded in using the core drill to locate hidden structure for nearly a year before the scouts of other companies caught on to the method we had been using."

Not all geologists and oilmen will agree with him in this statement, but it indicates his pride in the discovery of a new technique.

When he finally got the seismograph from Germany, he could experience a sort of ecstasy, since here he had one of the modern devices which was all mechanism, and therefore highly satisfactory. The seismograph was used by the geologists of Europe to work out the intricate structure of the Alps. An explosion was set off, and the three types of waves sent out from the explosion center, through the strata, could be charted. The speed with which they traveled determined the type of rock through which they passed. Then, when they were deflected back from some formation, the time it took the return wave to be recorded indicated the depth of the obstructing stratum, thus giving a wave contour of the subsurface.

When van Waterschoot van der Gracht came from the Dutch Shell to the Marland Oil Company, he became a vice president. He knew about the seismograph and its use in the Alps, but E. W. was apparently the first to put it to commercial use. He and E. W. imported a complete seismograph crew from Germany. This crew was used in Oklahoma, East Texas, and on the Gulf Coast, in 1924 and 1925.

Marland geologists played with the seismograph on the Gulf Coast. They tried the explosion above the ground at differing heights, then on the earth, then buried just beneath it, in order to find the best place for the explosion.

E. W. gleefully said, "I had nearly two years' start on the

industry in the use of this geophysical method of locating favorable structures. I must have ruined half the settings of eggs and soured half the milk on the Gulf Coast with my miniature earthquakes before other geologists learned what we were doing."

One of the first things he did, naturally, was to establish a scientific research department, whose geologists and physicists subsequently studied the value of back pressure and repressuring out of which his company began to use gas in repressuring some of the failing wells. It was fairly well known then, even among laymen, that natural gas, which is always associated with petroleum, is the ally and conservator of the latter. It provides the force which makes oil wells flow naturally, it keeps oil moving through its natural catchments or traps, and it holds back, by its pressure, the ever-threatening underground seas of salt water.

Not only the bright young men back home from the war in France came to E. W., but General William L. Kenly joined him as an associate in the Marland Oil Company. General Kenly had been a part of the United States Air Service on the French front. He arrived when E. W. became interested in aviation, as he had in many other instruments of mechanical progress.

The chief interest at that time was in lighter-than-air craft. Everyone had been impressed by the Zeppelin raids over London. E. W., like most of the other people of the nation, was interested in German progress with the great dirigibles bearing the Zeppelin name, and his enthusiasm was the reason for General Kenly's joining the company.

Helium had been discovered in the gas from wells in the Osage, and in Kay County, and in wells in southern Kansas. In 1917, the United States Bureau of Mines had sent a railroad laboratory car to Ponca City. Bureau officials had George G. Shallenberger, one of E. W.'s bright young men, gather samples in gas bombs, which they furnished. Until after the war, no one was informed of the helium content of these gas wells. E. W. assumed it was adequate and planned a big helium plant at Ponca City. He had already made moves in England to furnish helium to that country, when the government by an act of

Congress appropriated all the helium in the United States. His plans were balked and his enthusiasm wilted when his company finally got a report from the Bureau of Mines that the helium content from his gas wells was only a small fraction of 1 per cent.

However, his belief that lighter-than-air craft were very important to war and transportation of the future kindled a new fire. The navy had built a plant at Fort Worth for wartime production of helium, an operation which the government would keep running, since President Harding was asking for funds for that purpose. Then it would establish other plants, not at Ponca City, certainly, but perhaps at Amarillo. Anyway, the government would encourage the development of dirigibles for transportation, and a group of citizens might form an organization with governmental approval and not only make profits but have continental, inter-American, and transatlantic service mature and ready for the military in the event of war—in the event of war, but no one was really thinking of war.

Such a corporation was founded, with a capitalization of $50,000,000, and E. W. and General Kenly were among the incorporators. The others were John H. Kirby of Houston, W. L. Mellon, president of the Gulf Oil Company and cousin of the secretary of the treasury, and Franklin D. Roosevelt, former assistant secretary of the navy and a recently defeated Democratic candidate for the vice presidency of the United States.

Bascom N. Timmons, the Fort Worth *Record* staff correspondent, became interested in the future of this idea. He quoted Benedict Crowell, formerly assistant secretary of war, head of the American Aviation Mission in Europe, and president of the Aero Club of America. Mr. Crowell expressed the dream of the incorporators.

He told Bascom Timmons: "Our aim is to provide rigid airship service in America first, and as time goes on, link this continent with the rest of the world by aerial routes; a service supplementing existing methods of transportation, one which will traverse space in a minimum of time and supply a means of travel both safe and comfortable.

"Later, service will be opened up to South America and to

Europe and across the Pacific to the eastern countries. Plans for the aerial routes to be used on these lines have been entirely completed. The ships will be about 1,000 feet long, with accommodations for more than one hundred passengers and luggage, and nearly fifty tons of mail and freight. Luxurious lounges, promenades, libraries, and salons are planned. State-rooms will be patterned after those of the most palatial ocean liners. Every means will be taken to provide for comfort.

"One of the most important points of construction will be the fact that the ships will be practically fireproof. Noninflammable helium gas will be used entirely."

This was the dream of 1922. In 1926 E. W. sponsored an air field for Ponca City. The flying field was to be a part of the area northeast of the city which he had bought and dedicated to a playground for the people of the city. E. W. was "desirous that a proper field be located at Ponca City so that it may have air mail facilities at the earliest possible date as well as make this city an aeronautical center."

While he was building his integrated oil company, dreaming of the world's beauty that he would bring to Ponca City, envisioning great rigid air liners with passengers in luxurious lounges floating high over the earth, he never forgot his workmen. He was proud of their spirit and interested in every detail of their work in the field and about the refinery. He would go out among them and watch them at work, quite often unrecognized.

During the frequent building of extensions to the refining plant and additions to the big office building, there were work stoppages because of conflicts within the unions or between union and nonunion members; but E. W. could boast, as his father had done back in Pittsburgh, that there were no strikes against him because of unfairness.

E. W. was absent from Ponca City when a dispute arose between local union workers and men sent down from Wichita, Kansas, with whom E. W. had a contract, because Wichita had open shop. Sam Collins, Jr., who was in charge during E. W.'s absence, was soon flashing Irish anger. He sent for the sheriff, but as he awaited his arrival, E. W. returned from his trip. Sam with anger and emotion told what had happened and what he had done. E. W. said, "Sit down, Sam. I know what you're up against, but we are dealing with men. We might convince them, but we won't force them. I wish that every laboring man belonged to a union and could have a vote—and that there were sincere leaders. You have to look out for the ambitious leaders. The men are all right."

As early as 1919, E. W. had protected his employees by insurance policies, all premiums being paid by the company. There was life insurance, payable to any named beneficiary, from one thousand to five thousand dollars according to length of service. Compensation according to Oklahoma state law provided for hospital and medical bills. He supplemented the Oklahoma laws with sickness and accident policies, paid for by the company, covering sickness from any cause and accidents not provided for in the state laws. This insurance was carried by the company without expense to the employee as long as he remained with the company. For the permanent employee, the company paid full salary, supplementing the insurance, during sickness or recovery from nonoccupational accidents.

In the summer of 1925 Ponca City had difficulty with the various local industrial unions. After delays and misunderstandings, E. W. urged members of the Chamber of Commerce and delegates from the local unions to meet at his offices for a conference.

He said, in opening the conference, "I give it as my firm conviction that we generally want to be fair and that the industrial differences of the community may be settled amicably and with fairness to all if and when they are submitted to a group of representative citizens who are gathered for the purpose of studying the conflict and coming to an agreement.

"There are three interested parties to every industrial dispute: labor, the employer, and the public. Some may think industrial progress depends upon the activity of labor leaders and the strength of the union; others may think that such progress depends upon the enterprise and cunning of the employer.

138

There is ample evidence in our industrial history to justify the belief that sound progress depends upon neither of these two great forces, but rather upon public opinion, which demands that both forces pull in the same direction and in the interest of the community." He said he believed that the working man ought to have not only a "living wage but a saving wage."

He set aside one whole floor in the new office building for shower baths, locker rooms, lecture and reading rooms for the exclusive use of his employees. There were clinics where physical and dental examinations were given without charge to employees. He believed it would take a genius among labor agitators to talk these things away.

When the Ponca City Chamber of Commerce was establishing an open-shop bureau, he substituted his Industrial Council Plan, wherein representatives from the unions and the Chamber of Commerce would meet to balance interests of the three parties, the union, the public, and the employer.

This idea was publicized in the state papers as "Marland's Golden Rule" arbitration system, and caught the attention of the Commissioner of Labor Statistics in the Department of Labor in Washington.

It was a simple plan, one that an adult might hear on a playground for children. The fact that so simple a plan could be "discovered" suddenly by the statistician in the Department of Labor, and be received so enthusiastically by other communities of the United States, causes one to wonder what men were thinking and doing in the 1920's.

E. W. remembered what he had learned from Rugby Colony in Tennessee and from his father about the rights and dignity of the common man.

It was said that E. W. was a national Republican and a state Democrat, which was true until after he lost his oil company; then he became a Roosevelt Democrat with enthusiasm, both nationally and locally. He began to make contributions to Democratic candidates early in his career in Oklahoma, just as the orthodox Republicans from Pennsylvania, West Virginia, and New York did when such support seemed necessary for the progress of their plans. If a Democrat is sure of election, naturally one is not inclined to bet on the local Republican, no matter where one's political heart and conscience might be. Some of his friends thought E. W. was a little stupid in his lavish support of candidates before he was sure that they were anything but dark horses. One close friend said, "Hell, E. W., why don't you wait until after the Democratic primary? Then you got a sure thing. Why do you waste your money on dark horses? Because they happen to part their hair in the middle, and look good?"

E. W. came out with a statement on November 1, 1922, when at Ponca City he introduced Oklahoma's aged, blind former senator, Thomas P. Gore. All good Democrats were speaking for their successful gubernatorial candidate of the 1922 primaries, one Jack Walton. In introducing former Senator Gore, E. W. said, "I am an Oklahoma Democrat. Since my position has been in doubt the last few days, I will state that Walton was not my choice, but that I believe the party is wiser than myself in its selection. I will vote for its choice, for Walton and the whole Democratic ticket."

He had just contributed to the national Republican campaign for Warren G. Harding. He said, "I am an Oklahoma Democrat," and that is exactly what he meant. In the state's 1922 gubernatorial campaign, he put his money on a dark horse, one R. H. Wilson, who had been state superintendent of public instruction and a member of the School Land Commission in 1912, and lost. Some of the other oil men of the state supported Jack Walton even during the primaries. Two oil men from Tulsa, one a Democrat, C. J. Wrightsman, and the other a Republican, Waite Phillips, one of the noted brothers of the Phillips Petroleum Company, were betting on Walton before he was selected as the Democratic candidate. E. W. supported him after the primaries, and his fifteen-hundred-dollar contribution was used by Walton to entertain the members of the legislature during the January, 1923, session. E. W., with his Roxana and Dutch Shell friends, donated $73,000 to the Democratic state campaign.

Later Jack Walton met E. W. on the latter's private railway car at Oklahoma City, where they talked about Walton's difficulties, one of which was his desire to have a home fit for the governor of a state. There was no governor's mansion at that time.

There was a house for sale on Seventeenth Street in Oklahoma City by one Walter D. Caldwell, and Jack Walton wanted to buy it, but lacked $30,000 of the $48,000 which Caldwell asked for it. Walton had assured Caldwell that he had friends who would buy the six notes representing the $30,000 balance, those mentioned being C. J. Wrightsman of Tulsa, E. W. Marland of Ponca City, and C. L. Page of Sand Springs and Tulsa. E. W. took the six notes, which were to pay 5 per cent, and Jack Walton got his house.

This was just a deal between men who had need for each other. But the committee on investigation and impeachment of the state House of Representatives listed twenty-two specific charges against the newly-elected governor, Jack Walton, so that during the proceedings which impeached Walton in the autumn of 1923, E. W. was again connected with state political scandal. This time he was a wealthy man, a veritable prince of the Southwest. His name brought respect and his most trivial actions were interesting. When the charges against Walton were published, in October, 1923, Article 4 stated that "corruption was shown in his [Walton's] purchase of the residence of Walter D. Caldwell, for which he gave $30,000 in notes, and which were sold to E. W. Marland, the oil man, who then had large dealings with the School Land Commission, of which he [Walton] was ex-officio chairman."

This was a blow to E. W.'s pride. Jack Walton was not his friend in any sense of the word. Walton and E. W. both opposed the Ku Klux Klan, which had become disturbingly important in Oklahoma, just as it had in other states in the frenzied 1920's. But this was not a sufficient bond between them.

He, E. W. Marland, had to appear before these unimportant members of the state government at a definite time, and had no choice. E. W. Marland, whose name was known and respected all over the Mid-Continent, in Mexico, in New York City, and in London, must submit to these fellows. There was no question of haughty dismissal by means of his don't-bother-me-with-details attitude.

"Marland entered the Senate chamber leaning on a cane, and holding his hand on his back as if in pain," wrote a press observer. The top galleries, which held the largest crowd since the early days of the trial, sat tense as he walked to the witness chair.

E. W. said that the transaction was a business deal. "I received 5 per cent for the use of my money and the satisfaction that the governor of our state had a decent home to live in as long as he was governor." One of his enigmatic smiles would have been a better answer.

After E. W.'s testimony, there was a demand that the total amount of the contributions by Marland and the Dutch Shell to Walton's campaign be given and placed in the record. The Democrats of the legislature objected to this, but said they would acquiesce if the Republicans would divulge the amount of the donations made to their party by the Standard Oil. Glasser, to whom this challenge was given, had once introduced a bill which, if enacted, would have driven the Royal Dutch Shell Company and other corporations owned by European interests from Oklahoma.

E. W.'s flirtations with Dutch Shell were watched very closely. His visit to Sir Henri Deterding in London and his evident admiration of the men who ruled the Royal Dutch Shell were talked about and speculated upon. This company, like the Hudson's Bay Company and the old East India Company, was far more romantic to him than Standard and the American enterprises of the dollar-princes. They were baronial powers, backed by their strong governments. They were governments within the government.

Even without his inherent Anglophile tendencies, he loved the Anglo-European atmosphere of Dutch Shell, the dignity, the quiet efficiency, especially in the period of clatter in the 1920's, when Americans seemed to be making so much more noise than sense about their efficiency.

The Dutch Shell had interests in Russia, Roumania, Egypt, Central America, and the East Indies, and was represented in Mexico by the Mexican Eagle Oil Company and in the United States by the Roxana Oil Company. It was well known that Dutch Shell would be a very serious rival of the Standard companies, once it got a better foothold in the Mid-Continent field, where the independents, for the moment, had broken Standard's control of the nation. The old monopoly with which Standard had controlled the refining and the transportation of oil from western Pennsylvania, cutting the producers off from the Atlantic seaboard, was not effective in the spacious Mid-Continent.

When the news came that E. W., the head of the Union Oil Company, and the head of the Producers and Refiners Corporation were in London at the same time, the newspapers hinted of a coming battle of the giants. Keith J. Fanshier of the Wichita, Kansas, *Beacon* wrote with restraint on September 3, 1921: "The vision of a Mid-Continent competitor of the Standard Oil, able to take care of itself, give blow for blow, with millions of dollars in reserve and no desire to be bought or stop fighting, is in the process of becoming reality.

"Official admission of this fact has at last been made by the Dutch Shell interest, and negotiations are now under way in London for the purchase by the powerful British and continental organization heads of vast producing, refining, and marketing properties in the Mid-Continent and Rocky Mountain oil fields of the United States.

"The completion of the transaction will mean the consummation of a deal of such size that other petroleum deals of recent years, even those involving tens of millions of dollars, will be dwarfed.

"The essence of the proposition is that these British financiers . . . are trying to buy out the Producers and Refiners Corporation of America, and that negotiations also are under way looking toward the transfer of all Marland interests to the European power. In addition, the powerful Union Oil Company of Delaware is the object of a deal, hanging upon a proposed transfer of a majority or at least a large portion of its stock to the Dutch Shell."

A president of an independent company in Kansas and a stockholder in the Producers and Refiners Corporation said that if such negotiations were completed "it would mean a real fight." It was thought that the Standard "would not mince matters."

Keith Fanshier went on to write in conclusion, "Periodically the great majority of oilmen have hoped that a great, new independent concern will arrive and do battle with the Standard. Once this hope concentrated in the Sinclair; at another time in the Uncle Sam Oil. Both are still alive, but they for different reasons may be regarded now more on the order of smaller contemporaries rather than of threatening adversaries of Standard."

Thus fear of the Standard was creeping into the free Mid-Continent, while E. W., the Anglophile, with his Osage and Tonkawa and other fields, his strategic position on the plains, was said to be flirting with the powerful Dutch Shell. Newspapers carried stories about strange men from London visiting at the big house on Grand Avenue in Ponca City. They made much of Dr. van Waterschoot van der Gracht's change of allegiance from the Dutch Shell to E. W.

Later, in an article for *Brass Tacks* magazine, E. W. confirmed the rumor of his flirtations with the Royal Dutch Shell Company: "In 1920 I organized the Marland Oil Company and took over into that company all my oil and gas interests, which had become so extensive, as well as valuable, that they needed the type of management that only a centralized, corporate control could give them. I did not organize this company for the purpose of increasing my personal fortune or to sell stock. Long before that I had all the money I wanted and had ceased trying to make money for myself.

"I was ambitious, however, to build a completely integrated oil company that would take its place in the petroleum industry and compete for markets with the Standard Oil companies.

"Previously, when I organized Marland Refining Company,

which became a subsidiary of Marland Oil Company, I gave to my associates who had been with me during the years of the growth of my company large blocks of stock, representing a considerable interest in the company. This stock they exchanged for stock in the Marland Oil Company, when it was organized, and I made them directors and officers of that company. At the same time I made a very large number, if not all, of the employees of the company substantial stockholders, by furnishing them the opportunity to purchase stock on easy terms.

"The year 1921 was a year of outstanding success for Marland Oil Company. We had discovered and opened the Burbank Field in 1920, and discovered and opened the Tonkawa Field in 1921. These were two major pools, each making over one hundred thousand barrels daily, in which we had very extensive holdings of property.

"In the summer of 1921 I visited Sir Henri Deterding in London and organized the Comar Oil Company, which was owned equally by the Royal Dutch Shell and the Marland Oil Company. This little company, in which we never had more than one million dollars invested, made for Marland Oil Company's half interest from the production of oil over twenty-five million dollars in the next five years. I made the contract which founded this company after studying the exploration and development methods of the Royal Dutch Shell Company in Mexico and South America, and after coming to the conclusion that their scientific advancement was away ahead of any American oil company.

"By 1923 our production had grown to such a large amount from our various fields that it far exceeded the requirements of our own refinery, and I made a contract with the Standard Oil Company of New Jersey for the sale to it by Marland Oil Company of thirty-thousand barrels of crude oil daily for a period of several years. This contract was made with Walter Teagle, who at that time (February, 1923) believed that there was an impending shortage of oil and was glad to secure all the oil he could for his Standard Oil Company of New Jersey refineries.

This contract and others made with East Coast refineries furnished us with a market for crude oil which was very profitable to our company and, since these contracts gave Marland Oil Company a pipe-line gathering charge, we assumed a very important place in the petroleum industry in the United States.

"Our broader markets made it necessary for Marland Oil Company to build pipe lines and tank farms for the delivery of this oil, and for storage of surplus production for future delivery. This required a considerable, immediate outlay of money and I borrowed from all the banks with which I had business connections in Oklahoma, Kansas City, St. Louis, and Chicago, and one bank in New York City. I established lines of credit with these banks for current borrowings of five million dollars, which was not a great amount, considering the fact that we were having a gross income of that much, or more, per month."

He began to think like a Rockefeller. He talked of building his own pipe line to Chicago, largely because he had uncovered a rail transport problem. He had only the Missouri, Kansas & Texas Railroad to play against the Santa Fe Railroad when he thought that his shipments of refined products, especially gasoline, were being restricted by the freight charges of the Santa Fe. He had paid a total of $1,013,060 during 1921, and he had let this railroad know that the Marland Refining Company had contributed to the success of the railroad in the state of Oklahoma.

E. W. had no doubt that the refined products could be shipped as successfully as the crude had been shipped since the day of Cherry Creek in Western Pennsylvania. He was ready, he informed the Santa Fe, to build the pipe line.

He also planned to build a railroad so that his products could move west and east as well as north and south, complementing his drive for greater outlets to the Gulf. He realized that he must have life lines to water, and that he must not be at the mercy of the railroads or the ubiquitous pipe lines of the Standard companies. He could, perhaps, build a pipe line to Chicago for his refined product, and build a railroad, in association with other men of Ponca City, which would give him an outlet to the west, perhaps connect with the Rock Island or the Frisco railroads.

John D. Rockefeller, when he was building up the Standard, could not afford to be at the mercy of the railroads, so he played one against the other and got his famous rebates and "draw-backs," later setting out to control the Atlantic seaboard termi-nals and the pipe lines feeding them, to obtain a complete mo-nopoly of the oil business without becoming a producer.

E. W. and his associates in Ponca City and the Oklahoma Corporation Commission, a state control agency, recommended to Washington that permission be granted them to build their railroad.

The Santa Fe management presented a letter of protest through the railroad legal counsel, James Cottingham, and of-fered a petition to be heard before the Interstate Commerce Commission, to prevent E. W. from building his Ponca City Oil Field Railroad from Ponca City to Billings.

The Santa Fe management contended that their road was furnishing all the required facilities and that E. W. was looking at the earnings of the Santa Fe in Ponca City for the year 1922, which amounted to $4,611,880. E. W. got neither his pipe line nor his Ponca City Oil Field Railroad, a matter which his proto-type, John D. Rockefeller, would have deemed necessary to his existence.

14

THE EARLY 1920's, which saw the beginning of E. W.'s phenomenal "arrival," were the beginning of the decade of circuses and a partial reversion of the country to barbarism. Only the development of mechanism indicated that man was actually progressing. This was the beginning of the breakdown of standards of morality and decency, induced, perhaps, by the feeling of disillusionment over Woodrow Wilson's failure to materialize an impossible dream for the people of the world. The people of Europe seem to have conveyed their hopelessness to America, where it was expressed by the abandonment of gentle Victorian restrictions and by a free interpretation of God's laws. The thought that thousands of bodies were decaying in the fields of France without the manifestation of divine wrath may have contributed to this expression. Perhaps there had been no war in all history from which the details of the battlefield had been brought so vividly to the people. There was something about machine killing which suggested an animal's end—and oblivion.

It was the beginning of the decade of flagpole sitting, ocean flying, hip-pocket flasks, bathtub gin, and home brew.

It was the beginning of the little gods who were deified because of their millions. The decade was watched over by a little pasteboard god who occupied the White House after the death of Warren G. Harding. Three of the little gods dispensed with the customary oracles and spoke directly to the American people. The god of Detroit could speak because he was the richest man on earth according to American computations. The thin, pale, lonely man who was Secretary of the Treasury could also speak thus because he was one of the richest men on earth. This man from Pittsburgh had been built up by his propagandists as the benefactor of the branch of mankind residing in America, and the thoughtless hordes began calling him "Uncle Andy."

The little god in the White House could have been a Caligula, instead of a blown-up Marcus Aurelius, and the people would have cared not at all. They desired nothing from their government, since they believed that the good things which they enjoyed were merely sponsored by their government. It was paradoxical that their sly, orthodox, penny-wise President, with his New England outlook, should have become the symbol of an extravagant, childishly excited nation.

The early years of the 1920's saw the beginning of the little god of the Cherokee Outlet, lost in the frenzy of the nation, but with his light none the less bright on the Red Beds.

E. W. was never smugly contented, like some of the still-faced boys who kept careful account of their property and carefully guarded it. He refused to compute his wealth. His energy and genius had extracted wealth from the earth where "no one lost what I gained," and his intelligence had delegated the care of it to others. If a million dollars were not there when he needed them, then it was up to someone to produce them. If he had the whim to make a donation of several thousand dollars, he would write a check, often without consulting his staff, who never knew when they might be compelled to rush about to find funds to cover. He was with his staff like a spoiled, irresponsible woman who makes no attempt to keep check stubs on her allowance, and whose husband must sweat to keep her account straight. He depended upon his name and his ability to take care of all matters of temporarily confused finances. If there were insufficient funds in his personal or company account—and he never cared much about drawing a sharp line between them—

he would assume complacently that everyone must know that he was still there as the fountain from which all this plenitude had come. If uncontrollable little winds had whipped the fountain's jet about for a time, leaving a pool to the windward to dry up momentarily, one would know that the depression would be filled again when the wind changed.

But sometimes it was beyond the power of Seward Sheldon and Bob Clark, his young assistant treasurers, to refill the sack into which he had plunged his hand. Leases must be sold, or other arrangements made, to meet the terrific expenses of the company's operations, especially the weekly payroll. E. W. and his "lieutenants," as he called them, would sit around a table with men who sensed his needs, and the bargaining would be uncomfortable. At such times, E. W., annoyed that such discomfort should come to him, might give too much in order to be free from the annoyance. But his young men would obstinately attempt to make a better deal. When the discussions were most troublesome he would excuse himself and lie on the office couch and pretend that he had gone to sleep. His feigning sleep would kill the unpleasant day through adjournment of the others.

When his company reached the stage where, by its very size and wealth, it could more or less take care of itself, E. W. seemed to be searching for a way to express the energy which was no longer needed from him for its maintenance. He handed stock on silver platters to his associates and gave them unheard-of salaries and bonuses. When John Hale, who had transacted some business for him in Toluca, Mexico, returned to Ponca City, E. W. said, "John, you've made me some money, now I want you to have half of the profits that you've made possible."

Within the decade of the '20's he gave money to all denominations whose churches needed furniture, property, or a new building, to the Boy Scouts, Girl Scouts, and the American Legion Orphans' Home. He financed the publication of a dictionary of the Osage language by the Smithsonian Institution, and gave money for the building of the student union and the stadium at the University of Oklahoma.

For Ponca City he set aside grounds, just west of the company's office building, for an athletic field, clubhouse, and grandstand. Here Ponca City's own baseball team would play. He specified that the team would be a city team and not a company team. Here also would be a quarter-mile track and a field for the football games of the Ponca City High School.

He gave to the city a tract of land 100 by 140 feet and a cash subscription of one hundred thousand dollars for the erection of a building to house the Alfred Marland Masonic Blue Lodge and the local American Legion Post, as well as to provide facilities for a young men's club like the Y.M.C.A. He had urged a strong Y.M.C.A. organization for the city for several years.

Sometimes as he sat in his apartment in the Plaza Hotel in New York City, he would think of something additional he might do for the children of Oklahoma, and soon he would be dictating a wire offering a donation. But he had no desire to mingle with people and talk with them; children seemed almost to bore him. He once said that the trouble with the ordinary person was that there were "always too many of him in one place at the same time."

He also expressed himself in play. He liked conversation with some, and he liked to drink Scotch and soda. Just as he continued to love horses and dogs and hunting, he continued to love to play poker with deep concentration, except that now he could afford to lose or win as much as seventy-five thousand dollars.

Every species of animal that defends itself, or depends upon the overtaking or destruction of others for food, must spend much time playing. The play of such animals is utilitarian, since in it they re-enact the manner in which they defend themselves or the craft by which they take their prey. A cougar plays with a saddle blanket lost by a pack outfit in the mountains, and the house cat attacks a dead mouse or a ball of yarn. Rabbits and squirrels, the hunted, play at chasing each other and taking refuge.

Acquisitive men usually play those games wherein they

151

seem to be keeping bright their power to remain in the struggle. Poker is one of those games.

Many a night E. W. and his lieutenants and friends would sit until daybreak keeping their swords of wit and armor of trickery bright for the struggle of life. They would open their collars and allow their ties to fall awry. The ash trays would pile up into pyramids of cigarette butts, and there would be half-empty glasses at hand.

There were hundreds of private poker parties during a year. Sometimes there were lavish affairs at the Arcade Hotel, or at some private home, with Filipino boys in white jackets and glistening Negro cooks in the kitchen, and, perhaps, wild duck or venison from some private estate, or beef or guinea or turkey. Ponca City, like St. Louis, Houston, and New York, had never recognized the state of prohibition: there was always plenty to drink.

There was such a celebration to honor the fact that the land department of the Marland Oil Company had made a two-million-dollar profit from a ridiculous investment of two hundred thousand dollars. After the second or third cocktail, the game started. All night they played, the dinner lay untouched.

When dawn came there were checks under piles of treasury notes, and silver dollars in stacks all over the place. The floor was soiled with cigarette ash, and there were burnt spots where cigarettes had been allowed to die without attention. There were complacent faces, like E. W.'s, haggard faces, careless faces, and faces that glowed even through their greyness. There were those, sanguine and greedy in victory, who wanted to talk about the details of the night in voices hoarse from cajoling the dice. At one party a player saw one of E. W.'s lieutenants "cold deck" him for fifty thousand dollars.

E. W.'s love of horses and wildlife was reawakened by the plains. Horses, first brought to the plains by the Spaniards had given to the Plains Indians a distinct culture. It would have been rather difficult for anyone to remain uninterested in horses, with the 101 Ranch constantly in his consciousness and the plains all around, where a man on foot was as insignificant as a beetle.

He soon developed a love for hunting and for the companions of the hunter, hounds and guns. Like the true sportsman, he became interested in the conservation of wildlife. He had a three-hundred-acre tract northeast of Ponca City fenced with six-foot high game fence. Here he made lakes and planted trees and raised grain to be harvested by the birds. He stocked the lakes with fish, and the whole preserve with pheasants, mallards, geese, swans, and peacocks.

Later he offered to stock areas all over the state with his surplus. Through his magnetism and enthusiasm, he inspired conservation of wildlife in a region where not long before buffalo had been slaughtered for their hides and prairie chickens had been shot daily for the market.

He left large islands in the lakes of his preserve and planted them with flowers and cover so that his swans could nest there. He converted the old rock quarry, the source of the stones for his buildings, into a swimming pool. He allowed the public access to his preserve and the natural swimming pool, just as he permitted it the use of the pool which was a part of his private estate on Grand Avenue. He had roses planted along the fence in each span of the game preserve fence, so that there were miles of roses bombarding the traveler along the public highway.

In a grandiose effort to entertain his directors and friends, E. W. established a hunting camp on December 1, 1922. He had a tent city built, glorified with electricity, a sewage disposal system, and running hot and cold water, on a big horseshoe bend of the Arkansas River southeast of Ponca City. This was a section of the 101 Ranch called the Bar L and was still in its original state, with the exception of a lone oil derrick, whose boiler puffed a steam cloud into the air.

He put his associates, McFadden and "Press" Lowrance (the latter then mayor of Ponca City) in charge, and he invited people from New York City, St. Louis, Kansas City, Tulsa, Wichita, and Oklahoma City. McFadden brought his hounds and E. W. furnished horses and guns. The guests could hunt behind bird dogs for quail, shoot ducks along the river, hunt raccoons at night, or run coyotes across the river on the Osage prairie.

153

Teams were kept busy hauling up great logs for the fire at night, a fire that sent its tongues of yellow flame high above the trees and could be seen for miles.

There was jazz music from a primitive radio in the tent put up for the purpose of dancing. Guests could sit and talk about the fire, drink, play poker, roll dice, or dance. In poker, the sky was the limit, and during the eight days of the encampment it was perhaps exceeded.

To make the scene more picturesque, an Indian village was erected near the camp, with a Ponca chief as host, and Colonel Joe Miller of the 101 Ranch arranged for Indian dances. McFadden brought a pair of black bear cubs and a pair of young cougars from his last hunt in the Rockies.

E. W.'s surplus energy soon found expression in the building of stables and kennels: stables for hunters and for the breeding of polo ponies, and kennels for his packs of Walker and beagle hounds. The cowhorses used on the ranches of the Southwest, short coupled and well muscled, able to turn with the trickiest calf or stop with their hind feet dug into the turf like hook brakes, were good basic material for the breeding of polo ponies. His polo ponies were of the best. They were available for anyone who wished to play. He had several polo fields prepared, on which his "yellow" and "red" teams played against each other. A team chosen from the players of both played as the Marland Oil Team. They played against the Ft. Sill Artillery Post team, against teams from Wichita, Kansas, Wichita Falls, Texas, Kansas City, Missouri, and Ft. Reno, Oklahoma.

The hunters E. W. imported from England, and with them a real M.F.H., Major Don Henderson. The Major agreed with Siegfried Sassoon's old huntsman, whose idea of hell was "the coldest scenting land I've known, and hounds would never get their heads down; and officers from barracks overrode 'em all day long, on weedy, whistlin' nags that knocked a hole in every fence."

E. W. had the best hunters available, so Don didn't find it necessary to suffer from "weedy, whistlin' nags," but hell was generated every day the hunters took the field. It was the Marland executives and employees, not "officers from barracks," who overrode the hounds.

Across the savage prairie of the Osage and the undulating plains of Kay County would stream the field, on imported hunters, following imported hounds, on the scent of imported foxes. In Kay County they might find only a few limestone fences and Osage orange hedges too high to clear, but they also found Bohemian and German farmers, whose inherited ideas of thrift were not modified by the wild, open plains, and the huntsmen had to respect the farmers' crops. In the wild Osage, where there was nothing but staring, dumbfounded cattle, the field could go galloping after a bewildered fox that had just been turned loose.

Where the game of hunting has tradition, dignity, and taboos, especially in England, it would seem that each side—the hunters and the fox—knows the rules. But in the primitive Osage, where the coyotes chant to the moon and leave musk messages on limestone rocks, fence posts, and Geological Survey pins, the imported foxes knew something the huntsmen didn't know: that the coyotes of the Osage were warning the foxes to leave; they wouldn't allow them to encroach upon their domain.

It didn't take Major Don Henderson long to realize that foxes wouldn't stay across the Arkansas River in the coyote-dominated Osage country. When the next hunt was formed, he had Louis Soldani, the French-Osage son of one of the region's prominent families, haul the fox in a car to the Osage prairie and turn him loose, then the hounds would be allowed to find the scent and the field would be off.

The field assembled, their coats as red as the native sumac, and the fright-erected tails of the Hereford steers disappeared like whips over the distant prairie ridge. But Henderson was unhappy. It was enough that he couldn't hold his field back when the fox was viewed—his face was red and he felt, as he said, "sick to my bloody stomach" from shouting and swearing at the people who were overriding the hounds and bumping up and down like colored sacks of flour—and now the bloody hounds had lost their nose.

One hound mouthed mournfully, then the pack, with their heads down, made a circle and came back to the car which had hauled the fox, where they reared up, braced by their front feet, and sniffed. Henderson was about to swear in the shame of defeat because the pack was back-trailing. He rode closer to the car. There on the front seat, blinking contentedly, was the fox. He had made a short circle and then had come back to his old playmate in the red coat rather than endanger his life in the range of the coyote.

A large canvas of the field, as it was composed on a certain day, was painted for E. W. by Randel Davey and hung in the mansion which E. W. built later in the game refuge. Former members of the hunts go there to point nostalgically to each one, recalling the days when E. W. brought the world of Bucking-hamshire and Oxfordshire to the people of Ponca City on the Red Bed plains of the old Cherokee Outlet.

E. W. was proud of his lieutenants and his employees in general. He was not aware, however, that all the people who took part in the hunts were not filled with an appreciation of the new fields for enjoyment opened up to them. E. W. chose to believe that he had opened the doors to a sort of earthly heaven by making fox hunting and polo available to the people of the plains.

What he did, of course, was to make a vogue of both. Un-accustomed men soon learned the parlance of polo, if they never quite adjusted to hunting, and soon, in the spirit of the poker table, they began to trade in ponies and pay fancy prices for them. They discussed each other's ponies as they might discuss golf handicaps.

It was the thing to do, to watch the men play polo, and the women sat in their cars talking about clothes and servants or playing cards on their knees until the field followed the ball up to and by their position. Then there was always one to say, "Here come the men!" and they would look up to follow the play with interest, ready to applaud, hoping to be able to ap-plaud.

E. W. thought that the gift of freedom implied happiness. He didn't realize that the high salaries which he paid his executives and heads of departments freed men who didn't know how to use freedom. His company officials, having no economic fears, expressed their natural urges rather freely. But they soon satiated their appetites, and there was nothing else. Even the Mecca of all inlanders, New York City, became dull to them as they made frequent trips there. The women of New York suffered a fading of their glory with familiarity, and so did whisky and champagne. Fantastically dressed and rhythmically kicking choruses became commonplace. Even the noted people of the headlines and the gossip columns became just people in the smoky, dimlighted speakeasies of the decade.

One night, Spot Geyer and Jack Vickers, the latter an oilman and polo player from Wichita, Kansas, found diversion in tossing dollars at an ash can at Forty-fifth and Sixth Avenue. And one night, Spot Geyer, Jack Vickers, John Alcorn, and John Hale, sat on the curbing at Forty-second and Broadway, long after the New Amsterdam Theatre was closed, and talked with Will Rogers about polo ponies and the worthiness of certain players.

E. W. could express himself through the realization of his dreams for the pleasure of the people of Ponca City, but his young men did not have this outlet. Even making money seemed sometimes to pall, for they had many opportunities outside their salaries and interests in Marland Oils. There were little companies formed where they might take acreage and then sell to the parent company with profit for all. There was the Southland Royalty Company, the Northland Royalty Company, and other activities which might have absorbed all their acquisitive interests. The Southland Royalty Company, which absorbed the Marland Employee's Royalty Company and the Crescent Royalty Company of Colorado, had as its field Texas and New Mexico. The Comar Oil Company, it has been suggested, was organized for the purpose of evading the Department of the Interior's restriction of acreage in the Osage to 4,800 acres to each operating oil company. It was to the advantage of

E. W. and his associates to hold as much acreage in the Osage as possible.

There was excitement and maneuvering, and the chance to make money; there was polo, and poker, and visits to New York, Kansas City, and to the hospitable and frenzied Texas cities. And there were women everywhere, with short dresses and shingled hair, who, barbarically binding their breasts, attempted to look like shapeless young boys. They dressed and undressed without grace or beauty, and drank from silver flasks as coal miners drank from their pint bottles of moonshine on Saturday night.

There was no prohibition as far as E. W. and his young men were concerned. They had the best bourbons and ryes, and they got their Scotch and champagne "right off the boat." Many a long-haired prig became a shingled "bottle baby," and many a Sunday-school boy became "a quart-a-day man" in the delirious decade. It was the bottle that remained the one subject of interest when money and luxuries palled for many of the Marland lieutenants, whose capacity for the utilization of freedom he had characteristically overestimated.

But while life was becoming dull and commonplace for his lieutenants, his employees in general were happy, loyal, and hopeful. John Duncan Forsyth built them houses of sound design, new additions were opened, streets were widened, and flowers were planted. Jack Forsyth brought Spanish colonial architecture to Ponca City from California and New Mexico. E. W. gave land, close to where the rival settlement of Cross had originated, for the building of a hospital in the Spanish colonial style. It is like a tranquil *hacienda's casa grande*, the picture being enhanced by the black-robed nuns who walk sedately in the cool corridors. The atmosphere is that of an eternal siesta.

E. W.'s Japanese gardener, Hatashita, brought to Ponca City and cultivated scores of flowers that would grow in the Permian soil. When a friend built a new house, E. W. was interested. Soon his gardener would appear to plant flowers from the Marland gardens and advise in the landscaping. He wanted everyone to have flowers and space for gardens, and, when they should desire them, thick rugs and oil paintings for their interiors.

When Sam Collins, Jr., built his house on Central Avenue, E. W. came to visit. The large comfortable room where he sat was beautiful and restful, but E. W., after looking around, said, "Sam, you ought to have Persian rugs on your floor. You ought to have a good oil painting there above the fireplace—you ought to have two or three oil paintings."

"I know," said Sam, "but I don't want oil paintings, and I can't afford expensive rugs. What's the use of having expensive things you don't want?"

"You want beautiful things—that's what makes life worth while," said E. W.

"I know," answered Sam, "but I like it the way it is. I don't intend paying out a lot of money for something that I don't like just because it's beautiful and expensive. Maybe I don't like expensive oil paintings. These carpets are good enough for me, too."

"Yeah," insisted E. W., "you better let me send my man around with some pictures."

Sam was his brother-in-law. He had been with him in West Virginia, had walked with him in Pittsburgh in 1907 and 1908 when they didn't have car fare, and he was independent-minded. Others usually acted upon "Ernie's" suggestions.

E. W., when asked about his determination to bring the good things of the world to the plains, said:

"Maybe I did all this because I subconsciously remembered my narrow escape from the ranks of the employed. Or maybe my so-called philanthropies were just intelligent selfishness—'good business.' Who can tell why we do some of the things we do? I spent money like water on my people and my town—and they flourished and bloomed like the rose.

"They were a contented, happy company, and they made money for me at a great rate. Good fortune may have spoiled a few of my lieutenants, but not many. The town was too small and everybody knew everybody else too well to permit anyone to become 'high hat' or 'stuffed shirt.' This was the land of opportunity. The employee of today might become the employer of tomorrow. Hope and confidence and the realization that there was an opportunity for everyone were in the very air they breathed. Mutual respect between officers and men made the hardest kind of work a joy.

"Bonus plans, premiums for discoveries or improvements, and big pay for good work were also responsible for this atmosphere and helped to solve many a technical problem. Marland Institute, a school for employees, gave everyone a chance for improvement, and, above all, the security of employment was responsible for their happiness."

In the twenties, the people of the plains felt liberated from the mores of plodding and prayerful early exploiters of the area. They felt a kinship with people pictured in slick magazines at play in well-known clubs and cafes, on the beaches, and at the spas of Europe. They, too, felt smart. They had their hunting habits made in London, they dressed in the right manner to watch the men play polo, and they had their bars and their white-jacketed Filipino house boys. However, in their leisure they never followed a cult of unfettered freedom. While they might pick up the mores of San Sebastian or Cannes, as they picked up the newest fashions, they often took their *bons mots* from the comic sheets, the cinema, and later the radio. They were fresh and interested in being alive. They could be thrilled by their own inhibitions and the consciousness of their own well-being.

Beneath all the artificiality, there was the courtesy, friendliness, and graciousness of civilization made convincing by the sincerity and generosity inherent in the atmosphere of the plains.

Naturally, being a very important figure and a very active man in the community, E. W. was not admired by everyone, and not everyone was loyal or grateful. His imperialism was not appreciated by his competitors, especially.

He incurred criticism from conservative businessmen of the community for his drunken-lord spending on hunting, polo, golf, private railroad cars, yachts, flowers, sculpture, and paintings, and for his pampering of his employees and union men. They shook their heads and said that he was a poor businessman, and a few talked of him as self-righteous wives talk of a woman who is misbehaving with men. They resented his being given publicity and credit for accomplishments for which he deserved no credit.

Some of the oilmen who had come from Pennsylvania, lured by his luck, or men associated with him in his first ventures later considered him as a rival in struggle and, therefore, became bitter and contemptuous of his well-advertised activity.

This enmity among oilmen was not unusual. Many a pair of angered oilmen had stood palsied with wrath, their soft bellies almost touching, their veins swollen in their necks, and with tender fists circling ridiculously against a background of marble and potted palms.

Naturally E. W. would never play a part in such a scene of impotent anger. He might have become white-faced with rage, but he said nothing when he heard a rumor that "E. W. Marland's guts would be dragged down Grand Avenue on a meat hook."

E. W. had a temper, but it was strange to see the effect which his early home training had on his expressions of it. Indelibly written on his consciousness were the strict admonitions of his English father that gentlemen did not show their temper by loss of control. It was trained into him until it became a part of his nature, so that when he was aroused he became cold, incredibly angered, but silent.

E. W. traveled much during the decade; he seemed to have business to attend to wherever he went.

He spent much time on his yacht. He had bought the *Georgiana II*, which he rechristened the *Whitemarsh*, from Mr. E. Stotesbury in 1921. He was very proud that "more people went down to the waterfront to look at her than saw the Derby." It was said that the *Whitemarsh* was the first seagoing craft to dock at Louisville. He weighed anchor after the running of the Derby. Virginia was with him and he had as his guests his old

161

friend, Dr. J. A. Crisler, Mr. and Mrs. W. H. McFadden, Lydie Roberts Marland, and a friend from her school, Oaksmere.

The party sailed leisurely down the Mississippi to New Orleans, and thence visited the Gulf ports before going on to Tampico and up the Pánuco River to visit the leases at El Limón.

A man from the *Commercial Appeal* of Memphis described the *Whitemarsh* as "probably the most magnificent floating home that has ever been in the local port, not even excepting the palaces of the bygone days of river supremacy in travel and transportation."

E. W. liked to combine business with pleasure, taking associates along with him, as well as other guests, when he traveled either on yacht or in his private car. During the period in 1923 when California was flooding the Atlantic Coast with oil shipped through the Panama Canal, he made several trips to California. After he had leases and oil production there, his private railroad car shuttled back and forth between Ponca City and Los Angeles. He might have Dr. van der Gracht, Spot Geyer, M. G. Gulley, Earl Oliver, from Marland of Mexico, and C. C. Osbon, of his economics department, with him, or he might have John Alcorn, W. H. McFadden, one or more of his geologists, John Hale, and perhaps his friend, Jo Davidson, the sculptor.

He would set a limit to his winnings at poker; when that limit was reached, he would leave the table and sit looking out the window, watching the sand wastes of New Mexico and Arizona slip by. He liked the great expanse of land and the romance of the far-away blue mountains. He could enjoy this savage land, he said, when his thoughts turned to it from the worries, which he shared at this time with the Mid-Continent oil producers, over the oil from California flooding the eastern markets.

It was on one of these transcontinental trips that John Hale won two thousand dollars from Jo Davidson, and, in lieu of an I.O.U. took a beautiful bronze torso, which he prized very much. Later he gave it to E. W.

E. W. visited both London and Mexico City on business. He liked both cities. He had business to arrange in London, and in Mexico City he had business to protect. He had pipe-line trouble in the Pánuco field. He found himself cut off from the Gulf. His manager, Chester Westfall, ran into bandit barricades in the jungles near the village of Guerrero. He was never sure whether the trouble was local bandit-leader temperament or big-company influence. Chester and General Kenly seem to have managed Marland affairs as well as might have been expected in this land where one had to depend upon the legerdemain of intrigue rather than the machete of direct action. E. W. was contented in the end to sell his production to Doheny's Huasteca Oil Company, to Sinclair and others.

E. W. also spent much time in London, to which he often took Virginia and Lydie when he traveled. He was an Anglophile and thought that England had the highest form of civilization, his loyalty and pride as an American notwithstanding.

Not that the cheap exhibitionism and noise of America in the twenties disturbed him—the people were happy. The self-sufficient government that turned its shoulder to the world, put up higher tariff walls, and felt smug and secure in complete dependence upon hardheaded businessmen, suited him perfectly. The wild spending and excitement of the people, he interpreted as happiness attained in the sensible progress of the nation. He was pleased that ordinary people, as well as the hitherto privileged big boys, could play the stock market. It was democracy, and he could see no end to the gaiety and the freedom. He would sneer with his faint little smile when anyone suggested that the circus would end, just as he smiled at the memory of Walter Teagle of the Standard of New Jersey who had feared that oil might be exhausted.

This had been characteristic of the Standard, he believed, this worrying about the exhaustion of oil and good things, ever since John D. Rockefeller used to lie in bed worrying about the exhaustion of oil before the Pithole field came in to give new hope to the early oil producers of western Pennsylvania. This was the spirit in which the Standard official had stated in the 1880's that he would drink all the oil found west of the Mississippi River.

But this characteristic fear and caution of the still-faced boys of big business was no longer characteristic, it seemed, when they represented the people. Andrew Mellon was really the head of the government; he saw nothing to fear. The great engineer and international businessman in the Department of Commerce, Herbert Hoover, seemed to have no fear either.

E. W. believed the decade of the 1920's was the fulfillment of the American promise. The mad decade was the decade of the people's glory and the madness was only an expression of freedom.

15

THE RED-TRIANGLE SYMBOL and the name of Marland became known over the country. E. W.'s luck and energy flooded him with oil for which he must find outlets. He had, moreover, to build more facilities for handling it, because existing facilities had become inadequate. He was more and more in need of money. He borrowed from banks in Kansas City, Wichita, Oklahoma City, St. Louis, and New York, and when his need seemed to be urgent he went to the Dutch Shell to arrange a new contract, or to sell acreage. His company was very important in the Mid-Continent field, not only as a well-nourished independent company, but in its position as the balance of power between two of the world's largest oil companies, the Standard Oil Company of New Jersey and the Royal Dutch Shell Oil Company of London and Amsterdam, Holland.

The Standard Oil Company became interested in E. W. about this time for three reasons. One was that his company was a full-blooded, lucky, healthy youth with a future. Another was that, in its growth, the Marland Oil Company needed money and more money. The third reason was quite obvious: the Standard did not like the Marland flirtation with the Dutch Shell.

It can be assumed that the Standard Oil Company would, at the propitious time, take advantage of the first two conditions presented by E. W.'s company to thwart the further development of the third condition, his courtesies to the great overseas interest in Amsterdam and London.

There was a little organization called the Continental Oil Company which had set out with hope in Montana but had soon become anemic for lack of oil. E. W. suggested that it had become moribund. This company had come under the control of the Newmont Mining Company of Montana and Colorado. The latter was the property of either J. P. Morgan and Company or of the Standard Oil Company. It is difficult to know exactly, but apparently something like this happened: J. P. Morgan and Company had put the Standard down for so much stock in the Continental Oil Company, or the Morgans were caught with the stock they were attempting to sell. Whatever the situation, either the Morgans or the Standard were stuck with the Continental Oil Company.

This is pure supposition, but one can be assured that Morgan and Company would merge a sick company into health if they happened to have such a company on their hands, and they would certainly look about for a full-blooded, lucky, healthy youth with a bright future for a marriage partner for their anemic child. Like all good, interested parents, Morgan and Company would investigate the field—the Mid-Continent field, where so many cocky, wholesome youths had sprung up. Their investigation need not last long. E. W.'s Marland Oil Company was the youth they would be looking for.

One day in the autumn of 1923, E. W. received a telephone call in his hotel room in New York City.

Mr. Charles Sabin of the Guaranty Trust Company of New York was on the telephone. He wondered if Mr. Marland would be coming downtown that day. E. W. assured him that he had business downtown that day. Why? Mr. Sabin said that he would like to have Mr. Marland stop in at his office and see him if Mr. Marland found it convenient to do so.

E. W. called at the office of Mr. Sabin, who said that he had been talking with Mr. Morgan of Morgan and Company just the day before, and that Mr. Morgan had expressed a desire to meet Mr. Marland—as a matter of fact he had asked if he, Sabin, could arrange the meeting. Mr. Morgan had expressed a desire, said Mr. Sabin, to talk over the general situation of the oil business with Mr. Marland, adding that Mr. Morgan had told him that he was especially interested in talking over the business with Mr. Marland because he understood through a mutual friend, Mr. A. C. Bedford, chairman of the Board of Directors of the Standard Oil Company, that Mr. Marland was really well informed about the conditions in the Mid-Continent oil field. Then he asked E. W. if he might arrange a meeting with Mr. Morgan.

E. W. replied that he would be very glad to meet Mr. Morgan at any time. Thereupon Mr. Sabin telephoned to Mr. Morgan, then took E. W. over to the Morgan and Company offices, where he was introduced to the son of one of the great little gods of his boyhood and youth.

Mr. Morgan and his partners gathered around Mr. Marland. They later had lunch together in the bank, and as they lunched there was the usual friendly chat and a show of great interest in this famed Oklahoman who had honored them. They told E. W. that they had taken very little interest in the oil business, but the business was of such great importance to the country that they felt they must take a more active interest in it and learn something about it; that their sole financial concern with oil up to that time had been as bankers and underwriters of an issue of the Standard Oil Company of New Jersey; that they had no affiliation with any oil company; that they had expressed a desire to Mr. A. C. Bedford to inform themselves about the oil business and that Mr. Bedford had recommended Mr. Marland as a man of high character—"one who was a student of the business and who had developed a very important unit in the industry."

Mr. Morgan sat forward in his chair. He wondered if his firm could not possibly be of some help to Mr. Marland by establishing a line of credit for him in their bank and in the Guaranty Trust Company of New York to, one might suggest, take care of his current needs. Why not let them, the Morgans, become his banker and the banker for the Marland Oil Company. It would be more convenient for him. He wouldn't be compelled to worry about visiting the banks in Chicago, St. Louis, and Kansas City to keep his lines of credit open.

In other words, the Morgan partners implied that it was all very well to have regional loyalty, but a man splashing a big canvas with vivid colors and bold lines shouldn't be disturbed with details like borrowing accounts of five million dollars scattered over the Middle West and Southwest, which he personally had to visit periodically in order to keep open.

The offices where he sat were really the ganglion of the financial world, especially since the war of 1914-18. London might be dying hard, but facts were facts. He felt that he was a part of the affairs of the world as he sat there. Certainly the masters of the world were around him, seeking, deferring, pushing the cigarette ash tray closer to him so that he would not have to reach, giving over-the-shoulder nods and curt orders so that they could give complete attention to Mr. Marland, who was telling them the fascinating story of oil in the Mid-Continent field.

He talked and the international bankers listened. And as he talked he saw himself as a world power, too.

The arrangements were made whereby Morgan and Company would become the bankers of the Marland Oil Company of Ponca City, Oklahoma. Then the Morgan partners seemed to read his thoughts and suggested that he would certainly want to expand. E. W. said that he had, as a matter of fact, been very anxious to get into the producing business in Texas, California, and New Mexico, and to make further extensions of the refinery at Ponca City. He said that he would like to have five million dollars to invest (open up new fields) in California, five million dollars to invest in Texas, and two million dollars to make extensions to the refinery in Ponca City and to start in New Mexico. But, he said, he would not really feel safe in borrowing such a large amount for permanent investment, because it might take him two or three years to realize on such an investment.

The gentlemen could see, from his explanation of the nature, discovery, and production of oil, how this could be.

Well, that could be taken care of, they suggested. Why not buy stock in the Marland Oil Company to that amount?

E. W. got the Marland stockholders' approval and twelve million dollars' worth of stock in the Marland Oil Company was sold to J. P. Morgan and Company.

In announcing to the stockholders of the Marland Oil Company the sale of shares to the Morgan company, E. W. wrote, "I have no doubt of the wisdom of thus strengthening our financial position and our financial connections at the same time. This action will enable the company to take advantage of present favorable opportunities for investment and to pursue an aggressive policy in the development of its properties."

Then at a stockholders' meeting in January, 1924, E. W. was given authority to make a sale of unissued stock to the Morgans. The sale to the Morgans included 3,000,000 shares at $30 per share payable in cash, and an option for them to buy 335,000 additional shares at $39 per share. This option was to run until February 10, 1925.

A rumor sprang up that the Morgans would control the Marland Oil Company, but this was denied by the Marland executives. Then the rumor came that Standard Oil was getting control of the Marland Company, and this was likewise denied rather strenuously.

At a meeting of the directors of the company held immediately after the first agreement, at the request of Morgan and Company, Mr. George Whitney, one of the Morgan partners, Mr. W. C. Potter, president of the Guaranty Trust Company of New York, and Mr. Charles F. Smithers, president of F. S. Smithers and Company, an investment banking house, were elected members of the board of directors, which was composed of the Marland young men who were operating heads of the various departments, and large stockholders. There were fifteen of them.

George Whitney and W. C. Potter were very happy to sit at E. W.'s feet to learn about the very fascinating oil business.

They would learn, through E. W., about production, refining, and the working in general of an oil company. In exchange for this tutoring in oil, they could certainly be of use to E. W. with their advice on financial matters. The Morgan members of the board of directors of E. W.'s company pointed efficient fingers at an obviously inconvenient by-product of the Morgan–Marland arrangement. Why should all the fifteen Marland members be compelled to leave their work and make expensive trips to New York for meetings? Why not form an executive committee, which would have the powers of the board of directors, and they could meet in New York. Then only E. W. himself and two others to be appointed to the executive committee from the Marland Company need come to New York.

An executive committee was elected consisting of the three Morgan representatives and W. H. McFadden, Vernon F. Taylor, and E. W., of the original Marland board members and stockholders. From this time on Morgan and Company dominated from New York City the Marland Oil Company of the Cherokee Outlet of Oklahoma.

"The influence of Morgan and Company upon my executive committee was, of course, dominant," said E. W. "The other members of the board of directors, men who had grown up with me in the oil business and who had theretofore been active in formulating and directing the policies of the company with me, attended directors' meetings thereafter only when necessary, and they voted 'aye' to every suggestion of the executive committee. In this manner the Morgan influence became supreme—and the builders of the company lost control of policy direction."

The company had always developed and sold oil properties for the purpose of financing company extensions. This policy was common in the oil industry. A wildcat well was often partially financed by one or more companies or individuals for the purpose of proving new acreage, and leases were often sold for the purpose of further financing. It was not until later, when petroleum engineers could make estimates of the oil left in the sands after primary production, and after the successful employment of secondary recovery methods, that bankers would become interested in the oil producer's hopes.

Even plunging, self-assured E. W. and his optimistic young men didn't like the "suggestion" from the Morgan members of the executive committee that when they needed money they borrow it from the Morgans. "Why," said the Morgan members, "should there be further need to finance ourselves by the old method? If a property is good enough for one of the major companies to buy, it is good enough for us to keep." They vetoed the suggestion that the company sell part of their property in West Texas and in Southern California, two years after they began operations there, "at a price that would have given us all of our invested capital back. We were offered twenty million dollars for our Seal Beach property, and turned it down under our new policy."

E. W. talked with his old associates about this new policy forced upon them by the Morgan men on the executive committee, and they sometimes tried to convince him that the need to sell part of their valuable property to extend exploration, or to finance expansion in general, no longer existed—that the Morgans were right. With the House of Morgan behind them, they could grow to be the largest company in the Mid-Continent, a tremendous plant sending its roots into Texas, California, New Mexico, sucking the substance of other growths until they, the Marland Oil Company, could cast a shadow like that of the Standard. Just as Standard had expanded from Ohio, Pennsylvania, New York, Kentucky, and West Virginia, now Marland was expanding to Colorado, Kansas, New Mexico, Texas, and Wyoming.

For a time he was filled with confidence again. Especially when he discovered a new field in the Los Angeles Basin, the Seal Beach field. And the New York headlines predicted that the Marland Oil Company would become the greatest independent oil company on earth, with the sale of 750,000 unissued shares of the company's authorized 22,000,000 shares of stock. There was encouragement in the statement by W. E. Fitzgerald of Potter and Company, party to the deal. "The Standard Oil

Company is not involved. The banking syndicate has acted for itself and is acquiring the stock as investment and not for speculation."

E. W. had done very well with the siren Petrolia: the Congo field in West Virginia, the Ponca City field and other spots in Kay County as well as in Noble and Pawnee counties, the Burbank field in the Osage, and now the Seal Beach field out on the West Coast.

But why rest on his laurels? Petrolia had secrets yet unrevealed, and she favored the men who had the courage to seek them. E. W., flooded with oil as he was at this time, was still the lover of Petrolia, still fascinated by her whimsies. He was still the wildcatter with a wildcatter's dreams.

On one of his many trips to London he made arrangements to sell his refined product, gasoline, in England and in the dominions. He also made another of his blanket leases, this time with the great Hudson's Bay Company. He was to furnish the technical knowledge and the material and undertake the expense of exploration, and the great company would share to the extent of 50 per cent of the gross production. Thus he became a partner with a second empire of his romantic dreams. Both the Dutch Shell and the Hudson's Bay Company were gratifyingly British.

Since the time he was embarrassed by having only coal leases on the Congo field, E. W. had associated himself only with empires, so to speak: with the 101 Ranch, Oklahoma school lands, the Republic of Mexico, and large acreage in the Osage obtained by circumventing government restrictions. Now he was a partner with the romantic empire, the Hudson's Bay Company.

He had millions to manipulate and the world's greatest bankers back of him. He was glad to hear his old associates remind him of these things. But misgivings and a feeling of uneasiness came to him when he had long hours to himself as he returned from executive committee meetings in New York. There were still no cynical little smiles on the faces of the Morgan members of his executive committee, and there were no expressions of grim caution, no lizard eyes, which he associated with the still-faced boys. There was only courtesy, graciousness, and culture in which one had confidence. But they smashed his dreams at every meeting as one smashes a butterfly on the pavement, not in wanton cruelty but in the cold carelessness of absorption in business. He kept his temper before these gentlemen, but he had periods of disillusionment after each meeting. The Morgan members consistently squashed his plans for selling certain acreage and "getting on velvet," and for the laying of pipe lines from developing and developed properties.

He couldn't see how men worth millions, sitting on the boards of many enterprises, could be so stupid that they passed over the value of the obvious fact that you could lay pipe lines and make the full profit of your property, instead of selling oil at the wellhead to other pipe lines. He actually began to wonder if they were such big men after all. Almost any of his subordinates in the operating departments could see obvious advantages to a producing company. Maybe they were right, although he felt sure that they were wrong, in not allowing him to sell off acreage in discovery and developing fields in order to finance still further development. But there was no doubt about the pipe lines—there couldn't be any doubt.

But he expanded with the Morgan backing as he had planned to do. In western Texas he became interested in the Reagan County production. This was the Big Lake region, where the plains are impressed with numbers of sinks or shallow depressions which are filled and made into large lakes in the seasons of rain.

He formed the Reagan County Crude Purchasing Company for the purpose of purchasing oil from the region's producers, and from the Texon Oil and Land Company and the Big Lake Oil Company. He put in his adopted son, George, as president of the Reagan County Company, and the Marland Oil Company had three of the five directors. Among them were Howard Drake, Charles Stephenson, and George Marland, and representing the Texon Oil and Land Company were Frank T. Pickrell and Levi Smith.

The two companies, the Texon and the Big Lake, controlled

the Reagan County production, which was about ten thousand barrels daily. This production had to have an outlet. Tankage had to be built and an outlet to the Gulf was a necessity. He sent Myles Kyger and others out from the Ponca City office to represent the pipe line department and made plans to build a pipe line from the field to Texas City on the Gulf.

Then he put the proposition to his executive committee in New York City. He showed them that the building of the pipe line would save three million dollars a year in freight, and the pipe line itself would cost only five million dollars. Walter C. Teagle, president of the Standard of New Jersey, A. W. Corwin, president of the Carter Oil Company, and W. S. Farish, president of the Humble Oil and Refining Company, came to San Angelo, Texas, with him in a special train. In the dining car W. S. Farish looked across the table at E. W. and said, "E. W., I'm not going to let you build that pipe line," and that was the end of that dream.

The Marland Company was forced to sell its oil to the Humble Company, which in turn delivered it to the Standard. J. P. Morgan and Company were bankers for the Humble Oil and Refining Company. E. W.'s company was paid a premium of twenty cents a barrel. It received $1.20 a barrel on a stipulated twenty thousand barrels a day.

E. W. became very angry with the Morgan partners over this incident and began to think seriously that they were incapable of understanding the oil business. He became more contemptuous of them and experienced a deeper fear of their faraway control through the manipulation of paper. When George Whitney of Morgan and Company asked him his reasons for wanting to spend five million dollars on a pipe line, he became pale with anger and said, "Do I have to go over all that again?"

But even at this late date he was attributing stupidity to them. In his own arrogance and in his self-satisfaction with his outstanding success in oil production, he thought that they were incapable of understanding, and he was annoyed that they seemed to distrust his *savoir-faire*. It was after the incident of the proposed pipe line across the state of Texas, from New

Mexico to the Mississippi River, that he wondered about his company's position as a servicing company to the Standard.

It was incredible how obtuse he could be, how his *amour-propre* could flood his reason and keen judgment. The obstacles with which his executive committee, controlled by the Morgan partners, seemed to encircle him like a progressively higher stone wall, only produced white-faced silence in his despair over their stupidity. "They can't see beyond their noses! They know nothing except market quotations, sleight of hand with other people's money, and figures—book figures! No vision whatever."

He appreciated as well as anyone the use of wits, the fast thinking, the planning, the compromising, and the eternal alertness that were necessary for survival. He should have been eternally on guard. But when he was filled with his romantic dreams, which seemed to anesthetize him progressively by working upon his egotism, he was like an emotional patron leaving the Philharmonic, oblivious to anything but the experience charged with fantasy.

Under the spell of his own dreams, E. W. would forget the wall of obstacles and again approach his committee with his bright idea.

One day he ran his stubby finger over the map from the Permian Basin in New Mexico, where he had production, across the state line into Texas, thence across Reagan County; from there his finger traced a line to Fort Worth, where he had refinery customers, thence across eastern Texas near Tyler, across the state line into Louisiana and through Shreveport, and thence on to the Mississippi River. Along this line he would build a pipe line; he would carry oil from southeastern New Mexico through western Texas to Fort Worth, to Shreveport, to the Mississippi. As he followed this line with his finger, Petrolia was at his shoulder, moving his hand when it swerved too far to the south or too far to the north, guiding it so that it passed through eastern Texas, through an unpromising area of sand and roses which a few years later was to become the East Texas oil field, the greatest in the United States. How diabolical of

Petrolia: he would not have the Marland Oil Company then! His pipe line, if built, would have been available when C. M. Joiner brought in the wildcat that tapped one of the world's greatest petroleum reservoirs.

He showed his executive committee that the Marland company was paying an average of fifty cents a barrel pipe-line tariff, which, with their fifty thousand to seventy thousand barrels of oil a day going to Standard-owned pipe lines, would amount to from twenty-five thousand to thirty thousand dollars a day. This they might keep themselves, besides establishing their independence. He drew their attention to the Marland balance sheets of over twenty million dollars in cash and United States Government bonds.

He gave them figures more often now, in his helplessness against their obstinacy. Perhaps if he dragged the fox scent of figures across his highway of visions, they might follow and allow him freedom to dream and work for the benefit of all.

When they turned down his pipe-line dream, he left the room in deep dejection. "Bankers," he sneered, "internationally famous bankers!" However, he brought up his pet dream every time the committee met, and every time he brought it up, the members turned it down. Then it seemed that for the first time something came into his mind that might have been taken for suspicion of his committee members. He suggested that the company build the pipe line in co-operation with another major company, thereby reducing the risk, and he specified that the other major company be not of the Standard family. When he was turned down this time, he felt no anger and no annoyance. He experienced only a feeling of weakness.

It is likely that he might have wanted to escape the now growing but intangible malevolence, and certainly it was rumored that he tried to sell his company to the Dutch Shell for $59,000,000. He should also have known that he would not be allowed to do that.

16

IT WAS during the period when the free flow of his accomplishments was dammed by the policy of the Morgan partners that E. W.'s energy was diverted into other channels—into the creation of ornamentation. He had continually to lose himself in some dream.

He began the building of a mansion in the game preserve. E. W. was fascinated by the colonial Spanish and the Pueblo Indian architectures, and originally a combination of these was planned to be the style of the new house. But the idea came under one influence after another, and finally, after someone had considered the driveway of the preserve, which was in imitation of Hampton Court, the mansion was changed into an English manor. J. Duncan Forsyth, a Scotsman, was the architect, and he took pleasure in translating E. W.'s dreams into stone.

E. W. had Jo Davidson and Jo Mora come to Ponca City to make statues for the approach to the manor. He commissioned other statues from Bryant Baker. These artists made for him statues of George Miller as a typical cowboy and W. H. McFadden as a pioneer, and others of a Ponca chief, a Ponca woman, and Belle Starr, the Cherokee "bandit queen.' He also had statues made of himself and George and Lydie Roberts Marland. Mezquita painted George in torn slacks as an oil-field roustabout. He painted Lydie as Carmen.

The stables were fashioned after a French billet where Major Don Henderson, M.F.H., had stayed during the war. There were gatehouses and a lodge, a garage, and a delightful building called the art gallery and studio.

But the building of the mansion was not enough to absorb him. He had collectors in Europe acquiring art objects for him —an activity which, however, did not call upon his own energy. He bought a plantation in Mississippi for $750,000 during a bear hunt conducted on a lavish scale. He then set out to build a model plantation for the two hundred and fifty families living there. He built cabins of two rooms with the traditional "dog trot" between the rooms. He built a community school and church, and a community cannery. He urged the families to grow their own fruit and vegetables. He built plantation stores where he allowed no scrip—a practice he hated because it kept the Negro in constant debt to the plantation owner.

One of his earlier and more utilitarian dreams became a reality during this time. The Marland Industrial Institute buildings were completed—a dormitory and general classroom building. There were provided in this scheme a dining hall, assembly hall, clubrooms, classrooms, a golf course, a tennis court, and a swimming pool. The educational work at the Marland Industrial Institute was to "fall into two classes: the first, a continuation of the educational opportunities now being provided for all employees of the Marland Oil Company; the other classification, for technical instruction and training, to be conducted largely by officials and operating chiefs of the Marland operating organization, for young engineers, graduates of technical schools, who wish to get into the operating end of the oil business."

The things he did for his young men to help them achieve pleasant living—hunting, golf, high salaries and wages, educational and cultural opportunities, gardens and flowers—could be said to reflect his own ego, giving back to him the full glory. But his feeling for the common man and his children was deep and sincere despite his vanity.

One of the many things he completed in the late 1920's was

the American Legion Home School. When the chairman of the Legion's state child welfare committee came to him in 1925, he became deeply interested in what he had to say and began to plan with the officers, and even ahead of them. He and W. H. McFadden, infected with the enthusiasm of these men, actually built the Legion's home for destitute children. The twenty acres upon which it stood would be tilled by disabled veterans. There would be varied training and education from kindergarten through high school. McFadden built a camp for the Camp Fire Girls, and the boys would go to Scout camp and have the privileges of the Marland Institute's swimming pool and recreation grounds. Shrubs were planted, and the inevitable trees and roses. The children would have access to the lakes and paths and flowers of the game preserve. There were to be no uniforms. E. W. would have no regimentation. Each child could choose his own clothes, with a little guidance and within certain limitations. He would be trained to work with his hands as well as with his head. Many of the children, E. W. hoped, might be brought someday into his organization.

Although E. W. seemed to live for the hour, he also had thoughts of immortality; not for benefits in an afterlife but for things he had created. He wanted to be associated in the memory of man with beauty and happiness.

But it was an idea conceived in John Alcorn's kitchen, according to one story, which he thought would preserve at least a small chamber in the memory of his neighbors, if not in the memory of man in general.

The 1920's were a decade of kitchen drinking, whether in the big red brick house of a vice president of Marland Oil Company or in an oil-field shack. The kitchen, during the period of prohibition, was a refuge from the sin of law breaking, an illusory deception, and a gesture to Puritan conscience. Also, it left the other rooms free from rum's contaminating influence.

In John Alcorn's kitchen one night the question was asked, "E. W., why don't you have Jo make a statue to the vanishing American, a Ponca, Otoe, or an Osage—a monument of great size?"

Women were sitting about in short skirts, putting their knees awkwardly together as they backed up to a chair to sit down, continually tugging at their inadequate skirts to cover an exposure of pale thigh. They shook their bobbed hair back like emergent swimmers, and lit cigarettes as if they expected them to explode. They saw the obscenity and missed the point in jokes, which, incidentally, were few and pale when E. W. was present.

E. W., in a pontifical manner which often offended those who didn't know him well, said, "The Indian is not the vanishing American—it's the pioneer woman."

Quite possibly he had not thought about this before that moment as he sat with his Scotch and soda in his hand. He assumed the attitude of "I tell you what I'm gonna do," and the idea of the statue to the pioneer woman was born.

He had models made by several sculptors, twelve in all, and he had them sent around the country at considerable expense so that people could see them and vote their choice as the best representative of the pioneer woman of America. Upon the chosen model, the heroic statue would be created and placed in faraway Ponca City, on the Red Bed plains of Oklahoma.

When the Bryant Baker model won by vote, Baker was commissioned by E. W. to create the spirit of the pioneer woman in bronze.

Thus, as the grey English manor house rose among the trees, lakes, and flowers of the game preserve, and the white clubhouse and other buildings of the Marland Institute, in Taos Pueblo style, rose on the heights above the Arkansas River, the orphans and destitute children arrived in Ponca City to take over their new home. The twelve models for the statue of the pioneer woman had traveled from coast to coast for the people's vote. His collectors were buying art, and he was having a table and chairs carved in the manner of Charles I of England. He was, in many ways, diverting his energy from the dammed channel of his business, to form marshes and bayous choked with beautiful, exotic growths.

Virginia Collins Marland died in 1926, after a long illness.

Her suffering, it was said, drew little sympathy from E. W.—at least, there was little manifestation of pity. Her friends hint at a Greek tragedy in which she played the most tragic role during the last years in the big house on Grand Avenue. Any attempt to discover her personality is repulsed by her partisans as an attempt to gossip.

E. W. always seemed to fear age. He refused to be without youth; it must be around him in the persons of others, since his own was gone. His attitude toward Virginia's illness and death impressed many as being one of hurt vanity. He seemed quite surprised to find himself an actor in a drama which the national public willed to be a Greek tragedy, wherein humanity, wealth, and power were the background, while interest centered like a searchlight on this bewildered man.

In 1928, two years after the death of Virginia Marland, the court of common pleas of Philadelphia changed the legal status of Lydie Roberts Marland back to the original Lydie Roberts. In July, 1928, E. W. and Lydie Roberts were married at Flourtown, Pennsylvania.

The story was ready-made for the Sunday supplements, replete with pictures of the millionaire polo player mounted against the new mansion in the game preserve. Pictures of the mansion and pictures of photogenic Lydie in some gay, insouciant attitude, or dressed in her hunting habit with her hunter hanging his aristocratic head over her shoulder. Even Trotsky, the beautiful Irish setter, came into prominence.

The text flirted with libel in its attempts to inspire the sluggish but willing imaginations of its readers. The rumors circled and sailed and dipped, rising and falling on motionless wings, casting disgusting shadows like vultures', but never quite settling to the feast.

It was about this time, so the story goes, that a Morgan member of his executive committee came to E. W.'s hotel room in New York and asked him what action he took when he found that he had too many polo players on the field during a match, or if he kept players on the field who contributed nothing to the game. He then suggested, rather ominously, that it might be time to replace the old, familiar, but high-priced and decorative players with new and less expensive ones.

There is no record of what E. W. answered, if in fact there really was such a conversation, but undoubtedly he got the hint. The Morgan partners were losing their patience over his high-salaried young men's duplicating each other's work. The end of the mad decade was near, even if the Great Engineer who was now president seemed to have no intimation of change. Mr. Hoover was the first president really to represent the mechanicale age. His hard efficiency seemed to ignore human frailty and relegate it to man's dark, chaotic past. He was both honest and able, but he failed to understand why smooth-running machinery could not be built up with reasoning men as the efficient working parts.

E. W. must have remembered the hint from New York. He called Chester Westfall in and asked him to make a survey of the Marland organization and make recommendations for improvement and "streamlining." This was a new word, picked up from aviation during the late war.

Chester got in touch with General Baird Markham and explained to him what E. W. wanted. "The way I see it," said Chester, "E. W. wants a picture of the situation as it actually exists; he wants no cover-up. He wants to know the worst."

Somehow the news got about that General Markham was making a survey, and the natural thing happened: the personnel in each department, from the head down to the janitors, began to pose for the "picture." The heads of the departments appeared with dangling eyeglasses, as if interrupted in their work. The lesser clerks became very busy, as though they scarcely had time to stop to be photographed. And pretty stenographers, some of whom, it was said, couldn't even take shorthand dictation, became busy at their typewriters, pretending to be swamped by work.

Baird Markham wanted to recommend the release of some of the employees, even some of the heads of departments, but Chester advised him that the authority to recommend changes had not been given to them.

Flush production of oil, when the market is favorable, will allow of almost any whimsey on the part of the producer and his organization, flooding the necessity for caution and conservatism. El Dorado was never as whimsical and capricious as Petrolia; never as wanton and as contributive to waste. E. W. and his young men were flush productionists. Under Petrolia's mad influence, they were protected in their lavishness by her seeming inexhaustibility and abundance. E. W. was inherently incapable of recognizing the stage of development which he hated most, the stage of balanced figures and profits computed in cents instead of dollars, when the demand for petroleum products should fall off. Success had made the imperious little boy from Mount Washington rather indifferent, when he could keep his thoughts away from the bankers in New York. And there is evidence that he was thinking less and less of the bankers as he directed his energy into creations which he could finally see fully formed and adorned.

Many believed that at this time he had assumed the role of English country gentleman and squire, and some went even further and suggested that he had assumed a rather haughty dukedom. His success was certainly due to his energy, his imaginative thinking, and his shrewdness, but there might have been the feeling in him that his glory was his divine right.

The conversation in his hotel rooms about the polo players and the necessity for their replacement by disciplined players more susceptible to teamwork impressed him for a period, but he soon forgot this warning.

The money from the House of Morgan acted as an underground stream to nourish the roots of the Marland Oil Company. Soon it was sending its roots out into Texas, New Mexico, Colorado, Wyoming, Kansas, and California. By 1926 the company had thirteen hundred persons employed in the Marland Company of Texas. This company had seven hundred thousand acres under lease, and 107 wells drilling. Its production was ten thousand barrels a day. It had acreage in the Amarillo area in the Texas Panhandle, in southwest Texas at Layton Springs, and in Wortham, Shackelford, and Archer counties, besides the purchased oil of Reagan County.

In 1925, Spot Geyer became president of Marland of Texas, and C. E. Hyde and Alexander Deussen became vice presidents. After Geyer's resignation, Van Waterschoot van der Gracht, the Dutch geologist, was sent down to succeed him, and one of the Marland young men from the University of Oklahoma, Alvin Moncrief, became a vice president under him. I. G. Harmon became head of the production department, and Joe McGraw, son of one of the early 101 Ranch Oil Company associates, was in charge of the land department. In the Amarillo area, J. V. Howell was in charge of geology.

Here were some of E. W.'s bright young men who had come to him fresh from the universities, now being placed in important positions as he expanded. He was taking the final steps, one supposes, toward his integrated company. His young men were loyal to him. They were alert and he listened to them because they were of his family—his handsome young men.

When it was found that the oil from the Texas Panhandle was heavy with paraffin and asphalt and would flow sluggishly through the one hundred and fifty miles of pipe line during cold weather, he took his young men's suggestion and placed his pumping stations at thirteen mile intervals instead of the regulation twenty-six. He also arranged to have the exhaust from his engines utilized in the heating of the sluggish, asphalt-heavy oil. Such alert interest in the company by his young men made him happy.

He had periods of happiness when he added 250,000 acres to his Panhandle holdings and leased the Canadian River bed from the state of Texas. He liked to have large acreage so that he could keep control in the event of an oil strike. He leased the large Bell Ranch in New Mexico, eighteen miles northeast of Tucumcari, and acquired a block of four thousand acres on the Notches Dome in Wyoming, which was already proven territory through the activity of the Midwest Refining Company.

Through his Marland Oil Company of Colorado, with headquarters in Denver, he got leases on the Hamilton Dome near Craig. When this little field was named for the town of Craig, the other little towns became jealous, with the result that the field finally carried the name of the romantic mountain railroad builder, David H. Moffat. E. W., George Miller, and Jim McGraw arranged for acreage near Ft. Collins, Colorado, to the extent of only 560 acres, but this was in the territory of big-company operations. He got a lease on the K-Bar-T Ranch on the Isles Dome in Rio Blanco County and made a test three miles east of Meeker, along the highway from Rifle to Craig. He was warned against this, because the Dakota sandstone outcropped here, but he sent his test down to twenty-five hundred feet and got production.

This was wild, free mountain country possessing scenic qualities which alone would have drawn his attention to it. The White River roared and foamed down out of Trappers Lake, high up under the flat tops. There were deer and cougar and elk here, and hungry trout lying in the icy waters of the river and in the many little lakes.

There was also a feeling of freedom and space in the flat, sun-hazy San Joaquin Valley of California. In the spring the poppies could lure E. W. from as far away as Ponca City. These wild California poppies, appearing like a lazy prairie fire from a distance, thrilled the lover of floral bombardments. He took acreage in the Valley wherever he could get it.

On Carl Beals's recommendation, he took leases on the Rio Bravo, along the Kern River, in the Buttonwillow and Goose Lake sections, and in the Kettleman Hills. He took fifteen thousand acres in the Lost Hills and got oil at 4,282 feet in the Dominguez field.

In the Los Angeles Basin he got leases on the Compton Dome and discovered Seal Beach "right under the noses of the boys of Signal Hill." By 1927 he was taking eighteen thousand to twenty thousand barrels daily from Seal Beach. He spent more than three million dollars there in building a stone wall seven feet above high tide to avoid pollution of the bathing beaches and the local water supply. He built a wall around his property, not because he was forced to go so far, but because he chose to do so. He knew how annoying oil could be to bathers.

He put Franklin R. Kenney in as president of the Marland Oil Company of California and named Carl Beals, the old Mexican hand, vice president, after Spot Geyer and John Alcorn had established the first contacts.

T. L. Golay, who had come to him from the Twin States Oil Company, was president of Marland of Colorado, and the very able and highly respected geologist, Alex McCoy, was head geologist. The Denver offices controlled activity in New Mexico and Wyoming. William D. Frothingham, his representative in Kansas, had come to him from Harvard. Chester Westfall managed Marland of Mexico, and Earl Oliver became general manager of that organization.

Dr. van Waterschoot van der Gracht and T. L. Golay had come to him from other companies, but for the most part E. W. placed his own men as heads of his other companies. He would control the Southwest as Queen Victoria controlled Europe in the nineteenth century. He had complete control over the subsidiary companies in which he had placed his young men as chiefs. But ever since he had drawn the line from southeastern New Mexico across Texas and Louisiana to the Mississippi River, only to have his dream dissipated, he had been unable to hide from himself the fact that he was becoming, or had actually become, a service company for Standard.

His losses in 1927 and 1928 made him realize that something might be wrong. The national oil picture was changing. California, even with her flush production being shipped by tankers through the Panama Canal to the East Coast, was no longer a threat to the producers of the Mid-Continent. Franklin Kenney doubted that California could supply her own needs in 1927 and 1928 despite the new, deeper sands of the Signal Hill pool which were now in production. The Texas Panhandle was just coming into its own now, only three hundred miles from Ponca City. But this didn't help matters. Something was happening to the demand.

The losses sustained in the years 1927 and 1928 were temporary, E. W. believed. He never dreamed that he might be compelled to garner profits from half a cent to a cent a gallon on his gasoline, that he might have to count pennies on each barrel of crude, and that he might be compelled to cut salaries and personnel to survive. If he did not do these things, the dinosaur that was his organization could never hope to survive economic temperature changes, even though it had some of the best food in eight states and in Canada and Mexico.

However, the curlicues and calcareous spines continued to grow. The lumbering beast was impressive. Its departments were strong and efficient, very much like the strong limbs and heart of a zoological monster. But the ironical trick which Nature plays on organisms by loading them with interesting but useless ornamentation as a prelude to their doom was plainly evident here. Only the adaptable can survive, no matter how great the apparent size or strength.

His treasurer, W. G. Lackey, was an experienced banker, and Lackey's assistants, Seward Sheldon, who later became treasurer, and Bob Clark, were highly efficient. In the all-important refining department, Walter Miller had a German efficiency that made things move like the parts of a smoothly running mechanism. Harold Osborn, the imaginative assistant superintendent of refineries, compared the efficiency and the conservatism of the Marland refinery to the Armour Packing Company and its amazing list of by-products. The packing company boasted that it used "everything out of the hog but the squeal." Osborn said proudly that "the modern refinery must, to compete successfully, extract from a barrel of crude 'everything but the squeal.'" He was proud of the many products that came from a barrel of oil, and especially of the utilization of petroleum coke, a product of the heavier oils coming from the process of gasoline production.

In March, 1927, E. W. could tell his stockholders a story of expansion for the year 1926 by stating that Marland Oil of Ponca City had a production of 13,137,048 barrels of crude oil for that year, with 7,528,196 barrels run through the Ponca City refinery and 5,603,117 barrels on hand at the year's close.

"The refinery extensions," he said proudly, "resulted in an output for the month of December of 715,181 barrels, or a daily average of 23,070 barrels." Thus did the company start the year of 1927 with a 30 per cent increase in refining capacity as the result of its extensions.

If E. W., under the consciousness of his restriction, doubted the importance of his expansions, he could get back from the headlines of *The Ponca City News, The Kansas City Star, The Daily Oklahoman, The Tulsa World, The Oil & Gas Journal,* and the New York financial journals a flattering image of himself. He was like a primitive worshipper who had charged a piece of obsidian or a wooden figurine with his dreams of God. The primitive worshipper could go to the symbol of his gropings and get the illusions with which he had charged it.

There were headlines constantly telling the world of his importance, of the greatness of his building. "MARLAND BUILDS HUGE REFINERY IN SHORT TIME: Growth of Ponca City Institution Most Wonderful in Oil Industry." Another headline: "A FINANCIAL ROMANCE," and again, " 'GAS' SHIPMENT OUT OF PONCA MAKES RECORD: Marland Sends Out 1,200,000 Gallons In Two Trainloads: FIRST TRAIN IS 80 CARS." A reporter wrote: "The train was two-thirds of a mile in length and, with the deep black cars of uniform design shimmering in the sunlight, made conspicuous by the four-foot red triangles on each car, presented silent testimony to Ponca City's and Marland Refining Company's pre-eminence as leaders in the petroleum industry."

In 1926, E. W. had bought the retail marketing departments of the Derby Oil Company of Wichita, Kansas, including about one hundred and sixty service stations in Oklahoma, Kansas, Missouri, Colorado, and Nebraska. This addition gave the company about four hundred service stations in ten states. The Derby stations added three states to his seven, forcing Sam Collins, Jr., to establish a new district. A year later he purchased thirty-five service stations from the Moberly Oil Company of Moberly, Missouri. The announcement of the purchase stated that the "new property will give the Marland Refining Company more than five hundred service stations in ten states."

Then came the headlines in 1927: "MARLAND WILL INVADE THE EAST: Oklahoma Company Runs More Than 500 Stations in 11 States." From the offices in Ponca City came the statement, "It is well known that Marland officials feel that there is no such thing as too many direct-to-the-public sales of the output of the Ponca City refinery."

Sam Collins, Jr., could shortly announce the purchase of the Gibson Oil Company of Ft. Smith, Arkansas, which included eighty-seven service stations and bulk plants in Arkansas and Oklahoma. There was a new sales division after this transaction. All told, there were now 550 service-station outlets for Marland products.

In 1928 came the headline: "MARLAND COVERS LARGE TERRITORY: Products Sold in Every State in the Union and 17 Foreign Countries." There were more than six hundred Marland service stations in the middle western states now, and five thousand dealers in the eastern states and Canada, selling red triangle products. It took five thousand Marland tank cars, with the four-foot red triangle and the magic *Marland Oils* across it, to supply the domestic market. At the terminal at Texas City, Texas, two large tankers slipped in from the Gulf to load Marland products for the foreign market. The tankers sailed for his beloved England where the gentlemen of the Sealand Petroleum Company, one of his subsidiaries with offices in London, distributed his products over Europe.

But his report to his stockholders concerning the expansions and the wonders of the year 1926 was his last princely statement to have a good, solid economic foundation. It was the last boast that would have anything more solid than his optimism to sustain it. In July, 1928, came the headlines: "TEXAS OFFICERS OF MARLAND TO PONCA: Executives of the Company to Come Here From Fort Worth." The text said: "Reports from Ponca City state that Marland is cutting down its losses very materially . . . that for the third quarter of this year they are expected to show somewhere in the neighborhood of

189

two million dollars. This has been accomplished by cutting down overhead to meet bad market condition."

In the same article E. W. was quoted as having pointed out with his usual compensatory enthusiasm that in southeastern New Mexico the company was the largest acreage owner, with four hundred thousand acres, and that two wildcat wells now drilling "are showing for big gassers" and were expected to get oil in lower strata.

After a meeting of the executive committee in May, 1928, E. W. wired Chester Westfall, who was now at the Ponca City office, a list of the officers for the coming year. He also wired the list of the directors for the coming year. There was no change in the membership of the executive committee, except that Arthur Lawrence of New York took the place of Charles Smithers, also of New York. Chester had no announcement of other business transacted at the meeting.

The meeting was not, however, a pleasant one for E. W. As usual, his committee crushed his dreams for 1929. The atmosphere had changed rapidly, leaving E. W. with a sharpened sense of fear as well as the old anger. He noted a colder courtesy from the committee, whose members seemed more like still-faced boys than they ever had before. They referred with courteous hesitancy to the thirty-million-dollar indebtedness of the company from the sale of 5 per cent bonds the winter before. They seemed to place the responsibility for such indebtedness upon him. He recalled that during the winter they had suggested to him that, since the bond market was very good, and since they had just sold some British 6 per cent bonds, and since they were having a land-office business in foreign bonds, the time seemed ripe to sell Marland 5 per cent bonds. He had been happy for the moment with the thought of the thirty million dollars in working capital; maybe they were having a change of heart. But he had soon realized that he would not be allowed to use any of it for further development.

As he sat there in the meeting he remembered the commission they had made on the sale of the bonds and how they had answered his question about the use of the money by saying proudly that the issue had been oversubscribed four or five times on account of the good name of the Marland Company. It took him some time to realize how empty this praise had been. He really had no need for the loan; the money had remained in their hands at a time when call-money rates were high. He couldn't lend on call or invest it in his own company.

He became afraid of these gentlemen that day. The old fear of the still-faced boys must have come over him. He could call up nothing to mitigate this fear. Almost in panic, he wanted to placate them in some manner not at all clear to himself. He approached W. C. Potter of the executive committee. "Bill," he said, "I want you to be perfectly frank with me. I have a feeling that there is a lack of confidence on the part of my executive committee in my management of the company. I want you to tell me honestly and frankly whether I am right in this, and, if so, why I have lost their confidence."

Potter assured him that they had not lost confidence in him; that they had lost no degree of confidence in his ability or his knowledge of the oil industry. But he felt that E. W.'s relationship with his junior officers was too cordial and friendly, and that, furthermore, these officers should not be directors of the company. It was all right for the president to be a director, but none of the other officers should have so important a post as membership on the board of directors. He said, just because these young men had helped build the company and were loyal as youngsters did not mean that they therefore had sufficient qualifications for membership on the board and should make the company's policy.

Paternalism, Potter suggested, was a fine thing, but such concern for, and arm-around-the-shoulder closeness with, the company's employees was not conducive of efficiency. E. W. could be chairman of the board, that sort of thing.

Later George Whitney joined W. C. Potter and E. W., and he agreed with what Potter had said. They said that Morgan and Company felt that there ought to be a hard-boiled president under E. W., and while they were on the subject they suggested, according to E. W., "that I should ask immediately for the resignation from the board of directors of all those men who had been with me since the inception of the company."

They told E. W. that he might begin to look for someone, the sharp, cold, executive type they had just characterized as hard-boiled, to assume the presidency of the company and become general manager. This, they said, would give E. W. free time for executive detail and time also to devote himself to major policies and mergers.

After this interview, John Alcorn, Jack Cleary, and Seward Sheldon came to him and resigned. He then appointed Charlie Brown as vice president and general manager of the company. He believed that Charlie was the most practical and efficient executive among his associates. But his executive committee said that Charlie Brown was not the type. He then suggested General Baird Markham, but they said they didn't know him.

They asked him if he knew D. J. Moran, vice president of the Texas Company. They assured him that Mr. Moran was the type of hard-fisted executive they had in mind for the company, and they thought he might accept if the position were offered him.

When E. W. talked with Mr. Moran, he found that he had already been approached by members of the executive committee and apparently had already decided to take the position. The contract was signed.

From Dan Moran's attitude, E. W. realized that it was understood between Moran and the executive committee that he was to supplant E. W. entirely, and he further realized that his position as chairman of the board on salary—a very large salary in fact—was clearly a "pension job." Later the executive committee hinted that the efficiency of the president, in what they intimated would be a house-cleaning job, might be impeded if E. W. continued to live in Ponca City. They told him that the blind loyalty which he had built up and the little-god worship with which Ponca City was burdened might make Moran's position with the subordinate officers of the company rather difficult. They told E. W. that Moran would not carry on if he continued to live in the headquarters town.

Because of commitments on his stock, E. W. had only his proposed salary. He once asked, when someone suggested he reinvest a $75,000 check from a matured insurance policy, "What can you do with $75,000?" He might ask the same question now about his salary. After the first shock of losing his independence was over, his vanity surged through him again and brought back the color to his anger-blanched face. He resigned his position as chairman of the board, with its niggardly "pension."

His officers wanted to resign with him but he asked them not to desert the company they had helped to build. He urged them to work with Dan Moran as they had worked with him. However, his old friend, associated with him in all things, associated himself with him in resignation; W. H. McFadden resigned his vice presidency.

Dan Moran called the operating executives to his office in New York and discharged some of them, then discharged others later by telegram. He discharged superintendents and managers of various departments who had grown up with the company. This was under order of the executive committee, E. W. believed.

There was deep discomfort in E. W.'s feeling that he was responsible for the summary discharge of his young men and his managers and superintendents. He had no ill feeling towards Dan Moran. He said: "It is hard to believe he liked the job he performed. His job was to eradicate any influence E. W. Marland might have in the Marland Oil Company organization, so that no one in the organization might be able to raise a voice against anything the banker management might want to do with the company." He recognized the ability and high character of the men Dan Moran brought to Ponca City to replace his own officers and department heads. His good wishes for them and the company were quite sincere. His lifelong fear-admiration of bankers expressed itself in vindictiveness toward the House of Morgan. He became obsessed with the determination to break the power of the great bankers.

Part IV The People's Voice

17

E. W.'s HEART was almost broken when he saw his
name, his magic name, painted out on the symbolic red triangles
on his filling stations over the land. Instead of *Marland* there
appeared the name *Conoco*. His old Marland Company had
been merged into the Continental Oil Company, the company
which he had called "a semi-moribund former subsidiary of the
Standard Oil of New Jersey." The old Marland Oil Company
was now the Continental Oil Company. The name *Marland*
was painted out and the name *Conoco* painted in on all the triangles, not just those on the filling stations—on every tank car,
truck, pump station, and company-owned building in the country. E. W. could not smile when he talked about it. "My name
disappeared," he said, "and Conoco was put in its place. The
old Marland Oil Company was a thing of the past. The House
of Morgan had merged it out of existence."

The old Marland Company substance was not "merged out
of existence"—only the name and the spirit. Its substance was
in the Kettleman Hills, Seal Beach in California, in the Permian
Basin of New Mexico and western Texas, in the Texas Panhandle, in the Osage, Kay County, Colorado, Kansas, and Wyoming, and in Mexico and Canada. The old machinery was
burnished, old parts were replaced, grease rags were picked up
from the floor. Duplications were scrapped, the numerous, in-

souciant, little-god-worshipping attendants were replaced by fewer attendants who knew how to say "sir" and "mister." The lumbering dinosaur was suddenly changed into a sleek lizard, fleet and protectively colored.

E. W. felt no real animosity toward the persons who were the instruments of his defeat, but he was uncharacteristically vindictive toward the condition which made their actions necessary. They were applying the laws of struggle, the same laws by which he had gained his own power. In the pattern of creative competition, however, the activity of the investment bankers was, to E. W., a malignant growth which ought to be eradicated, very much as a cancerous growth should be. He felt that he was a competitor who understood and lived by the laws of natural struggle; he believed that he was a gambler who knew how to lose; but he intimated that the lustiest competitive animal could not fight against a malignant growth. "Where in the natural processes can you find such a thing as the Money Trust represents?" he asked. "Can you tell me?"

When the news came out of New York City in March, 1929, that the fabulous E. W. Marland was starting a new oil company, hope was born again in many of his old worshippers. They gave little thought to the realities but were ready to follow the mystical genius. Of the formation of the Ponca City Oil Company, E. W. said, from self-induced enthusiasm, "It is because I am convinced that we must actively resist the attempt of the Money Trust to control the petroleum industry that I am organizing the New Marland Oil Company with most of my old officers and directors, men who made the first company a success, and who were forced out when the bankers gained control, as incorporators with me. We will direct its policies and management, and no investment banker will be permitted on its board. When I need capital I will go direct to the public for it. The price the investment banker exacts for enlisting 'other people's money' in any enterprise is too high for that enterprise to bear when it entails even the slightest degree of banker management. I will have no more of the banker-director trying to serve two interests—his own and that of the stockholders. The experience and knowledge gained by the builders of any industrial corporation are the greatest assets that corporation can have."

He wasn't really thinking of the public, as his statement might indicate: he was vindicating his hurt vanity. He seems to have forgotten his loss of independence under the soothing influence of his optimism. He was unable to appreciate his own limitations in the acquisition of wealth under the existing economic conditions affecting the oil industry. It would seem that he believed in his own mystical powers.

By April 1, 1929, the name of his new company was changed to E. W. Marland, Inc. His secretary, John Hale, became president, and G. W. Blackard, secretary. He made a financial report to the Oklahoma Corporation Commission for the year ending June 30, 1930. This report showed Charlie Brown as president, Alex McCoy, vice president, H. L. McCracken, secretary, and I. G. Harmon, treasurer, with H. R. Kent as assistant to both McCracken and Harmon.

In May, 1931, he assumed the presidency, and Charlie Brown and Alex McCoy became vice presidents. His son, George Roberts Marland, was added to the membership of the board of directors.

Earlier, in 1929, he had incorporated into one holding company all of his private land holdings except the new mansion and the thirty-seven acres surrounding it.

Before the autumn of 1929, the old Marland magic was strong and E. W. had little trouble raising money for his venture of vanity and optimism, but during the autumn of 1929 the national Mardi Gras ended and the season of injured national innocence and vindication began. This sudden dislocation in the economic machinery of the country was not called a "panic," but a "depression." The people of 1907 had been more dramatic but the people of 1929 were perhaps more exact in their term; perhaps unconsciously so, since it was really the invention of those who had been soothing the people with statements which proved clearly that all was well with the world. This term "depression" was a delicate euphemism which, by suggesting the trouble it connoted was to be short lived, served to save the face for those who had failed to warn the people against possible economic changes. However, the great common sense began to assert that, to say "depression" during this disruption beginning in the autumn of 1929 was like saying that little Nellie "passed on," rather than saying that little Nellie "died."

When vertical pressure is exerted, something that is not normal happens to that which is depressed, whether it be air, water, or the human spirit or human energy. Air or water, when not forced to contract under pressure, will escape through physical expansion, while the spirit of energetic man escapes in out-of-routine activity, expressing his urge to survive under the new circumstances. Like the substance of E. W.'s old Marland Company, his own optimism and energy were not "merged out of existence" with the name on the red triangle.

E. W. reacted to the depression much as the nation reacted. The people, deprived of their comfortable living and circuses, resorted to vindictiveness toward their government and were ready to gain their lost comfort by associating themselves with any group action which might serve their ends. They were eager to follow any Pied Piper or strong leader who promised a return to the "good old days."

There was no money to nourish E. W.'s ideas now. He might have played the role of Pied Piper himself to the people of the plains, obtaining leases and raising money for his ventures, if he had gone among them. His name was the very symbol of well-being, and his presence alone would have sold stock. But he sat in his room in the mansion or in his office in the new Spanish colonial building which he had just built on Grand Avenue. The promoter who had watched his ditching crew in West Virginia, the man who had pulled off his pants to aid workmen lay a gas pipe line across the Salt Fork, was now under the influence of a little god Dignity, who had put in his appearance during the years of glory.

But his energy was fluid and his spirit and optimism youthful. While he held money in contempt and had ever refused to recognize its absence, he never had more need for it as a tool than now. Its scarcity at the moment seemed to him to be the only obstacle to the carrying out of his ideas. He had set aside ample funds for Lydie and George but now he needed this money. He also went to his friends and former employees whom he had made rich and, by requesting that they invest in his new venture, placed them in a dilemma. Some took the attitude that, since he had been responsible for their affluence, they could scarcely in all fairness withhold such encouragement from him. Others realized that the oil market was extremely unfavorable at the time—oil had reached a ridiculous twenty or twenty-five cents a barrel. They could salve their consciences by convincing themselves, if not E. W., that by lending or advancing money they would be encouraging him to make worse his already bad financial condition. It was a difficult decision for some of them.

E. W. had borrowed some time previously $850,000 to pay his income tax, and he had pledged more recently his Marland Estate, Inc., as well as his stock in the Southland Royalty Company. It will be remembered that the Southland was the result of a merger with the Marland Employee's Royalty Company, one of the many royalty and producing companies that had sprung up around the mother company during the decade of the prosperous twenties. This company was very strong and was progressively becoming stronger.

He had nothing but his hope, his mansion, and its surrounding thirty-seven acres, free from obligation. He had hope of winning a suit against the United States government which would give him $1,600,000 in income tax refund. He hoped to get an income tax refund from the state as well.

His action to obtain a tax refund was based upon his sale of leases and other transactions affecting the state school land leases taken in 1912 and subsequently. He contended that, since the land was not taxable as state land, then the profits taken from the land should not be taxable, on the ground that to tax profits made from state lands might jeopardize the leasing of state land, thus resulting in an injustice to the children of the state. His interest in the children of the state was well known, but this specious contention of a frustrated, acquisitive man, whose now ragged mantle could not be expected to cover any public interest, failed to impress the court.

He often had to rob Peter to pay Paul. His difficulties were constantly appearing and he was constantly arranging to satisfy his creditors, believing always that his difficulties were temporary. Sometimes he was so pressed that he was compelled to do things which would have hurt his vanity and smudged his dignity if he had not convinced himself that the transaction was an emergency of a temporary nature, for the sole purpose of advancing a plan which would more than compensate for the unpleasant action.

In 1922 he had bought land north of town and divided it into two hundred one-acre tracts, whereon he had built houses for employees and others who appreciated space and gardens, a cow, chickens, and pleasant and secure living in general. This subdivision he financed and called Acre-Homes. In the tight situation of the now fast developing depression—apparently the American National Bank of Oklahoma City was pressing him— he started a friendly suit against the city of Ponca to recover approximately $78,000, which was the value he placed upon the water and electric lines and other properties in the Acre-Homes subdivision. After negotiations the city agreed to pay him $36,- 000 for the water and electric systems, etc., since Acre-Homes had been taken into the city as an addition in 1930.

In the days of his glory, he would have given these utilities to the city with a wave of the hand in a manner which would seem to say, "Is there anything more you'd like to have?"

If he had stayed in his room at the mansion and read Spencer and books on industrial America, or strolled in the tranquil beauty of his preserve, visiting with his friends, he might have served himself better. But under the stress of vertical pressure his constant activity drove him erratically against stone walls or to the edge of a precipice, like a bear who, having forgotten to hibernate, finds himself lost in an early winter blizzard.

On April 22, 1930, the statue to the Pioneer Woman was unveiled and turned over to the state. Governor W. J. Holloway declared the day a holiday. All the state offices were closed and the state's military organizations were lent to the committee in charge of the ceremonies.

Governor Holloway himself was present in top hat and cutaway to receive the gift in the name of the people, and E. W. was present in top hat and cutaway to make the presentation to Governor Holloway. The earlier venture of sending twelve models of the Pioneer Woman over the nation so that the public could make a choice had cost two hundred thousand dollars. It had been a magnificent gesture and because of it E. W. could now be the prince again for a few glorious hours.

The presentation took place on the anniversary of the "Run" into the Unassigned Lands in 1889, but the statue stood on ground staked by a runner who had gone into the Cherokee Outlet in 1893.

Patrick J. Hurley, secretary of war, broadcast his speech from Washington. Pat Hurley was the state's first cabinet officer and Oklahoma was proud of him even though he was a Republican.

Another son of whom the state was very proud was present. The great crowd craned their necks to see him and smiled happily to themselves. His very presence inspired good will and seemed to charm away the little troubles of daily life. His satire was hidden, like a rapier in the pantaloons of a clown. His earthy, Cherokee Hills, horse corral philosophy was appreciated by all who recognized their own inadequacy and inability to face life with a sense of humor. He drew aside the cloak of defense and bluff, and so laughingly lifted the masque of pretense from mass man that he offended no one. His subtle exposure of human frailties glorified the egotism of the unimportant and gave them equal weight on the scales of humanity with the conspicuous and the successful.

His head hanging as though in shyness, his smile indicating a consciousness of being guilty of presumption, he shuffled up to make his speech like a recently grounded cowboy.

E. W. was nervous. This was an occasion of the greatest dignity and importance to him, and he had refused to invite Will Rogers. But somehow, perhaps in the confusion of Pat

Hurley's inability to appear to make the principal speech, Will had been invited, and he had flown in from California to speak.

Will said something about coming all the way from California to undress a woman—this being an unveiling ceremony as well as a presentation ceremony—and E. W. winced. Then, while on the subject of women, Will told a story about a pioneer woman in the Cherokee country who had taken her corset off at a country dance and had spread over the whole width of the wagon seat going home.

The crowd loved this; they loved Will Rogers. They forgot their sore feet and their fatigue when they looked at him. Just looking at him gave them a warm feeling inside and brought smiles and laughter of which they were unconscious. But for E. W., the dignity of the occasion had been marred.

When the speeches were over, the crowd dispersed, leaving their popcorn bags, candy papers, deflated balloons, and cigar butts as a tribute to the Pioneer Woman. She was not a woman "who had endured but a woman who was about to venture." As Bryant Baker created her, she is young and filled with determination more than hope. She has a bundle and a Bible in one hand, leads a little boy with the other. She strides across the plains. You can almost hear the grinding of the grit and sand under her great clumsy brogans, and the folds of her ample skirt swish with her long strides and are molded by the winds of the plains against her hard, Junoesque legs. Her face is set as she looks toward the shimmering, indefinite horizon as she walks away from the mansion and the Versailles vista with its lesser statues. She turns away from stately pretensions, from the artificial lakes and the planted trees of the game preserve, and ignores completely the city of the plains, now smothered by the beauty of its own plantings. The woman "about to venture" looks intently, with some trepidation but with steady purpose, into the hazy distance of the beyond.

This was E. W.'s contribution. He had done something more than exploit the plains.

Headlines marked each phase of E. W.'s energy and the very wording of them seemed to assume that each new dream would crystallize into a lustrous gem of reality, so deeply had his career and his personality affected people's imagination. The end of his glory was never noticed through announcement. But there was an announcement, a symbol of the end of glory. It was a rain-faded, wind-agitated piece of drab paper tacked up at the corner of Fifth Street and Boston Avenue in Tulsa. There was no glow from the blurred name, "E. W. Marland," on the restless, faded paper. It was as profane and unemotional as a numbered tag placed on the inert form of a tornado victim.

The piece of paper advised those who might be concerned that "in pursuance with a consent made and given by E. W. . . ." the security which Mr. Marland had pledged against a loan was now foreclosed. The unpaid indebtedness was $157,163.92 —a small sum in the good old days but the margin now between solvency and a status E. W. had not known since his early years in Pittsburgh.

The property pledged was the Marland Estate Inc. At 11 A.M. on August 11, 1931, the pledged property was sold to the highest bidder, and W. H. McFadden was the highest bidder. He had already taken over E. W.'s shares in the Southland Royalty Company. His bidding in the Marland Estate was a gesture of friendship. Someday E. W. could redeem it, he felt sure.

While E. W. succeeded in getting some refunds from the United States government on income tax payments, he failed to get back the $1,600,000 paid on the profits from the school lands deal. He attempted to get $7,548 refunded from the state and failed. He was refunded in 1932, however, $60,523 on over-assessment on income tax and credited with $59,257 for the year 1917, the assessment for 1918 being withheld for investigation. In 1933 he received a total amount of $140,698 as a tax refund. It was said by political foes later that, after paying some debts, he lost the remainder on the stock market.

But he continued to make Olympian statements, many of which sounded like whistling in the dark but could have been statements of sincere belief. In 1932 he said, "I have never known a better time for the building up of a big oil company than right now." The Mid-Continent field was afloat with oil, and the East Texas field, the greatest in the United States, was in typical Petrolian frenzy. State and federal governments were worrying about conservation. But perhaps there were wildcatters who would have agreed with him; at least they could have picked up cheap property.

During this year, true to his statement about propitious times, he formed another oil company, the Marland Oil Company, and had as directors, John Alcorn, George Marland, I. G. Harmon, and Alex McCoy. It was the purpose of this company to engage exclusively in the production branch of the oil business. "Contrary to general belief," he said—and the belief was not only general but deep—"it is my opinion that the supply of oil which can be produced during the next five years from the fields now known and developed in the United States will not equal the demand for oil during that period. It is our belief that the petroleum industry, as it is overbuilt in its refining and marketing branches, with nothing but obsolescence to correct the evil, will find its profits in the future in the producing branch of the industry, and consequently, the reward of the successful producer will be much greater in the future than it has been in the past."

This was in May, 1932. That summer he was candidate for the Democratic nomination for United States congressman.

18

THE DEMOCRATS had first suggested E. W. as a candidate for the office of congressman-at-large, and he had imitated the coyness of ambitious politicians. Later when his name was suggested to represent the Eighth District, he could say, like a seasoned political flirt, "If they wish to nominate me, I will accept. But I am not announcing my candidacy for the position."

The Kay County Democratic organization indorsed him as a candidate for Congress from the Eighth District and Governor William H. ("Alfalfa Bill") Murray as a candidate for the presidency of the United States.

E. W. didn't like this, nor did the people of Kay County. They were for Ernie Marland all right, but this steamroller business they didn't care about.

Bill Murray was a poor man's governor, and Kay County was one of the richest counties in the state. He had made his campaign for the office of governor in 1930 on cheese and crackers. He was, in fact, the very picture of the political Messiah during the depression. He was not exactly the Pied Piper nor yet the great leader. He was an Oklahoma Andrew Jackson in a genuine but transplanted Jacksonian atmosphere. Unlike Jackson, he had no lingering malaria, no duelist's bullet in his chest, and no lung trouble or symptoms of bone deterioration, but like Jackson he had rage, vindictiveness, and bitterness against pomp and dignity and those who differed with him. His bright mind, his intensity, and his determination to impose his opinions and lead men caused him to look with contempt upon a world not of his own designing. Like Jackson, he placed a high value on personal loyalty. Under different circumstances and in the atmosphere of earlier times, he might have left a great impression on the people of his country. He had the mind and the determination required of those who find a place in history.

E. W. refused to credit Murray with Sir Thomas Hughes's ideals or to recognize the fact that Murray, too, had organized a colony for the underprivileged and the dissatisfied. While Hughes had come from uncomfortable England to the Cumberland plateau of Tennessee to express in practice his ideas, William H. Murray had left uncomfortable Oklahoma to plant his colony in Bolivia. But, like an astute politician, he had come back to the scene of his Constitutional Convention triumphs, during which he had acted as midwife at the birth of the state in 1907, just at the opportune time. The frustrated masses, jobless, vindictive, and seeking an escape from economic pressure, made a hero of this intense, able man who knew he was right.

Since his inauguration in 1931, he had made a good governor for the times. He had called out the militia to conserve oil. His activities raised the price of oil to a dollar a barrel from its previous market price of a few cents.

But because E. W. thought Murray lacked dignity, he could give him little credit for these things. E. W. had paced up and down his room in the mansion and dictated a letter to Murray, when the latter was attempting to restore the price of oil by proration, drilling shut-downs, and abandonment of exploration. It was at a time when Murray had placed men, sometimes national guardsmen, in the oil fields to guard against the running of oil above stated amounts daily. (That which was run secretly, through all types of evasions, ingenious and otherwise, was called "hot oil.") The letter which E. W. dictated to John Hale was to a certain extent an expression of his frustration. E. W. was not opposed to conservation; he wanted some type of control so that oil would not be wasted. But he felt at this time that conservation was serving the purposes of the Standard, just as it had done before. At this particular time, he said, the people who had given leases on their land should not be made to suffer through the withholding of royalties, especially the thousands who needed income more than ever before. In a mood of disgust he dictated his letter to Governor Murray. He entitled it *Call Out the Militia.*

"Nobody called out the militia in the days of Glenn Pool," he dictated, "when the producers of oil of the older pools of this and other states suffered a decline in the price of production from their stripper wells.

"Hardly had the survivors of that depression recovered a fair earning power when they were overtaken by a flood of oil from Cushing and the twenty-eight-cent price of 1915.

"The pumpers in the Glenn Pool were shut down.

"The new crop of producers at Cushing made a lot of money from their flush production and, with the return of prices, waxed fat on $3.50 oil in 1920.

"These again were caught in the flood of 1923. New fields everywhere—California, Texas, Oklahoma. Down came the prices. Weeping and wailing on the Cushing leases.

"But nobody called out the militia.

"Good times came again. Then 1930 with its discoveries and developments and resultant crash prices.

"Seven years from peak to peak of production—four times repeated.

"Every seven years a new crop of ambitious youngsters disturbing the old fellows in the enjoyment of high prices for the product of their old wells.

"Every seven years a new supply of oil for the use and enjoyment of the public, found by enterprising explorers of impossible places.

"Now the cry is: 'Call Out the Militia. This must be stopped —by law—military, if civil won't do it. The Standard Oil is now a producer.'

"Bayonets will be used if necessary to preserve values for the vested interests. They have six hundred million barrels of oil in storage. They must be protected from financial misfortunes resulting from their errors.

"Was not the president of the Standard Oil Company justified when, in 1920, he predicted a shortage of oil? Had not all government geologists previously prophesied the shortly coming end to our supply? Did not the vested interests put six hundred million barrels of high-priced oil in storage—for future use by the public—at higher prices, they hoped.

"They must not be disappointed in this hope. It was their mistake, but call out the militia and save them.

"Shut in Oklahoma! Shut in Texas! Let the vested interests get rid of some of their storage oil.

"What do we care whether these new producers and new royalty owners and the oil field workers eat this winter or not?

"Call out the militia and keep them from selling their flood of fresh oil at a nickel a barrel to the American public.

"The American workingman and farmer want to pay twenty cents for gasoline, not ten cents. They are prosperous and not stingy with their money.

"Mother Nature planted a billion barrels of oil in East Texas where the big companies—high-priced geologists—failed to find it, and Lady Luck sent some poor out-of-work boys over there who found it in this year of grace, 1931, just when cheap gasoline was most needed by our unemployed city folk and twenty-five-cents-a-bushel wheat farmers.

"A poor cotton farmer, with forty acres of five-dollar land in East Texas, six starving kids, and a lame old mule, leased his land to a bunch of the boys almost as poor as he—ex-employees, fired by the big oil companies—who borrowed a rig, casing, and tools and worried a hole down to a rich oil sand.

"Under every acre of that forty were thirty-two thousand barrels of oil. The farmer's one-eighth royalty was four thousand barrels. Four thousand barrels at ten cents equals four hundred dollars per acre, fabulous riches from the old five-dollar land.

"*Call Out The Militia!*

"He must not be permitted to sell it. He will ruin the vested interests of the petroleum industry with such a price. They have five hundred million barrels on hand that cost them more than a dollar a barrel.

"What matters if he wants to produce his oil this year? Buy the old woman a new dress, calico, of course; buy the kids some books and shoes and send them to school; give the old mule a full feed just once?

"No, he must not do it. It is his oil, of course. The law says so. But he must not produce it and sell it.

"The law says it is his—the law allows him to produce it and sell it at any price he sees fit.

"Ten cents a barrel—four hundred dollars per acre.

"Fifty cents a barrel—twenty-five hundred dollars per acre.

"There does not seem to be any law to prevent him from selling his oil at ten cents a barrel.

"And if he does so it will reduce the dividends of the vested interests.

"Every sound-thinking American must believe in conservation of an irreplaceable natural resource such as petroleum.

"Every citizen has an interest in the prevention of physical waste.

"Because he is concerned about price, present and future.

"If the military of our state government is to be used at the expense of the tax-paying public to prevent physical waste—that public is entitled to protection against unreasonable advance in price."

Thus did E. W. rave at Governor Murray as he paced his room dictating to John Hale. Then he dictated his last sentence on the subject of proration for the benefit of price, not of conservation. "Back up, Bill, on that dollar order before it makes a monkey of you."

Even to his loyal former lieutenants, his statements, which once were oracular, now were becoming contradictory.

He began his campaign speeches by expressing his own grievances, implying that they were the grievances of the people. His suits over income tax refunds had been long drawn out, and he, in his need, had been annoyed and inconvenienced. He promised to rectify the tax system of the government and investigate the causes of its casual administration and the resulting long, unjust delays in making restitution. Later he took his pet theme of the bankers' control of the nation's economy. He had in mind the Money Trust and, even more definitely, the House of Morgan.

The people, seeking a leader to symbolize the vindictiveness born of their loss of comfort, would attack the person or thing he might point out to them. He pointed out to them President Hoover as an international businessman who was more interested in faraway Europe than in the good and virtuous people of the plains. He pointed out to them, with straightened arm but always with dignity—he never pounded the table or raised his voice—the "wolves of Wall Street" and the tax system under the president who was interested only in international business. He was courteous toward his Republican opponent, Congressman M. C. Garber of Enid, who was associated with the Garber oil field. The race in November was between Ponca City and Enid, the two wide-branched oaks of the old Cherokee Outlet, but there was little rivalry between the two cities now. The rivalry in the state was between Oklahoma City and Tulsa, between the capital of the state and the city that grew up on oil.

During the first days of his campaign, E. W. didn't say much about the man who had been associated with him in the Zeppelin transportation venture, Franklin D. Roosevelt, who was the party's nominee for the presidency of the United States. He listened to the voice that came over the radio. Its tone, its inflections, and its localisms he respected as being from the East. He believed in this man, the second gentleman of the Roosevelt family aspiring to leadership. E. W. not only felt confident that he was a gentleman but thought his voice bore conviction and inspired confidence, even as it sounded the most obvious facts. Here was a determined man who knew exactly what he was going to do and was telling the people about it as though he believed sincerely in his proposal.

Then one day the magic of this man came to him as he listened to his radio. It came clearly and definitely, and he felt the whole power of the man behind a single phrase. He turned to John Hale. "How's that, John—'turn the money changers out of the temple'—how's that?" He had no fear of identifying himself with Roosevelt. Even the Republican Eighth District would follow him, he was sure. Everyone was turning his ears to this virile voice, vibrant with confidence. As he listened to this militant, inspiring man halfway across the continent, he began to project himself in a new, winning role out there on the plains.

All was friendly and dignified, this first venture in politics. The Garber name was important in the Outlet, but E. W.'s name was bigger. People were coming under the magic of the voice that came out of their radios, the voice that inspired as much confidence as a presence. Not only was E. W. identified with the voice of the vital presidential candidate, but he was among friends and admirers, and carried weight as a person who had accomplished much himself. The Eighth District had the same boundaries as the old Cherokee Outlet, save that Ellis county had been left out of it, and the long Panhandle, which had been tacked onto Oklahoma Territory in 1890, had been added.

The atmosphere was a family one. When E. W. won the primaries, Phil Ferguson telegraphed his congratulations, adding in the friendly, sardonic spirit of the plains, "You have the most neighbors."

This was what E. W. liked, dignity and friendliness. When he won the election, he had the honor of being the first Democratic representative from the only Republican district in the state. No work-and-win youngster could have been filled with a greater desire for worthy battle for the people than he.

Howard Drake, who was not one of his bright young men of the Ponca City Marland offices, but who had been with E. W.'s son George out in western Texas with the Reagan Crude Purchasing Company, had served as his campaign manager. "Pete" Drake was handsome and tall, and E. W. attributed political shrewdness to him, perhaps partly on this account. When he talked strategy with E. W. there was no chewed cigar in the corner of a distorted mouth, no wheezing, no flabby jowls. There was no stubby-fingered hand with dirty nails playing with a pencil to jar E. W.'s sensitiveness to beauty when he looked at Pete. Pete's strategy seemed good to him. If he had not lost his company, Pete might well have become one of his vice presidents one day.

He was happy to have an important office to absorb his energy. He had made no promises that were vain and empty, and he, E. W. Marland, with such a president as Franklin D. Roosevelt, would accomplish much. He had entered politics as a gentleman should enter it, quietly and with dignity. What really lay at the bottom of people's hearts, he believed, was an unconscious appreciation of dignity in their leaders. He had won the office by more than eighteen thousand votes, which was called a "sweeping victory." The incumbent, Congressman Garber, the oilman from Enid, had with great friendliness congratulated the people of the Eighth District on their choice. "To my distinguished successor," he said, "I wish the greatest good fortune in his future labors in Congress for the Eighth District, and I feel sure that he will endeavor to represent you to the best of his ability."

E. W. convinced himself that he was now a gentleman-statesman. He had no distinct plans, but he knew that the people would receive his full attention. He seemed to be extending his concern to the people in general now, but it is quite likely that when he thought of the people he still had images of people whom he actually knew. He had few doubts about his future in Congress. He felt a smug assurance that the people of the district would retain him in Washington.

In Washington, he was given his predecessor's place on the Committee on Interstate Commerce, which he knew to be a good one. It was a phase of national government with which he was acquainted because of his years in a big business which depended upon interstate transportation. He was accepted as an authority on the oil business.

He was a freshman and he felt like a strange boy entering a large, noisy school. The little god of the plains received no fanfare, but was assigned, figuratively, to a back seat, along with other freshmen. The older boys in the big school had their prerogatives, and the very atmosphere of brashness made him feel ineffectual.

He also found that there were many other important men in the Congress, where he had thought he might be conspicuous. There were men of great wealth, scholars, and men whom even he would recognize as gentlemen, besides the well-cured, highly-seasoned leaders and the "gallery watchers."

John Hale went to Washington with him and for the first time in years John could be assured of a salary. John, out of loyalty, had continued to stay with E. W. as his secretary without pay during the months when there was nothing with which to pay him. He had at first received a salary of five thousand dollars, then it had been raised to ten thousand dollars, but since 1929 he had had no real assurance of receiving anything.

John had smoked his special mixture in his big pipes, read books in Spanish, French, and English, stored facts, become cranky over misuses in written English, but had let nothing, not even lack of salary, affect his loyalty to E. W.

19

AFTER FRANKLIN D. ROOSEVELT was inaugurated, the people awaited with confidence his treatment for the national malady. The public became the calm patient of the great specialist. At times they thought of him as a social doctor, at others, as the earthly counterpart of the Archangel Michael, with flaming sword bringing confusion or actual pain and death to Satan's hordes of social, economic, and political evildoers who had imposed upon them. Even the big boys were listening with hope, not to the avenging angel, but to the man with the fireside manner. They would take their night sweats to the specialist with the hope of having them banished.

E. W. had said that the businessman himself would be the chief cause of revolution, if it ever came to America, because he was not able "to see any farther than his nose." He had also said that "a defeated big businessman is, ordinarily, the biggest crybaby in the world." There seemed to be no ray of self-revelation when he found himself blaming the House of Morgan and the Standard for his own defeat.

Here, then, was a gentleman in the White House who had the same feeling for the people that he had, and had the power to do for them what idealists had dreamed of doing for them for ages. The very fact of the Great Leader's existence, dramatized by a voice that spoke democracy, had left the mad agitators for blood and chaos without hope of revolution. They could only watch their potential disciples turn their faces to the White House. E. W. would aid the Great Leader with full heart in giving the people a chance to enjoy freedom and dignity, which were their rights in a rich and powerful country. He noted with pleasure that this Great Leader was not a bitter man, coming up from the coal pits or from the slums of the steel plants, carrying in his heart the poison of hate and the spirit of vengeance. He was also pleased that he was not a man of big business—a falcon, who, when unhooded, uses his perfect vision, his strong wings, and his swiftness to fly to the prey of selfishness.

This man in the White House was, E. W. believed, a kindred spirit, but he didn't realize their fundamental relationship. The Great Leader had also been a little boy imperialist, an only son. He, too, had been under the influence of a strong, adoring mother, but he had gained his liberal insight, not through a father's idealism but through physical handicap. His great energy, even his little-boy imperialism, had been dammed after a happy youth and young manhood by his physical handicap, so that his spirit and force were turned into the channel of ideas, some of them certainly ornamental, but some of them as inspiring to faith and devotion as the crucifix.

E. W. approached the President with the attitude, "Since you are a gentleman, and we believe the same things, you lead and I'll follow."

When he arose on the floor of the House to propose amendments to the hastily prepared bills which were to carry out the Great Leader's ideas, crystallizing them for the New Deal, he was fearful of lese majesty. He feared any action of his own which might throw the New Dealer off his rhythm.

But he wanted to be sure that the weapons, the social and economic measures which would aid the common man, were right-handed weapons of defense, not left-handed weapons of retreat, and he wanted to be sure the shining blade that looked like steel was in reality steel, not a clever imitation fashioned by the big boys, who were sure to be on the people's oil and finance committees.

He arose to address the House:

"I am a new member of Congress, and it is with the greatest reluctance that I rise to offer an amendment to a bill reported favorably out of the committee of which I am a member.

"The reason is this:

"That when I became a candidate for Congress it was because I believed that my experience in the business and the financing of a great corporation might be of value to Congress in finding a solution for some of the industrial and financial problems.

"I have had intimate, personal contact with many of our smaller investment banking houses over many years, and finally with the banking house of J. P. Morgan and Company, which latter experience lasted over a period of five years and until I was forced by them out of control of the company I had spent my lifetime in building.

"The amendment I will offer to this bill is that hereafter it shall be unlawful for any person to act as a director of any corporation which is selling securities in interstate and foreign commerce who shall be a partner of or financially interested in any banking concern buying and selling the securities of such corporation for profit."

Then, in support of his argument for the amendment, he quoted Woodrow Wilson: "The great monopoly in this country is the money monopoly. So long as that exists, our old variety of freedom and individual energy of development are out of the question. A great industrial nation is controlled by its system of credit. Our system of credit is concentrated. The growth of the nation, therefore, and all our activities are in the hands of a few men, who, even if their actions be honest and intended for public interest, are necessarily concentrated upon great undertakings in which their own money is involved and who, necessarily, by every reason of their own limitations, chill and check and destroy genuine economic freedom."

He then quoted from his favorite, Supreme Court Justice

Louis D. Brandeis's book entitled *Other People's Money and How the Bankers Use It*. "The investment bankers control the people through the people's own money—the fetters which bind the people are forged with the people's own gold."

After this quotation, E. W. offered his amendment.

He was running smoothly with the current here. But when he studied the National Industrial Recovery Act, he thought that perhaps he detected a tendency, in the reshuffling of the cards, to change the game from poker to slot machines, where the law of chance was restricted and calculated beforehand. He also thought that the enthusiastic academic reformers who had flocked to Washington might not have practical sense enough to detect "cold decking" by the cunning representatives of the big companies, also wearing the academic gown of public interest, but only for the purpose of disguise. He couldn't have expressed exactly what he felt at that time, but he remembered having seen intellectuals curtsy to him when he was a wealthy man, thereby manifesting the secret admiration which nearly all Americans had for great wealth and power.

He thought long about the N. I. R. A., and the more he thought about it the more it seemed to him to be a very dangerous weapon in the hands of human frailty. The danger was two-edged; the freedom of oil, the second largest industry of the land, might be curbed by the intellectuals or by the cunning of the big boys. He became emotional at the thought of either eventuality, losing his fear of lese majesty and the mighty power of the people's anger.

He dictated a speech that came straight from the depths of his feeling, not as a careful politician but as a romantic lover of the siren, Petrolia, his symbol of freedom.

"Mr. Speaker and Members of the House:

"Never before in the history of the world have a people of a civilized nation, such as ours, abandoned completely an industrial system that had prevailed among them for generations without attendant bloodshed and political revolution.

"This Congress today, representing the people of the United States, has turned its back on the highly competitive industrial system which has built this great nation of ours and which has been the life of trade during the centuries of progress from our European ancestors.

"We have not only abandoned an economic system which had its beginning in the dawn of civilization, but we have left it without knowing what system we are to follow in the future.

"No law has been written which so affected human rights, human happiness, and human destiny since the writing of the Magna Charta on the field of Runnymede, seven hundred and eighteen years ago today. It may mean that by the passage of this act we have repealed that great charter of human liberties which guaranteed government by law instead of government 'by discretion of royalty' which had theretofore prevailed.

"By this National Industrial Recovery Act we will confer upon the President of the United States wider discretionary powers of government than have ever been held by any but an absolute monarch. The saving grace to this renunciation of our constitutional rights lies in the fact that a national emergency exists and that the powers granted to the President shall cease to exist at the expiration of two years after the date of the enactment of this act."

As he spoke specifically about the oil industry, one could have seen the lover's interest slowly crystallize: "The individual enterprise, the initiative, keen competition, ability to endure hardships and disappointments have built this great industry. Its expansion, its physical progress have been due to the enterprise, the ability, the genius of the individuals engaged in it. Its growth into the first rank among the great industries of our country has been unequaled by that of any industry intended to be aided by this act."

He went on to say that the oil industry was built by free men of daring, with confidence in their freedom and the freedom of oil. He reminded the Congress that the late war had been won by oil and that civilization in peacetime depended upon oil. "What does the future hold in store for us under the new economic order about to be set up under the Industrial Recovery Act?" he asked. "Will individual effort, will initiative and enterprise, will inventive genius be smothered under the codes of fair competition written by trade associations and approved by the President?

"When the code to govern oil producers is written by an association or associations financed and controlled by interested corporations, will it provide that the President or his administration say when, where, and how a man may drill a well for oil?

"And if he find oil, when, where, and to whom, and for how much he may sell his oil? Will the code limit his possible profits when he is lucky and ignore his more frequent losses? Will the code compel him to sell his crude oil to existing refineries or may he build a refinery of his own and sell products to the customer? Or, if he is permitted to build his own refinery to refine oil, must he forego the privilege of marketing the products direct to the consumer and, perforce, sell them to some existing marketing agency?

"There is nothing in the act to say what he may or may not do. He will be governed under it completely by the discretion of the president.

"It is to the President that he must look for the determination of his rights and privileges and future conduct of his business.

"Mr. Speaker, it is my intention, as soon as this act has been passed, to notify my friends in the producing branch of the oil business of the United States to assemble and write a code to govern their future activities, and present it to the President for his approval.

"They must not permit the great integrated companies to write a code for them. A major company engaged in producing, pipe-line transportation, refining, and marketing cannot be expected to write a code that will be fair to producers not engaged in other branches of the industry.

"The great integrated companies, with their enormous profits accruing to them from pipe-line operations, are not so much concerned about establishing a price for crude oil to meet the cost of production.

"Nor can they be trusted to write a code that will be fair to each of the several oil producing states when their producing interests may be entirely in other states.

"Mr. Speaker, I would like to impress upon the President and the agency he sets up to administer this act, insofar as it relates to the petroleum industry, the importance of the facts: that, in the past, the independent producer of oil, the individualist, has found nearly all of the oil fields that have been found in this country.

"That he must be depended upon to do so in the future; that his incentive must remain; that his initiative must not be ruined; that he must not be turned over to the tender mercies of the great integrated holding companies, whether they be Standard, Mellon, Morgan, or Dutch controlled."

He suspected the young, earth-alienated intellectuals who had swarmed to Washington in the hope of making over the country to fit their dream designs. Their views, which they lumped together as liberalism, did not spring from some inherent quality of altruism in themselves, but seemed to have been induced by their detached theorizing and by their reaction to the overbearing, shortsighted, hooded-falcon philosophy of the acquisitive-struggle survivors. The simple arrogance of successful businessmen, often without cultural background or other indication of civilization, and the very fact of their recognized and effective power, inspired a rather precipitate eagerness to discredit them on the part of the intellectuals from the smug atmosphere of the great universities.

E. W. resented their influence in the President's bill "To relieve the existing national economic emergency by increasing agricultural purchasing power." Debate had been limited under the rule governing its consideration and no amendments were permitted. In the two minutes allotted to each member, E. W. said:

"Mr. Speaker, I will vote for this bill.

"I will vote for this bill intended by the President to relieve agriculture. But with great reluctance, because I believe it will not have the desired effect of increasing the farmer's income sufficiently to permit him to pay his taxes and mortgage interest and support his family.

"I believe this bill, if it becomes a law, will increase the farmer's difficulties by giving him two bosses where he now has one—adding the political enforcement officer to his present banker boss.

"I do not believe that the bankers of my district want to curtail production. Nor do I believe in the necessity of curtailing [the farmers'] production if the markets of the world are open to them by the remonetization of silver, and the purchasing power of the people of this country be enlarged by the re-inflation of current credits.

"I will vote for this bill only because the President has asked Congress to give him the opportunity to experiment with the agricultural problem, and because he has promised to give up the experiment as soon as he discovers it is unworkable.

"However, it is my firm conviction that nothing will help the farmer pay his taxes and mortgage interest and hold on to his land, except a revaluation of the dollar."

The applause he received must have sent warmth through his body.

He believed that, as far as oil was concerned, the President really felt as he did, but having had no practical experience, and no advisers except experts whose advice was colored by their company interest, he might need counsel. The President at this stage was readily admitting that he was experimenting. However, the little-boy imperialism of the man from Hyde Park did not take such bluntness kindly, even as early as 1933. On the other hand, the little-boy imperialism of the man from Mount Washington, even though he had lost his cloud seat in Oklahoma, had little practice either in tempering his expressions of will, his desires, or his emotions born of hurt vanity and defeat.

There was certainly no enmity between them. E. W. would never feel anything but admiration for the Great Leader, even though the latter might have a very good memory in recalling such phrases as "by discretion of royalty," and later favor less belligerently opinionated men.

E. W. visited the White House to discuss phases of the bills written in scholarly eagerness and perhaps occasionally in breathless hurry, and he wrote a letter to the President expressing his fears.

"I would like to express to you my opinion that the ills of the producing branch of the petroleum industry are not due to actual overproduction, but are due to proration as now controlled by the major purchasing companies, themselves controlled by, or affiliated with, pipe-line companies. Honest proration, rateable taking, as between states, as between pools in states, as between wells in pools, to limit production to market demand, had never been given a fair trial.

"In my opinion, the ills of the petroleum industry are not due to unregulated production of petroleum by independent petroleum producers but are due, largely, to the unregulated operation of pipe-line companies controlled by holding companies, which are also the owners of producing companies.

"May I respectfully suggest that while 'the enactment of emergency legislation divorcing oil pipe lines engaged in interstate commerce from other branches of the oil industry' may be necessary to prevent monopoly, such divorce might be long delayed by legal procedure and that much can be done immediately toward curing the ills of the petroleum industry by requiring the Interstate Commerce Commission to assume the duties already placed upon it by the Interstate Commerce Act to fix fair compensatory rates for the transportation of oil, and to regulate the amount of oil taken and the manner in which oil is taken in the various fields in the several oil producing states in the United States."

The President, when not occupied at Albany, had become adept at dreaming and learning at Hyde Park. By physical inactivity he had joined what most men miss—a chance to think—so that the torrent of his energy was diverted and sought strange depressions and canyons, to form placid bayous where new growths in the form of ideas were nurtured.

When this metaphor was suggested to E. W., it in turn suggested his own years of struggle, with a resultant philosophy which seemed similar to that of the President. But he insisted on going further and suggesting that his natural survival-struggle had given him much that a thinker could never learn. Life, he believed, was like poker. A New Dealer had no chance with the professional sharpers unless he knew all the tricks. There had been many a slick new deck, unwrapped in the presence of all, that had contained five aces.

The term New Deal to a poker player had deep meaning, and E. W. thought it apt. But when he thought of the great oil companies and their poker tricks, and of the Standard monopoly that had been built upon transportation, both railway and pipe line, he feared the big companies might be able to hold on to this control through their ownership of pipe lines.

In the poker game that was the oil business, the high rates of the pipe-line companies, controlled by the big oil combines, provided the "kitty," demanded of the independents and the small operators. In this game, the proration of production and any losses which the producing departments of the big companies might suffer were more than compensated for by the pipe-line take. E. W. pictured the representatives of the big companies as "cold deckers" and card markers.

"One hot afternoon this week," he wrote, "I walked into a room of an uptown hotel in New York called the 'Roosevelt,' by coincidence, for a gathering of the greatest gamblers in America—and that means the world.

"The players for the Rockefellers, the Morgans, the Mellons were there; presidents of Standard and other great oil companies, along with a lot of smaller fry—fixing the cards for the new deal in the oil game. Writing the new rules to govern the players and calling it the 'Code of Fair Competition for the Petroleum Industry.'

"They had their coats off—sweating over the problem. Worried looks on some faces—tongues in the cheeks of others—many with hands on the table—others with the fingers of one hand crossed underneath the board.

"This code had to be approved by the President of the U. S. —and there might be jail sentences and fines for the violators— no wonder the perspiration.

"Two years to play the new game. No fear of Federal Anti-trust Acts. What a splendid break of luck that was. Of course they had to keep one eye on the attorney general of Texas—a hope for grace from that quarter.

" 'Open covenants, openly arrived at' was frequently quoted. They seemed to like the sound of that. They were safe. Hadn't the customers—over one hundred trade associations representing thousands of members—95 per cent of the oil industry— adopted the code in the big meeting in Chicago? Weren't they in good faith compelled to adopt the code the customers wanted?

"Hadn't their committee seen every association in the business and sold them the idea of approving this code? Of course, there was nothing that this meeting could do but approve it and transmit it to the President of the U. S. for his approval.

"No more secret rebates—no more unfair practices—prices must be posted in the future—several such inconvenient provisions. No dealing from the bottom—in fact, no cheating at all. That's what the code said.

"Hell of a game for men to play who had enjoyed the advantages of marked cards and cold decks all these years.

"But let's hop to it and thank our lucky stars the fixers had not thought to monkey with the kitty.

"Their takings from the pipe-line kitty were good for $150,-000,000 a year anyhow. Been good for $125,000,000 for the past four depression years.

"That was plenty of advantage, after all. No amount of fair dealing could offset that edge.

"No one had ever talked about it, so why should they mention pipe lines in the code.

"President Roosevelt would probably forget what he said in April about pipe lines, that time he sent the letter to the governors of oil producing states:

" 'The report of the Independent Association Opposed to Monopoly recommends the enactment of emergency legislation by Congress divorcing oil pipe lines engaged in interstate commerce from other branches of the industry. I am of the opinion that this is a reasonable request and that such legislation should be enacted at as early a date as possible.'

"That's what the President said—but he is so busy now with so many other problems that if we play this new deal right he may forget it.

"I want to assure them that Congress is not going to let the President forget what the President said about the reasonableness of divorcing pipe lines; not unless they cut the big fat kitty at least in half before Congress meets again."

Oil-company poker and oil-field poker were the same, E. W. thought. The players had to realize that you knew all the tricks and had the power to enforce fair dealing, then there would be no more difficulty. He said the fixers in the Roosevelt Hotel in New York were like the gamblers he surprised in one of his oil camps in western Oklahoma. It was a very hot afternoon. He pushed open the door of the "office" of an oil-field shack "club." He wanted to investigate the report that his workers were being robbed of their very substantial wages by sharpers. "Found half a dozen men inside in their shirt sleeves, sweating over the job of marking cards, stacking decks, carefully opening new decks, inserting an extra king, abstracting an ace, resealing the pack."

He sent for the gambler who ran the place, and when he appeared he told him that he wanted his boys to have entertainment, and he didn't care if they lost, but he wanted them to have a chance to lose fairly. He didn't threaten him. The gambler knew, however, about aroused oil field workers. He knew what they might do to his "club" if they got in the mood. He knew that E. W. would build a club for them and hire someone to run it, if he found it necessary. He also knew of E. W.'s fairness.

The gambler looked him in the eye and said, "How much take-off for the kitty, E. W.?"

E. W. replied, "Oh, about half that," indicating the unreasonable percentage of the take.

The gambler held out his hand and said, "You're on."

Life was like that. Adequate force had only to present itself. E. W. wanted to make sure that the New Dealers, with the power of the aroused people behind them, could recognize the tricks of the wolverines of the oil game. Everyone was afraid of the power of this physically incapacitated man in the White House; the tremendous power delegated to him by the disturbed, vindictive people whose collective voice sent a chorus echoing over the world.

He introduced in the House a bill "to raise revenue by prohibiting oil pipe-line companies from filing consolidated returns and to increase the income tax on such companies." He introduced a bill to "aid the states in the conservation of crude petroleum and to prevent the transportation in interstate and foreign commerce of crude petroleum which has been unlawfully produced," and a bill "to preserve and protect the correlative rights of the oil-producing states; to assist them in the proper enforcement of their oil conservation laws; to assure the conservation of crude petroleum and natural gas and preserve the same as national resources; to regulate the transportation and sale in interstate and foreign commerce of natural gas, crude petroleum, and the products thereof; to prevent waste in the production, marketing and use of such natural gas and petroleum; to invest the secretary of the interior with the power to carry out this act; and for other purposes." He introduced a bill "to provide for the control of the flood waters of the Arkansas River and its tributaries to provide irrigation, electrical power, reforestation of the watershed, and for the well-being of the people in general."

But this business of being just a member of the chorus, the great New Deal chorus of responses to the Great Leader, seemed to be like hiding one's light. He felt vaguely that he might be wasting his time and his proven ability by remaining a member of the chorus.

In the autumn of 1933 he made his farewell speech to Congress, stating that he would not seek re-election in the summer of 1934. He spoke of providing the unemployed with subsistence homesteads and of the condition of the farmers. He spoke of the need for co-operation between the officers of the national and state governments on many social and economic problems which affected the people of his state, Oklahoma, so importantly. Then he said,

"Mr. Speaker, I will not longer detain the House with a discussion of Oklahoma's economic problems.

"I will only say that I am leaving the House, where I have enjoyed my work and my co-workers, to run for governor because the financial and economic situation of my state is so grave and requires business leadership."

On January 15, 1935, E. W. wore his top hat and cutaway again. This time he rode through Oklahoma City to the state capitol to assume the office he had won in November, 1934.

Crowds jammed the sidewalks as he rolled along in a big car. This man in the high hat had been, because of his wealth, a minor oracle in the twenties, and everyone had heard of his princely lavishness. But certainly he was not the people's man; no Andrew Jackson, "Alfalfa Bill" Murray, or Jack Walton. The applause was dignified.

A man financially ruined but certain of the support of the people of the old Cherokee Outlet might have hesitated to leave the Congress with a salary of, at that time, $8,400, for the governorship of Oklahoma, a post conceded to be one of the most difficult in the nation, with a salary of $6,500. But what was money to E. W. compared to a position as leader again?

There were faces at every window, and little girls ran alongside the creeping car with arms full of flowers, their little ready-made speeches garbled in excitement.

W. H. McFadden, the big game hunter, tall, hard-twisted, and ruggedly handsome, rode Major, the piebald from the old 101 Ranch show troupe, as grand marshal. The Oklahoma Military Academy band pranced behind McFadden. Behind them came the cavalry troop from the same Academy at Claremore, proud, as all horsemen have been through the centuries. Behind them crept the car carrying Howard ("Pete") Drake, campaign manager and chief of staff, and the little boy from Mount Washington, replete with emotion that inflated him visibly. Behind their car came scores more.

The national guardsmen swung along behind: the cavalry, the inevitable caisson of the field artillery, and the infantry, followed by a cavalcade of plains cowboys, some with belts straining to accommodate life-of-ease stomachs.

"Uncle Sam" was there in stars and stripes and chin whiskers whipped indecorously by the crazy little winds of the plains—offering perhaps a double symbolism.

The A. & M. College band from Stillwater came along, less fervent than at football games; the University of Tulsa band, and the University of Oklahoma band playing "Boomer-Sooner," the pep song of the playing fields. Inevitably, symbolizing the nympholepsy of a nation, came the cuties, dressed presumptuously in the kilts of the glorious fighting male of the Highlands of Scotland. They were the famed "Kiltie Band."

" 'And thick and fast they came at last, and more and more and more'," quoted an Oklahoma City reporter. "More than twenty-five bands and drum and bugle corps blared and drum-ruffled their way out to the capitol. Seventy-seven official cars rolled along in the procession, which took seventy-five minutes to pass a given point.

"College groups, reform school groups, business men, laborers, farmers, the very old and the very young, the rich, the poor, the professions—all strata of the state's social and economic society—were there.

"Everybody was present but Governor Murray . . . ."

There were banners, "Poverty Must Be Wiped Out" and "$50 Old Age Pensions." There were banners crying for a "30-Hour Week" and one assuring the people that "Those Who Till the Land Should Own It."

"Elect Me and Bring the New Deal to Oklahoma," had been E. W.'s slogan. He had no doubts about the good will of the people of Oklahoma or their judgment. He had told them that he would bring the New Deal to the state, and they had approved by electing him to their highest executive office. He had attacked the Money Trust and the big oil companies. He had obviously been one of the Great Leader's disciples in the preparation of the New Deal. He had helped frame emergency legislation for the welfare of the people, and the people of Oklahoma had approved of all these things. While in Washington he had lived quietly and represented the people of the Outlet with the dignity of a prince, a way of doing things which they liked —so much so that they had chosen him in the gubernatorial primaries over fourteen opponents. He had amassed a plurality of fifty thousand votes over Tom Anglin, a formidable opponent, who won second place. He took this to mean that, in choosing him over Anglin, who was Bill Murray's candidate, the people wanted dignity and were tired of "fire bells" excitement.

He had been gratified by the withdrawal of Tom Anglin from the runoff primary of July, leaving him as the Democratic nominee to face the Republican, W. B. Pine. He believed that this courtesy on the part of Anglin indicated the reasonableness of a gentleman, and he later asked him to serve on the Interstate Oil Compact Commission and on his Highway Commission.

This day, January 15, 1935, was E. W.'s climax. That is, this date seemed to him to mark a climax, but in fact it was only a brief hour of illusion in his anticlimax. He had been the little god of the Outlet, now he was the little god of the whole of the Red Bed plains, of the woodlands, the pine-covered mountains, the canyons of live water in the Cherokee hills, the short-grass country, and the swamps of the southeast where the white heron nested.

Just as he had been the executive lord of a great oil company during a time when all men were loyal, from tool dresser to vice president, when his word had been eagerly accepted as law by thousands of people, so now he would be the beloved chief executive of a state. He would enter with assurance the halls of the legislature, just as he had entered the meetings of his operating departments. He would reign at conferences, just as he had reigned where heads of world-important oil companies had asked his opinions; even as he had sat in the offices of Morgan and Company, the ganglion of the world's financial system. He would see again the faces aglow with collective pride in him as a symbol of well-being, and he would feel again great warmth as he acted to facilitate the pursuit of happiness by the people of the state, as he had done for the people of the Outlet.

During the campaign he had had moments of dejection and perhaps of fear. After his marriage to Lydie, the "shine-light" of the poacher had picked him up in the nocturnal forests of domestic privacy, but this annoyance had not lasted long; the poacher had turned to other game. But during his campaign for the gubernatorial nomination, and later as the party's nominee, there had been many hunters in the forests flashing and firing at him, and some of the shots had wounded his dignity if not his self-esteem.

He was supposed to have written a letter to Grover Blackard, the manager of the Marland Estate, Inc., suggesting that it would be a good time to sell 240 acres at $2.25 an acre to the government for home sites for the financially on-the-brink industrial workers. He wrote this letter in August, 1934, from his vacation spot in New London, Connecticut, and he had ended it with, "I believe I can get this approved as a starter." The W. B. Pine forces got the letter and published it. E. W. defended himself, saying that he had no interest in the land, since it had been sold for the mortgage, and that, anyway, he had originally paid much more per acre for the land than the $2.25 asked by the seller. On the other hand, it was generally understood that W. H. McFadden had bought the land, along with the other property of the Marland Estate, Inc., at the Tulsa sale, with the understanding that E. W. might redeem it when he became able. The Pine adherents said that E. W. had been collecting rentals from it.

This was a clumsy situation for the nominee.

This, and other snipings at his character and whispers to discredit him, made E. W. realize that being a candidate for the office of governor was quite different from being a candidate for office from his own community, where people remembered that he had been the benevolent source of much of their joy.

E. W. recovered from the hurt just in time to feel the sting of another sniper's bullet. He had to answer the charges again concerning the Jack Walton notes and the purchase of the house from Caldwell back in 1922. The old school-land leasing deal came up again, and many a detractor got out his pencil to figure his supposed profits in the millions to prove that the school children of the state had been deprived of their birthright by his shrewdness.

Someone found that he had never completed payment of principal and interest on state land, Section 13-R26N-T2E, in Kay County, which he had purchased in 1926 from the School Land Commission at an auction in the county seat, Newkirk. Apparently there had been no ad valorem tax assessments against it, and there had been nothing paid on it either in principal or in interest since 1930. This discovery had inspired an investigation of the School Land Department by the lower chamber of the legislature which was played up by his opponents during the campaign. The interpretation of this situation was not too difficult for his supporters. He had been financially unable to take care of all his enormous obligations after 1929. Who, they wanted to know from the people, could be expected to pay his obligations after the crash, steered by the big boys of Wall Street? What, they asked, could an honest man, attempting to do the right thing, do in the face of Republican Herbert Hoover's policies? Were they not all victims of the "wolves of Wall Street"?

The "Dear Grover" letter was by far the most difficult charge to explain, the facts notwithstanding. But persons were induced to follow him on his campaign tours, whispering, insinuating ugly things supposed to be secrets of his private life. This tactic got them nowhere, since a rare expression of his sense of humor made the slander ridiculous.

It was said that the Anti-Saloon League had been told by him to "go to hell." This was true. It was said at the time by others less forthright that no seeker of office in the state of Oklahoma had ever before evinced such magnificent courage. This courage, they said, should have been much more important to the virtuous people of Oklahoma than the puerile discussion and side-taking on the question of whether a citizen could drink what, when, and where he wished. Perhaps many people did appreciate the incredible and inspiring courage of this man.

When he was a candidate for the office of representative of the Eighth Oklahoma District to Congress—and this was one of the unpleasant incidents of that campaign—a man came into his office with a questionnaire, demanding that he fill it out and sign it. "This I declined to do," E. W. said. "I said I recognized no right of the Anti-Saloon League to pledge me to any course of action, regardless of my conscience, as the price of their support in the coming election.

"This man told me that if I did not fill out the questionnaire and send it in, the Anti-Saloon League would be against me.

"This, I think, would arouse any man's anger. I told him he could go back to whoever sent him and tell them that I said they could go to hell."

Later E. W. said privately that he was sorry that he had used such language. "There was no need for that," he said, "for such language."

This incident happened in 1932, and it was brought up to discredit him in the campaign of 1934. Naturally, only the terse statement was taken from the matrix of modifying circumstances to be held up for the people to see.

He had many unpleasant experiences as a contender for the office of governor of the state. This goal of political ambition inspired many intense but ephemeral loyalties based upon small vanities and personal interests. There were times when E. W. was actually weak-willed and tractable, even humble and shy and timid.

He stood before the Osage Indians after a feast at their village. He turned to a friend and asked in a whisper, "What shall I say—I don't know what to say. Tell me what I ought to say."

George England, who later became, along with Wendell Johnson, one of his secretaries, drove for him during his campaign tours.

They drove silently late at night through the Osage, where in the dark one feels the space one is able to appreciate in the daylight hours. As they came to the top of the last ridge before reaching the Arkansas River, E. W. asked George to stop the car. Across the river the myriad lights of the old Marland Refinery, now the Continental, spoke of the virility, the force, the overbearing importance of big industry. Outside the brilliance of mechanical progress was the dim outline of the plains. A cluster of lights high on a tower illuminated the dark line of river trees and revealed the rows of storage tanks melting into the darkness of the plains. The great headquarters office building lights made a wall of brilliance.

E. W. sat for some time and looked at the lights. There was only the slight hissing of activity and a lazily panting locomotive to be heard. He looked over the planted trees that now hid the many pretentious homes, where just twenty-five years before there had been nothing but a few houses and shade trees, alone under the limitless sky.

He turned to George. "Well, George, there it is. The work of my life. It must mean something. Anyway they can't take that away from me."

And there were times when he completely forgot the flesh wounds from the guns of snipers, and his old arrogance would return. His attitude seemed to say, rather briskly, "All right, it's up to you. I've told you what I want done; you carry it out —never mind the expense. It's up to you fellows to get the money."

He made a sincere play for the women's vote, and he promised them that he would make state offices available to them. He had a deep respect for women and their power. The opposition papers called him "Pioneer Woman Ernie" and "Lord Ernie." His sincere interest in women, his proponents could not, and his opponents would not, fathom.

But he was bored by gatherings of political women. Like the common man, there were always too many of them in one place at the same time. Immediately after a speech he would escape from the fawning, cajoling, committee-busy women, often without ceremony, and go to his room for a drink.

During periods of arrogance, he would assume that E. W.,

the executive, might take time off from his campaigning to lie on his hotel bed and think, or talk with friends, but he demanded that his supporters keep busy.

One of his friends left during October for a two-weeks' bear hunt in New Mexico. When he returned he rejoined the campaign party. "Where you been?" E. W. demanded, with his faint, cynical smile.

"Bear hunting. Got some good pictures."

E. W. looked only at the top one. "Huh," he observed, "I've hunted bear."

Raising money had been difficult. Certainly no one could accuse him of getting money from Standard or Dutch Shell. The fact that he had attacked the big companies had been good political sauce for the public, but it didn't serve as political advantage to himself. It was said that W. H. McFadden had given $50,000 to his campaign fund. Certainly "Mack" spoke like a true rabble-rouser in his behalf.

At the beginning of the campaign, E. W. had called B. S. ("Cheebie") Graham, the man who had come to him for money many times in his fund-raising activities. E. W. pulled out a list of donations he had made, amounting to $681,000, then turned toward Cheebie, smiling, and said, "Cheebie, you've chiseled me out of $681,000 in donations to your various funds, now I want some reverse English." Cheebie Graham joined Pete Drake as money raiser, campaign manager, patronage dispenser, and general adviser.

It was difficult to keep E. W. in expense money during the campaign. Once when he and Cheebie were staying at a Tulsa hotel, they found on the day they chose for checking out that they had only five dollars between them. Across the breakfast table they considered their plight. E. W. said with his Olympian air, "It's up to you fellows to get the money," and as he arose he left the five dollars as a tip for the waitress.

Traveling over the state, he was always interested in his old filling stations which now had the word "Conoco" across the big red triangle. He seemed to know a little of the history of every station, and when the indicator needle moved toward empty as he rode in his car, he would say to his driver, "Pull over to that Conoco station. Maybe an old Marland boy is bulk agent here—maybe the boys on the drive are old Marland boys."

One hot afternoon in western Oklahoma, he made a speech outdoors. The spring and summer of 1934 were a great drought period, productive of dust clouds which, floating like crystalline fog over the land, had inspired national concern. Picked up by furious winds from the semiarid lands of western Oklahoma, the Texas Panhandle, New Mexico, and eastern Colorado, the dust was carried far over the Southwest. Sometimes, after playing furiously with the dust fog, the winds seemed to tire of their mad game and left it to float, to creep, black and menacing, to disembody the voices of starving cattle. But when the winds played with it, it buried ranch buildings and lonely little farm homes, covered wire fences, stopped windmills, blinded prairie chickens, and caused men to shout raucously at God.

As E. W. talked the dust got into his eyes. He inspired images in his listener's minds of a New Deal heaven for which he assumed priesthood's role. The faces, worn, dust-powdered, and unresponsive, were turned to his glowing words of hope. Some allowed their mouths to open slightly, as though they would lose no word of hope, no hint to nourish after he left them. There was a visible catch in E. W.'s throat as he talked into the upturned faces.

When he had finished his speech he turned abruptly and started for his car, ignoring a brown, cracked hand extended toward him. He left those who would shake hands with him, climbed into his car and sat looking at nothing, waiting for his companion.

As they drove away there was silence. His companion wanted to impress him with the nature of the terrible thing he had done in ignoring outstretched hands, but miles passed before he could decide on an opening sentence. His warning formed, he looked at E. W.'s face, then he, too, looked intently down the dirt road where the dust played before the wind like rolling smoke-puffs from the smoldering earth.

But now, in January, 1935, as E. W. rolled down Main Street

in Oklahoma City on his way to the capitol which stood high on the Red Beds, domeless but substantial, the campaign was forgotten in the emotion of rejuvenated glory. Forgotten were the bullets of the snipers. The exigencies of the earth he had learned about through forty years of acquisitive struggle were pushed back into the wings of the new stage where he would play his beloved role. What need had he for prompters? He thought of himself only as the bringer of happiness to the people; the prince in a new, well-supported role who would recover for them their lost freedom. He would be the bringer of plenty, the conserver of their resources, the builder of subsistence homesteads, and the champion of their natural rights to enjoy the beauty and the fruits of the earth, common property of all.

He was probably the most sincere, the most naïve, the most imaginative, the most able man, or at least one of the most able men, who ever entered high office in the state.

20

Cheebie Graham raised $75,000 for E. W.'s "Good Government Fund." This fund was contributed to by the citizens of the state who desired to have a part in the new enthusiasm. The fund was to finance a survey of the state government by the Brookings Institution of Washington, D. C.

The mansion in the game preserve became preinaugural headquarters. Here E. W. met with his several citizens' committees who were to work with the Brookings Institution. Here in the paneled dining room now converted to a conference office, he would rest with his back to the great fireplace, button the lower button of his coat, and discuss the plans for the people's welfare. Standing before his committee members, he said, "I tell you what I'm gonna do. I'm gonna have the Brookin's people in to tell us what we need for a complete reorganization. I want you to work with them. I've appointed you because I believe in you and I want you to study your fields and make your own recommendations. If you get into trouble, come to me; but it's up to you. That's why I appointed you.

"We'll establish civil service—no more spoils system. We'll take the schools out of politics. We'll open public office to women. We'll bring new industries into the state—why, we produce enough in this state to feed ten million people, and yet our people are starving. We'll put roofs over their heads, and we'll see that every man has his own bit of earth that belongs to 'im, with a house and a cow and a garden. We'll put a severance tax on our precious capital, oil and gas, in order to build up our other capital, soil, and conserve both. We'll give every child in this state an equal chance with every other child for an education, and we'll give security to their teachers through tenure. We'll give pensions to the aged and the widows in need. We'll take care of our blind and crippled children and our orphans. We want more than a living wage for our people: we want a saving wage. We'll use the people's money for the benefit of the people. Any questions?"

He appointed committees on taxation and revenue, education, public welfare, highways, law enforcement, state police system, old-age pensions, state conservation, and on natural resource industries. These committees all came, at different times, to the mansion at Ponca City to confer with him. Some of his committee chairmen had offices there.

He had conferences with the speaker of the lower house of the legislature, and with the president pro tempore and the floor leader of the senate. He gave a luncheon for members of the House and Senate. At a subsequent luncheon for a special few from the legislature, consisting of the leaders, he revealed startlingly the characteristic that was his eternal nemesis. The speaker of the house, Leon C. ("Red") Phillips, introduced across table a member of the House committee on appropriations. Instead of recognizing the introduction, E. W. said gravely, "Mr. Speaker, we follow the English custom here, we dispense with introductions."

To an Oklahoman, this was not a simple statement of mansion custom.

During the luncheon for members of the legislature, the mansion was filled with people studying the vistas, the grandeur, the pictured story of Marland on the ceiling of the banquet hall. They wandered through the spacious halls and up the majestic stairways. They examined the carved furniture, the shamrock curvings of the swimming pool, the refrigerator room, and the heating apparatus that had cost eight hundred dollars a month to run.

E. W. spoke to them at lunch in the great dining hall. He said he wanted them to wait for three months before asking him for jobs for their friends and supporters. He told them that he must become organized first.

His heart was not in it. There were too many of them in the same place at the same time. He was happy to be their host and he wanted them to enjoy themselves, but he didn't want to talk with them.

He left the hall and climbed the wide stairs to his old room, which was his preinaugural office. In the middle of the stairs he stopped and turned to a friend and said, "Come on up and have a drink."

He sat and looked out of the window upon his gardens. He looked at the statue of Lydie by Jo Davidson. She swirled in formal skirts as whimsical and as challenging as Petrolia—youth and beauty preserved in stone under his window by the great sculptor.

"E. W.," the friend said musingly, "do you realize that you are a paradox?"

"How?"

"By nature. Your ambition was to build an integrated oil company to compete with the Standard companies. In Congress you seemed to consider such companies enemies of the people. You have always been vehement about the complete freedom of oil, saying, I believe, that overproduction crises always worked themselves out. Now, this Interstate Oil Compact of yours, by which you want only sufficient oil produced to fill the market demand—in the name of both conservation and waste. If I didn't know you, I'd think you were making political adjustments to fit your changing roles, but your changes are definitely not political. Isn't it a public servant's duty to stand on the position that seems to insure the most benefits for the most people? You take sides."

He took his gaze from the statue, the gardens, and the trees that now, without their leaves, revealed the cold glinting of the lake waters. He poured a drink, then looked at his visitor. "I'm governor of the state—I'm not an oilman any more."

Downstairs, one of his "street smart" supporters was chewing his dead cigar in agitation. He moved it to the other side of his mouth with his tongue and mobile lips. "Jeez, what's he doin' up there—prayin' to himself in the lookin' glass? Hell of a note. Goes off and leaves these burr-heads that-a-way." He waved his hand at the splendor of floor, ceiling, and walls. "They're eatin' it up—jeez, what a chance. What's he think they are—a bunch of fillin' station boys? Hell, they're the representatives of the people! Don't he know that?"

The day after the inauguration he read his message to the legislature. He looked over the assemblage of law makers, just as Franklin D. Roosevelt might have done, and began with the same confidence and the same attitude of belligerent protector of right. He assumed that everyone knew there was an emergency.

As he stood before the members of the legislature, he was the old executive and these men were his loyal employees. He had no doubt that they could see the soundness and the importance of his proposals. To him, Claud Briggs, president pro tempore of the Senate, was the head of one of his operating departments, and Senate Floor Leader Jim Nance was another head, or an important assistant head. Big Red Phillips, speaker of the House, was a division manager, who, though able, had not learned about the ethics of co-operation in the corporation family. He had had some difficulty with Red over the speakership. He felt that Red might be a mild menace in the future. But as he stood there before the Fifteenth Legislature, he saw Red only as a responsible officer of the big corporation that was the state, and House Floor Leader F. N. Shoemake was his assistant. The faces of the others, the indefinite smear of faces, were assembled salesmen, perhaps, in from several divisions for a meeting on change of company policy that would be worked out by the heads of the departments, the directors, and himself. He had spoken to such assemblages many times—not individuals, but a mass of necessary men, assembled to hear their chief executive's message.

He outlined his New Deal program with confidence and a cold detachment that created a sort of echo, "I shall want you to do thus and so," behind the actually spoken, "I shall propose." The very way he looked up over his glasses, as though he would see whether they were able to understand clearly what he was ordering, created unconscious resentment over the chamber.

Then, with the attitude which assumed that all reasonable men would certainly understand, he let them have the full force of his plan for the reorganization of the state's government, and outlined to them his plan for raising funds through taxation to carry it out. Since his Brookings Institution report could not be finished in time to be used for study of the state's needs and the proper legislation for the fiscal year, 1935-36, he asked them to consider revenue measures for only one year.

He also told them that the President had decided to drop from the federal relief rolls all but the able-bodied destitute unemployed. This would leave about 35,000 cases, out of the 150,-000 on the federal relief rolls, which would need the immediate attention of the state. For the support of these people, he asked the legislature to pass a general and service tax law, increasing the amount from 1 to 3 per cent. The problem of the destitute touched his heart and he mentioned it as the most important emergency.

He asked for co-operation with the national government in order to receive full benefits of the public works programs. He called for the establishment of certain state boards: a planning board of fifteen members, a flood control board of three members, and a highways board of three members. These items were "must" legislation, the executive told his sales meeting, or better, his new policy meeting.

He proposed, with the echo, "I want you to . . ." behind it, a severance tax of two cents a barrel on crude petroleum, two cents per one thousand cubic feet on natural gas, and one cent a gallon on gasoline sold in the state. He proposed the retirement of the Murray administration debt of twenty million dollars by paying off $2,500,000 a year, and he wanted authority to issue short-term notes to retire the outstanding deficiency warrants. The depleted treasury, he said, was one of the emergencies. He asked that the sales tax be upped from 1 to 3 per cent, the tax income to be used one-third for schools and two-thirds for relief. He wanted the passage of new tax laws to raise revenue for the general revenue fund and suggested as sources for such revenues, taxes on incomes, insurance premiums, inheritances, cigarettes, salaries, and income from rents. The mere suggestion of new loads on some of these items was politically dangerous.

There was silence, except for the sporadic scraping of shoes on the floor and an occasional cough. The galleries were packed. There had been perfunctory, courteous hand-clapping as he entered the chamber, but there had been no applause when he stressed a point and looked up over his glasses. There was no applause when he ended his speech with, "I urge, in the name of suffering humanity, prompt action on these emergency measures."

When he left the chamber, there was a repetition of the decorous applause that had greeted his entrance. He didn't mind this. At company division meetings men were never quite sure when they should applaud the big boss, so they remained quiet unless some emotional sycophant stood up, beat his hands together, and looked expectantly over the meeting. E. W. was accustomed to applause upon entering or leaving only, applause that was like the raising of one's hat.

Pencils came out; legislators figured and reporters from the press figured and they came to an awful conclusion: not counting ten million dollars, the then state income, the new Governor was asking naïvely for thirty-five million dollars. He seems to have spurned figures in his speech, except for a few items. It was the need he saw, and this only. Just as the money had always come from his loyal and sometimes sweating personnel of the great oil company to support his ideas, he assumed that it would come from the great and rich state. His attitude seemed to be: "I am your governor and these things I deem emergencies. It's up to you to get the money. Don't annoy me with such trifling, mundane affairs."

The headlines began to appear on the same day: "CITIZENS FACE TAX INCREASES TO PAY RELIEF: *Mr. Average Man May Be Forced to Foot Bill Under New Plan.* MANY DEPARTMENTS AFFECTED: *Services, Gasoline, Gas, Oil, Salaries May Be Hit by Levies.*" Then again the same day, another headline: "STATE IN ARMS AGAINST BOOST IN TAX LEVIES: *Tax Payers Deluge Capitol With Telegrams and Phone Calls;* LEGISLATORS ARE AWED: *Predict Modification of Marland Plans.*"

"We went in the hole some $4,000,000 trying to raise a $21,-000,000 budget these two years," said the Republican floor leader of the House. "I don't see how we can raise $35,000,000 for one year." Red Phillips, speaker of the House, said, "I think it is evident to everybody that we must do something for relief of distressed people. It remains to be seen where we'll get the money." And Sandy Singleton, chairman of the House appropriation committee, said, "If the legislature passes a law to raise that much in appropriations, it's all right to me. We're not going to appropriate it unless it's raised."

Pete Drake needed no reflective light from his chief. He had his own importance. He moved more in the reflected light of the great political entrepreneur, Jim Farley, but when he put on Farley's voluminous mantle, it dragged in the dust of the capitol floors. He was the suffused boy coming out of the cinema, blinking in the light of reality, but in spirit still the cowboy on the white stallion.

He couldn't maintain his chief's idealism in the amazing tragi-comedy of capitol politics. As master of patronage, he began appointing "old Marland men," immediately discrediting E. W. and his sincere dream of civil service. Then he began to yield to superior *savoir-faire* and appointed erstwhile Marland opponents. "See Pete," became the slogan of the job hunters. Soon E. W. knew not his own official family.

Then the attacks came. At first E. W. couldn't hear them

through the hum of his own *amour-propre*, but they eventually came through. He never did learn about the nature of the "flood of telegrams and phone calls." He believed each one to be from some interested citizen following in detail the varied affairs of his state, and it was the criticism expressed by the "flood of telegrams" that dumbfounded him. He could never understand why he was being attacked.

He had led his dream before the people's legislature, full fleshed and admittedly beautiful, but with the voraciousness of a giantess. The very magnificence of her frightened the people when it was whispered to them, or shouted to them, with mock concern that they would be the ones who would be compelled to support her.

It would seem that the people had not thought of that possibility. The support of this magnificent creature clothed in humanitarianism would be their responsibility. Where was the mystical magician from Ponca City who had created her? What had happened to "Pioneer Woman Ernie" or "Lord Ernie" and his princely concern for the common man? The beautiful ideas of the humanitarian accepted by the voters were suddenly being called "crazy" by workaday citizens.

While the "flood of telegrams" baffled E. W., he refused to believe that the members of the legislature were not misleading the people for the express purpose of embarrassing him. Like a wounded animal, he turned on the first object within view. He didn't seem to realize that whatever whispers or shouts or activities had created the people's attitude, the fact of the attitude was of importance to their representatives in both chambers of the legislature. The legislators had few doubts about where they should stand.

The job hunters lolling about the lobby and the halls of the capitol annoyed him. He felt angry about the legislature's delay in passing his proposed bills while they carried on text-book adoption investigations. The news correspondents annoyed him with their stories, often carrying facts that he refused to consider.

He thought only of his great plan for facilitating the people's pursuit of happiness, and anything that slowed its progress toward complete expression exasperated him.

He went to the people for approval of his bills, believing that they had been misled, but he had not the histrionics of "Alfalfa Bill" Murray in his "fire bells" campaign. He was sure the people would understand, once he presented his proposals directly to them, but they listened with cold respect.

He got some of his legislation. He got only a 2 per cent sales tax for the aged, the blind, and dependent children; he got homestead exemption from full taxation, and the gross production tax raised from 3 to 5 per cent, based upon the price of oil. He got his state highway patrol, which turned out to be a monument to his public service. He got his planning board and state aid for weak schools, but not his proposed reorganization, and only parts of his other proposed legislation.

The legislature co-operated with him in the attainment of one of his beloved objectives, the Interstate Oil Compact and the commission to implement it, which gave the oil states control over the conservation of their petroleum resources. The realization of his idea came after a series of trying conferences at Ponca City and Dallas after his election in 1934. He clung long to his contentions concerning what the compact should cover, against the fiery opposition of Governor James V. Allred of Texas.

Neither E. W., Governor Alfred M. Landon of Kansas, Governor Allred of Texas, nor any of the other representatives of the southwestern, middle western, or western states wanted federal control. Secretary Harold L. Ickes of the Department of the Interior had hinted at such control.

The Standard had been interested in conservation, he felt, not for the benefit of the people but for their own business purposes. The Standard had urged co-operation on the part of the early Pennsylvania producers, through shut-down of drilling, proration, and exploratory activity. The producers had little success with the enforcement of their association's regulations. The Standard made protective moves. It controlled production, through its monopoly of Atlantic outlets, transportation, ownership of refineries, and, when necessary, through infiltration into the producers' protective organizations. The Standard had stepped in to control production when the region's producers failed to control it.

E. W. believed that the old conflict was renewed, only this time the federal government would do the stepping in, perhaps not only to conserve oil through proration, but to set prices.

The shadow of Secretary Ickes was behind the chairs of the representatives from Oklahoma, California, Kansas, Louisiana, Colorado, New Mexico, and other oil producing states, but he was not behind the chair of Governor Allred of Texas. Governor Allred informed the meeting proudly that Texas, the Republic, had come into the union of states by treaty, and because the United States had refused to assume the indebtedness of the Republic of Texas, it had allowed the new state of Texas to keep control over its lands, mines, and minerals.

E. W. and Governor Allred argued about the meaning of the compact-to-be. E. W. wanted determination of market demand for oil, and then proposed allowables for each well and each field to suit the demand. Production above the market demand, he believed, would constitute waste. He believed also that the price of oil ought to be high enough to allow the continued operation of stripper wells, the kind which produced little oil after years of pumping. These quite often belonged to the little men and could not produce five barrels a day. Allred wanted no price-fixing; he was concerned only with the prevention of physical waste.

Against Allred's vigorous insistence on his point of view, E. W. became weakened and uncomfortable and finally gave in. He had selected Pat Hurley as his legal counsel in the series of conferences on the making of the compact. Pat had called upon the aid of Northcutt Ely. They had come down from Washington, D. C.

Over dinner E. W. discussed with Pat the rather gloomy outlook for an effective meeting of the minds between Allred and himself. Pat said, "What's the matter? You want your compact, don't you? Well, get Allred to recognize the necessity for the compact by statement. Then you've got your idea over, you see? It's the compact you want, and you might lose it if you prolong your argument over some of the measures. Get the compact, then you can work out the details later."

The Interstate Oil Compact Commission was shortly born. That it has survived to become one of the most remarkable control agencies in existence is of lasting credit to E. W. and his advisers.

E. W.'s dreams generally were not materializing as he had planned, however. He began to fear failure, but his fears brought the shrewd, struggle-experienced man back to displace the dreamer. Periodically he requested that the door to his office be left open when he was not having a conference. He looked up from his desk at faces with a question in his own now, and asked his secretaries for more information about casual visitors. But even when he was on the alert he could say to a friend who had inquired about the reasons for his asking another friend to resign, "Why the people approved of it—look at the telegrams." And he could say to Cheebie Graham, who told him that a certain group of people were misleading him to attain certain ends, "Huh?" Then, after looking at Cheebie as his anger grew, he said, "Grown men don't lie." As he said this he pretended to arrange papers on his desk, as an invitation for Cheebie to leave.

His fears grew with the growing number of obstacles placed in his way, but the bright spots came after longer and longer intervals. One bright spot was his successful fight to lease the state land around the capitol for the production of oil. The capitol sits high on a long swell of the Red Bed plains, the core of which is the buried ridge of an ancient mountain. Along its flanks, at some six thousand feet, the oil was found which gave birth to the fabulous Oklahoma City oil field.

E. W. had argued that wells drilled *around* the state's property would capture, by drainage, the oil *under* the state's property, and that the state was therefore forced to lease its land in order to recover its proper royalty share of the oil beneath its buildings.

Modern steel derricks began springing up about the capitol

like the very symbols of mechanical progress, and from the royalties the state built a much-needed office building for its legislators.

The roar, the shouts, and the clanking were music to the old wildcatter. The odor of crude oil, as it came into his windows on the capitol grounds, was like perfume to him and possessed the power that scents have to bring back emotions and recapture incidents of the past associated with them. He had grown tired of the screeching and grinding of the street railway cars that came up past the capitol. He was glad for the relief which familiar and competing noises gave. He might have felt like the important governor of an oil state now if he had not felt less and less like a governor recently. His fears were like sharp little pains that cause perspiration.

There was an air-cooling system in his office that seemed to do little more than preserve the animal odors of the people who came and left during the day. One day he sat at his desk as though he had succumbed to them. He had a slump of the shoulders that had just recently joined his other characteristic physical mannerisms. His face was grey. The door was ajar as he looked up and saw in profile one of his younger friends in the anteroom. He called to him, and as the young man approached, he said, "Sit down." The visitor waited, then asked, "Did you want to see me, E. W.?"

"No, no—I was looking at you through the doorway. I was just looking at your beautiful head. Nothing important."

There was a silence, and E. W. seemed to slump a little more. He put the ends of his fingers together and looked out of the window toward his home, the governor's house. The shrubs and flowers he had brought from his estate in Ponca City were flourishing where his predecessor, Bill Murray, had had his onion garden. He had once experienced a cynical pleasure in comparing this beauty which he had donated to the state with Bill's vegetable garden, just as he had experienced pleasure from contrasting his top hat and cutaway with Bill Murray's falling socks and old muffler. But now, as he looked across to the big house that had once been so stark, there were no humorous contrasts to lighten his thoughts.

When he looked back at his visitor his eyes were like those of a spaniel who can't understand why he has been threatened. He looked out the window again as he said, "They're going to impeach me."

But the next day E. W. had recovered. He had become angered and defiant. He was the guest of honor at a luncheon given by the Democratic women leaders, before whom he abandoned his prepared speech and demanded extemporaneously, with hurt dignity, of the nice chairwoman, "What do you mean by sending boys to the mill. Why don't you go yourself?" I seriously fear you won't get the government you want until you do. The utilities and big business are planning to elect a legislature to defeat your program, defeat me, and then impeach me." He said this with anger. "You sent me a legislature, a lower house of 120 members, 80 of them hardly out of their teens. They had no business experience, no professional experience. I got part of my program over, but I was able to do only some of the things you had promised." He used the phrase, "you had promised," not the usual pronoun "I." He was asking them what they were going to do about "their" program.

He mentioned the failure to get his police-pension bill through, his old-age pension measure, and satisfactory school reform. He continued, "The young men—they were entertained, wined and dined, given night parties, bedroom parties, by the utilities, the oilmen, the bankers, and the special interests."

There was ample ground for his fear of impeachment in the history of the nine governors who had preceded him. Of the nine, two had been impeached, and rumors and actual charges had made others very uncomfortable. The governor's seat was a saddle thrown onto a skittish bronco. You not only had to know much about broncos to stay in it, you had also to examine your saddle blanket for cockleburs every time you saddled up.

But there was no danger of impeachment for E. W. The

Senate had now become the governor of the state, taking over that part of his range of power and influence which it wanted and leaving the crumbs of power to Pete Drake and Cheebie Graham, making of E. W. the state's chief clerk. Certainly the Senate would not be interested in charges against him. Red Phillips of the House said his chamber didn't want to impeach him. "The heat's bothering him," he remarked. He said E. W. was throwing the beam of publicity on the rumor of impeachment "to draw attention away from all the political hiring he has done." Red was overestimating him—that is, actually attributing political shrewdness to him. Certainly E. W. knew the uses of the red herring, but his self-respect would never have allowed him to drag it through the citadel of his honor and dignity. He might have dragged it around the citadel, but never through its halls.

Now when he went to Ponca City to sit out the hot week ends at the studio on the preserve—the very attractive lodge-gallery-studio to which he and Lydie and the setters had moved when they could no longer afford to live in the mansion—he noted the paucity of callers, both social and business. He was not annoyed with job hunters and fawners now. He sat long hours with a drink in the breeze-swept area between the two long wings of the studio and yielded to the monotonous chant of the cicadas. An occasional coarse shout from ornamental water fowl, like a petulant protest against the heat, could be heard, or a tentative midsummer chorus of the frogs by the lake.

His old Ponca City friends came sometimes to talk and swim, and he would put on his bathing trunks and sit among them as they splashed about in the swimming pool.

There were incidents to make him unhappy. Some of the ministers of the churches to which he had made substantial donations had seen fit to criticize him for his "go to hell" statement to the representative of the Anti-Saloon League. Their criticism hurt him, as indeed, did criticism from any source. He had said that he would carry out the laws of a theoretically dry state, because such laws existed, and he did cause a raid to be made in his own county. But it was said by the fervent drys

that this raid, and others, had the sinister purpose of forcing re-
peal of the dry laws.

Often during periods of fear and dejection, E. W. realized
that he had alienated the interest of old friends and supporters
for whose resignations Pete and Cheebie had urged him to ask.
They would assure him that these people were not supporting
him as they should. In his anger he would dictate curt notes to
them. The resentment of these people and their friends stung
him. At Ponca, he felt the absence of the old gaiety and close
friendships of the past.

E. W. and his advisers decided that he should be a candidate
for the United States Senate in 1936, even though he had two
years to go yet as governor of Oklahoma. This was not his
original plan, but an office of such great dignity would suit
him; it presented an escape from the governor's office, an escape
for which he longed. He would actually "run" for the office of
United States senator.

There was money to be raised, so Cheebie got busy. There
were powerful blocs and interest groups to connive with, so
Pete got busy. The spring and summer of 1936 were another
drought period. The dust fogs rolled again, to stifle, to blind, to
impoverish both land and men. Pete and Cheebie built their
machine on dust, special interest groups, and the ambitions of
active men.

No governor had yet been able to escape from his office in
Oklahoma City to the United States Senate; the capitol machine
was as yet inadequate. It was good only for sure second place
in the important elections. This meant nothing to Pete and
Cheebie, nor did it mean anything to E. W. when the very
thoughts of escaping brought back his old confidence and sent
his fears into a comatose state. He knew that a tap on the shoulder from the White House in the presence of the people would
be almost as much as he might need to win the office. After all,
he could count himself as one of the Roosevelt-favored. He had
followed the Great Leader, not as a tail-wagger or a hand-
licker, but as a companion, traveling in the same direction but
keeping his independence. In that he was right, but in his as-

sumption that the President would tap his shoulder to impress the people, he was wrong.

There were three candidates for the office of United States senator from Oklahoma that summer; three candidates who interested the Great Leader in the White House. There was his old friend E. W. Marland, who had been loyal and co-operative. There was the Fifth District Representative, Josh Lee, who had been a veritable Saint John among his disciples, and there was incumbent, Senator Thomas P. Gore, who had only the light of his own heart and brain as he struggled in the eternal darkness.

Senator Gore would be eliminated immediately, since he had called the President a "panty waist" in private and had intimated the same in public. He understood only the fundamental necessities of struggle; he believed that a man must ever depend entirely upon himself, having confidence in his unconquerable spirit. He had fought his way up in complete darkness to his position of importance in the nation through his will to survive. In the light of his heart and mind, the only light in his cave of darkness, he reconstructed life out in the sun through the actions of men about him, and in their frailties he saw humor, while he, in the dark cave of complete blindness, clung tightly to the stalagmite of his convictions. He was, in his person, the very symbol of the unconquerable life-force, and even in darkness he had neither asked for nor received aid. He, therefore, must color the imagined condition of men out under the sun with his own experiences, with his own philosophy.

He thought the President was a pampered dreamer who had been dressed in Swiss laces and who had imperiously waved his silver spoon. Paternalism in government, to the blind Senator, softened the people of a nation that needed strong men more than any other nation on earth.

This left E. W. and Josh Lee for the Presidential tap on the shoulder. Josh received not the tap but a nod from the President at a reception in Washington.

Although E. W. felt no tap, he seemed not to worry about it. He felt assured of his friend's approval. When aid was really needed, it would come. He grew confident and almost cocky again.

Josh Lee came in first in the primaries, and E. W. came in a second—a second that was not encouraging but sufficiently good to place him in the runoff with Josh. He sat by the radio in the big room of the studio and listened to the returns. He lost little of his confidence, but had nothing to say about the results. Perhaps he was thinking that it was time now for the Great Leader to recognize his friend. Perhaps he reviewed his own speeches in Congress when he was so perturbed about the oil code. He might have thought with a start of his "government by discretion of royalty" speech. If he had these thoughts he didn't reveal them.

He lost the runoff election to Josh Lee. It must have been clear to him now that no aid had come from the White House. He sank back into immobility and waited for the senatorial campaign of 1938. He waited, as the chief clerk of the state, for the next try. Pete and Cheebie were sure that the machine could be perfected by then.

But in 1938 he lost again. This time the President not only tapped his opponent, the incumbent, Senator Elmer Thomas, but came into the state to do so. Pete and Cheebie boarded the presidential train at Fort Smith, and they met and talked with the President concerning support for their candidate. He knew E. W. and was very fond of him. Incidentally, how would E. W. like to be a member of the C.A.A. at $12,000 a year?

E. W. stood with the President and Senator Thomas before the people of Oklahoma at Oklahoma City. He must have felt like the gardener's boy whom the visiting princeling ignores to favor the tutor's boy.

He gave no sign of discouragement but worked hard to win. Even though he sensed after the presidential visit that he might be defeated, there was some relief, in that his fear of impeachment, imaginary or otherwise, was over. His term as governor would end in a few months.

In January, 1939, he wished Leon C. Phillips good luck in the governor's chair which he was vacating. This was not a politician's farewell, but a sincere one. He was glad to get back to Ponca City.

He half-heartedly promoted another oil company, but it died of anemia. He busied himself selling his mansion to the Carmelite Friars. He had told John Hale that he wanted to leave the mansion to some Catholic order, but, in his present condition, he could not afford to keep it, nor could he afford to make a gift of it. The tile roof had been damaged by one of the Outlet's wild hail storms, and many other repairs were needed. The native growths crept onto the diminished preserve to reclaim their own, overwhelming the pampered plants and exotic trees, which could not protect themselves against these virile invasions.

It was said that he sold the mansion to the Carmelites for $66,000. This dream that had cost him millions of dollars, made corporeal in the form of a grey-stoned English mansion, might live, like the dreams expressed in Gothic cathedrals in medieval Europe, through the nourishment of the church.

Since no woman could remain on the grounds after the Friars took over, the statue of Lydie by Jo Davidson had to be removed from the terrace and hidden in the shrubbery back of the other buildings, off sacred ground. And the statue of George was laid on its back in some wild growths along the terrace wall, where it lay eternally musing on the wide sky. The terrace, which had bombarded the senses with flowers, became a vegetable garden, attended by the brothers.

The paneled rooms of the mansion were now bare. Where there had been carved furniture, pictures, books, and beauty created by the centuries of man's dreaming, there was now ascetic austerity. In the rooms where luxurious beds had stood with their taffeta and silken coverings, there were now saw horses with planks laid across them, for which the imported paneling, from the days of laughter and worldly pleasures, furnished a dramatic contrast.

The swimming pool, where there had been gay splashing and laughter and hilarious play, was now silent. The wind sailed dead leaves across it, which were finally becalmed in the scum that had formed along the edges.

E. W. was periodically ill. He had had a slight stroke. He sat for hours, not dreaming now, perhaps, but with his mind ever busy, though it was powerless to inspire him to action. It is doubtful if he had many thoughts to spare from his own condition. Like most old and sick men, when incidents and men and life itself ceased to swirl about his own personality, he began to worry about his unit of society, represented by his nation—the unit which he had so blithely ignored all of his life. Everyone, his old friends and others for whom he had been the little god, were busy promoting their own affairs now. Things had changed —what were they doing? Some dark spirit seemed to be settling over the land, seeping into the hearts of men to make them indifferent to friendship. What he talked about, however, was another matter. He talked of people he had known and of events with which he had been personally associated.

He recalled his visit to Mexico when he was still governor, and the sincere reception he had received. President Cardenas had sent an official delegation up the International Highway to escort him to Mexico City.

Pat Hurley came by to see him, and they talked of the contract which Pat had made with the Mexican government as counsel for the Consolidated Oil Company—a holding company for Sinclair, Penn-Mex, Prairie Pipe Line Company, and the Sinclair Pipe Line Company. E. W., too, had been involved in this interesting incident of business diplomacy.

When the Mexican government had taken over oil lands and production of these companies, there had been some comic opera flourishes that were not in the least humorous to the foreign operators. Harry Sinclair called E. W. and asked him to go down to see what he might be able to do about it. E. W. could do nothing, since he was the governor of a state, but he called Pat in Washington, and he and Harry got together. Hurley arranged an agreement between the Mexican government and his client, whereby Sinclair and associates were compensated by the Mexican government by payment in kind.

Just as E. W. had called upon Carranza years ago when he got his leases, Pat had called upon Cardenas. He had walked into the office and bowed, then talked as one gentleman to another. There was no North American cockiness and hearty insincerity for a Latin-Indian to look through as though it were shabby glassware. Pat immediately recognized the section and article referring to minerals in the Constitution of 1917. There was no question about that—it was the law of Mexico. But why not confirm it, give it interpretation as a court might do, but in this case by making a contract based upon it. They came to an agreement. Ambassador Josephus Daniels said that much of their understanding was owing to the fact that Pat the Choctaw respected Cardenas the Tarascan, and vice versa. But Daniels neglected to note that Pat's histrionics are perfect, a part of his interesting personality. Nor does he have Choctaw Indian blood all the time—only when he needs it.

The days passed, the winds of spring seemed intent upon removing the soil of the plains from the earth. The warm winds came up from the Gulf, and the contrary winds above them pushed ragged clouds across the sky. The people, sticky with unseasonable heat, watched them, hoping against the elemental drama when the air from the Arctic would arrive.

The cicadas from the planted trees around the lake seemed to prolong the summer's heat by their chanting. The summer was very long.

E. W. heard the chanting from his bed, but his throat would not allow his swarming thoughts to pass, even in the form of broken words. Friends came to see him, yet he had that feeling that everyone was completely absorbed by his own affairs. They stood, his visitors, with their hats in their hands, as though they had left a pot boiling.

Jane Clark was constant, and the Soldani girls came often. He had admired Jane very much and had listened to her practical advice even in his glory. When she came to visit, he could overhear the conversation between her and Lydie. They were constantly giving the wrong name to the wrong man, misplacing incidents geographically as well as in time, but he must lie and listen, unable to correct them. And, somehow, it seemed very important to make such corrections at this time. Sometimes the urge was so great that he suffered the pain from speech for the satisfaction his corrections gave him.

Shy, uncertain people came to the kitchen door with baskets of food. Some of them offered money.

As E. W. lay there waiting, his futile worries must have given way to images from his life, sliding into each other, displacing each other, leaving no blank space on the screen of his memory.

The fox's brush held up by the second sons of Rugby Colony, the glistening wheels and the high-stepping horses of Pittsburgh, the library at Mount Washington, his spade-bearded father listening to his reading, the magnificent Henry Clay Frick, the frowning buildings and sinister half-lights of Pittsburgh, the smudge-faced coal miner, the well on the Brenneman farm, the menacing smog of 1907, the Ponca funeral scaffolds and the water pump with the voice of fate, the lights of his refinery on the plains, the long train of tank cars, the roses that bombarded the senses, the mansion in the game preserve, and hunters streaming over the prairie in red coats.

E. W. Marland died on October 3, 1941. From all over the region they came to pay their last respects. The representatives of Organization and Efficiency, the representatives of Politics and Administration came with polite and formal sorrow. But in the overflow crowd outside there was a genuine sense of loss, a resignation. It was the end of an era.

CPSIA information can be obtained
at www.ICGtesting.com
Printed in the USA
LVHW091332031219
639286LV00001B/63/P